The Grover E. Murray Studies in the American Southwest
Also in the series

between two rivers

between two rivers

PHOTOGRAPHS AND POEMS BETWEEN
THE BRAZOS AND THE RIO GRANDE

JEROD FOSTER and **JOHN POCH**
Foreword by **RICK BASS**

TEXAS TECH UNIVERSITY PRESS

This book is typeset in Minion Pro. The paper used in this book meets the minimum requirements of ANSI/NISO Z39.48-1992 (R1997).

Designed by Kasey McBeath
Cover photograph by Jerod Foster

Library of Congress Control Number: 2019934084
ISBN: 978-1-68283-038-3

Printed in the United States of America
19 20 21 22 23 24 25 26 27 / 9 8 7 6 5 4 3 2 1

Texas Tech University Press
Box 41037 | Lubbock, Texas 79409-1037 USA
800.832.4042 | ttup@ttu.edu | www.ttupress.org

Most rivers are 'people rivers,' in that their waters and the attributes of their shores have helped to shape human beings from primitive times on down, forming the ways in which those human beings have lived and labored and regarded the world.
John Graves, *Texas Rivers*

…To the place from which the rivers come,
There they return again.
Ecclesiastes 1:7

la la la li li li lend me your hand
there's many a river that waters the land
Texas River Song (anonymous)

contents

ONE first observes these photographs by Jerod Foster, and reads these poems by John Poch, with astonishment. There's nothing really fancy about the elegant simplicities of the photographs' composition—the stark contrast of water versus stone, and the horizontal versus the vertical—straight lines, seams, clefts, fissures, cracks; a horizon razored by sky, a river a scalpel in a canyon. And the poetry of Poch's conversational rhapsodies is likewise powerful in its lack of pretentiousness. In their cumulative, however, these photographs and poems, fueled by the aesthetics of celebration rather than those of morose lamentation, seem all the more bittersweet for the jaw-dropping beauty. Now and again we witness an iconic Texas view, acutely familiar to a deep or long-time resident—the Llano, the Rio Hondo—but often the photographs of water—so clean, and so much of it— seem as strange as if taken in Montana, Idaho, Wyoming, Colorado: land that was once the Texas territory, but no more.

And yet, what does it mean that we still have surface water, often little seams of hidden water, between the Brazos and the Rio Grande? Some of Texas lies to the north of this breadth of heartland, and some lies to the south. Across the years, political boundaries have waxed and waned in all directions, but the geology of the heart has remained constant, here in the center, between these two great rivers; and the water—which is to say,

life—is not all gone yet. Somehow, amidst so much rock, that remaining water seems—in these photos and poems—to be its truest self: a sight so strange we have almost forgotten what it looks like.

There is an open-heartedness in the poetry and photos here that is nurturing. These are the testimonies of celebrants, pilgrims, artists not lost in the wilderness, but reveling in their wandering; artists who know what they want, and how to look for it, and how to find it.

In reading the beguiling vernacular of Poch's poetry, and pausing long moments over Jerod Foster's photos, one is comforted further: these are artifacts of an intimate spirit, not an estranged aesthete or wayfaring stranger. This book is as full of residency as can be imagined: overflowing.

So many of these photographs are of the water I remember of my youth: water one could drink. How irretrievable that seems, with only a single generation gone-by. Nostalgia is always a danger—more so than ever, now, in a world that's burning, and burning hot—but I can't help but remember my youth of six decades ago, when I cupped water in my own hands, and drank. The loss of these little freedoms.

We likely won't see those days again, but perhaps this is only mild penance for all that is immense that we have failed to safeguard. It matters to me more now than ever that the other wild things—flora and fauna—still be able to sip this water, and survive, even prosper, even if we struggle as a result of our choices, or non-choices. Our inactions and failures to protect or conserve.

Make no mistake—these photographs of clear water—as Marty Robbins would croon, cool water—are revolutionary. The muddy stock tanks of north Texas and the blackwater swamps of East Texas, and the green veins of the Guadalupe on its way to the salt sea of the Gulf, are also our legacy—but in these photos of Texas' heartland of water, its strong veins still pulsing, I am reminded of how beautiful the world still is, and how noble an act it is to fight to protect such beauty. In beholding these images, and reading these poems—listening—we are drawn deeper into responsibility by the most noble of sentiments, love for something other than ourselves.

Rick Bass

PHOTOGRAPHER AND POET, Jerod Foster and John Poch, we both met fifteen years ago on the Texas Tech Junction Campus situated on the South Llano River. Jerod was teaching a photography class with mentor and Texas state photographer Wyman Meinzer, and John was conducting his first poetry course at Junction. Over the years, we have admired each other's work, and now we have come together to collaborate, to share our various arts in the one format of this book, and to praise and wonder among these varied, unique, and beautiful waters and landscapes of New Mexico and Texas.

The poems here range from love poems that use rivers and landscape as a symbolic or decorative backdrop to narrative poems that tell a kind of story. As well, there are linguistically reflexive ponderings and even more difficult surreal explorations of how a river can and cannot be comprehended. Some of the poems are descriptive, and others take a much more abstract, stylistic approach. A number of the poems are sonnets and more tightly wrought curtal sonnets (a form invented by the British poet Gerard Manley Hopkins), and just as many are free verse poems that organically find their own form, much in the way a river finds its identity due to the pull of gravity and the geological and geographical texture of the land which both obstructs and accepts or even needs its flow. Most of the poems aim to be as lyrical as Hart Crane and William Butler Yeats and as rhetorically clear and emotionally resonant as Elizabeth Bishop or Robert Lowell.

The photographs not only visualize and contextualize the words of the poems, they also bring to light additional, uncaptured descriptors and narratives about the waterways and the land that plays host to and inspires those cultures thriving nearby. The imagery mixes the art form of landscape photography with strong visual storytelling characteristics leaning toward the natural history and current state of the region's life sources. Likewise, the images evoke a visceral resonance with and recognition of the region's light, color, and romantic form. Indeed, they complement the text in helping to convey a sense of place and affection for these waters and lands. The photographs aid in establishing an origin story of the region these waterways populate, much in the way that seemed attractive to early settlers between the Rio Grande in the Sangre de Cristo Mountains of northern New Mexico and the Brazos River running the long course across the state of Texas.

Entre Dos Aguas is a flamenco guitar composition written by one of the world's most famous guitarists, Paco de Lucia. The words literally mean "Between Two Waters." The waters he refers to are the Atlantic Ocean and the Mediterranean Sea. Southern Spain, otherwise known as Andalucía, lies between these two. This land of flamenco is a large geographical region saturated by a culture, a feeling, a state of being or creativity that the Spanish poet, Federico Garcia Lorca called *duende*. Americans might consider this duende to be akin to our notion of "soul", but it is darker than that, connected to the culture of the bullfight that explores deep paradoxical tensions, perhaps especially the unexpected beauty that might be found in and after death. This understanding is also a Christian (for Lorca, *Catholic*) concept that embraces and worships the experience of Christ's passion, suffering, and death ultimately overcome by spiritual power.

It was a bold achievement for Paco de Lucia to portray Andalucian culture in a six-minute guitar composition. Emanating from this song is an authentic rhythmical and sonic arrangement, a familiar voice and imagery conjured in "Entre Dos Aguas" that anyone from Huelva to Cadiz to Granada would recognize as part of her own heritage and personality. There is a reason that as of this writing the 1976 video of Paco de Lucia playing "Entre Dos Aguas" has had over thirty million hits on YouTube. It is an immediately recognizable, defining arrangement of flamenco song.

In this book, the outer limits of our own "Entre Dos Aguas" are the Rio Grande River and the Brazos River. What lies between these two rivers is the land and cultural realm that reaches from the Texas Hill Country down to the Border of Mexico, across the Trans-Pecos and on up through Northern New Mexico into Colorado where we find the headwaters of the Rio Grande. The Mexican-American heritage of this area is fundamental to both our title and to the vision of this endeavor. The names of the two rivers that set the limits of our book are Spanish in origin, yet many English speakers might not think twice about them. The "Big River" to the west and "The Arms (of God)" to the east are natural borders that shape and help define this part of the world. The Rio Grande not only divides the United States and Mexico, but it also connects us. Linguistically and culturally, there has been a fruitful and meaningful cross-pollination available to our peoples, resulting in unique painting, music, visual art, and, of course, a cuisine known around the world. The multiplicity of our blended cultures has altered the simpler ways we might have seen things, making us who we are, more deeply human and artistically diverse.

The rivers and the land between the Rio Grande and the Brazos have generated a culture to be explored, pondered, and celebrated in song and image. Western songwriters have been mining this landscape and reflecting the beauty of her people for a long time. From Buddy Holly to Terry Allen to the Dixie Chicks, and for dozens of other extraordinary songwriters and artists, the wide open spaces of Texas and New Mexico have been a unique inspiration. There is a spiritual aspect to the region akin, perhaps, to what Lorca claims on behalf of the Andalucians concerning "duende". Anyone who visits the southern reaches of the Rocky Mountains, from the Enchanted Circle of New Mexico down through Sante Fe would admit that the Sangre de Cristo Mountains, the primary watershed that feeds the Rio Grande in northern New Mexico, exude a spirituality with which we yearn to reckon. And this reckoning has called a multitude of writers and artists to explore her territory: artists like Georgia O'Keefe, Ansel Adams, and D.H. Lawrence. For Texans, the Brazos River is a primary source, flowing from its often drought-stricken headwaters in the Llano Estacado down through the heart of Texas into the Gulf of Mexico, nearly cutting the state diagonally in half. John Graves's famous book, *Goodbye to a River*, takes place on the Brazos and its environs, and his narrative is a central text of the soul of the land for any Texan who knows her history. Our obsessions with the rivers of this particular region have resulted in photography and poetry, our own artistic visions and versions of image and song.

We hope that the combination of the images with the poems is beyond illustrative. The photographs shouldn't need help from the poems to situate their beauty, and the poems should be able to stand alone without the help of the camera's lens. Each art form provides its own sufficient language, though various members of our audience may be geared more toward the eye or ear. Yet our combinations presented in this book are attempting to complement each other, perhaps similar to how Bill Evans's piano or John Coltrane's saxophone might have added a dimension to Miles Davis's trumpet on *Kind of Blue*. This may be an audacious claim, but it is something to which any collaborator might aspire. Jerod's photographs in the West Texas Trans-Pecos region inspired John to write the poems "Independence Creek" and "Punctuation on the Devils River" among others. And John's poems about the rivers around the Enchanted Circle encouraged Jerod to direct his camera lenses on locations in Northern New Mexico where he hadn't yet traveled. We have spent a great deal of time choosing, editing, pairing, and organizing the very best of our work that considers, explores, and responds to this geography: river, land, sky, flora, fauna, and human presence.

The river is one of the defining metaphors of Time in literature and philosophy. The thought that a man can never step in the same river twice has been ascribed to Heraclitus. Furthermore, we can comprehend the philosophical notion that, like a river, everything flows (changes) through Time. While a river certainly changes, it remains the same somehow. We can see that the Brazos, high or low, upstream or down, is still the Brazos. Nevertheless, John Graves's *Goodbye to a River* is predicated upon the fact that, due to the damming by the Army Corps of Engineers, the Brazos he had known all his life would be changed forever. It is true of our selves, our souls or identities; we grow up and grow old, but we are still ourselves.

We cannot see the wind, but we can see its effects on the surface of an alpine lake or hear it whistle through the red willows along a shoreline. We cannot see Time, but we can see a river, and we can swim that river or fish it. Through our physical witness of this moving water, we have been "moved" to find and capture and order the words and images to this mysterious flow that so deeply has affected us and our lands. While our attempts might be to, in some definitive way, uniquely name or fix an image of a river or its riparian environs, we hope that the reader and viewer here will see the true nature of change in the shifting of the light and line in our work.

Art not only satisfies one's desires, but it intensifies these longings. Obviously, we have only addressed a small portion of the rivers available to us in these parts, and this book is no attempt to be exhaustive. And to write a poem about or take a photograph of the Rio Grande around Taos is not the same as if done all the way down along the Rio Grande in Big Bend. Even the much shorter Rio Hondo is radically different in its mountain heights than where it empties a few miles down into the Rio Grande. There are limits to knowledge, but you can't say we don't try to come to terms with those limits. In some ways, only art can test the limits of our mortal lives. In some ways, science or religion. Perhaps the limitations of our book will create possibilities for others to do their own good work and play, especially artistic, in such rich riparian environments.

Jerod Foster and John Poch, 2019

acknowledgments

Thanks to the editors of these magazines who first published earlier versions of these poems:

32 Poems: "Invasive Species"
America: "Rio Grande (South)"
Blackbird: "Independence Creek"
Carolina Quarterly: "Pot Creek," "The Little Rio Grande," and "River Prayer"
Cellpoems: "Lullaby"
Colorado Review: "Valle Vidal"
Gray's Sporting Journal: "Trout that swim"
Hampden-Sidney Review: "Love Creek"
Linebreak: "The Secret of Rivers"
Meridian: "The Cimarron River" and "Rio Fernando"
The New Criterion: "The Moon"
The New Republic: "The Llano River"
Orion: "Hill Country Drought Along the South Llano"
Poetry: "A River"
Sewanee Review: "Loving and Goodnight, Goodnight and Loving"
Sewanee Theological Review: "For the Christian Angler"
Shenandoah: "The Brazos"

Southwest Review: "The Rio Hondo" and "Punctuation on the Devils River"
Talking River: "The Vapor on Rivers"
Terrain.org: *"Entre Dos Aguas,"* "Red River (Hatchery)," and "Rio Lucero"
Thrush Poetry Journal: "Escape on the Sabinal," "Sonnet on Time," and "The Rio Grande"
Unsplendid: "Invisible Fish"

"Sonnet on Time" was also made into a poetry film by Alex Henery. Special thanks to the Texas Tech University Office of Research Services for a generous Scholarship Catalyst Program Grant which was used to complete the text of this book. Some of these poems were previously published in *Fix Quiet* (St. Augustine's Press, 2014).

Also, thanks to these individuals and organizations:

24 Frames/KTTZ
Joe Arredondo
Robert Bradley
Todd Chambers
Bruce Clarke
Grant Hall

Alex Henery

Paul Hunton

Doug Inglis

Kyle Jones

Mark and Pam Kirkpatrick

Karen Lopez

Wyman Meinzer

Jordan Messerer

Billy Moore

David Mullins

Corbin and Rebecca Neill

Rob Peaslee

David Perlmutter

Doug and Lisa Ray

Keith Rodgers

Kent Rylander

Lawrence Schovanec

Brian Still

Robert Stubblefield

William Wenthe

Bill Worrell

Lisa Wrinkle

LHUCA

The Nature Conservancy

Texas Parks and Wildlife

between two rivers

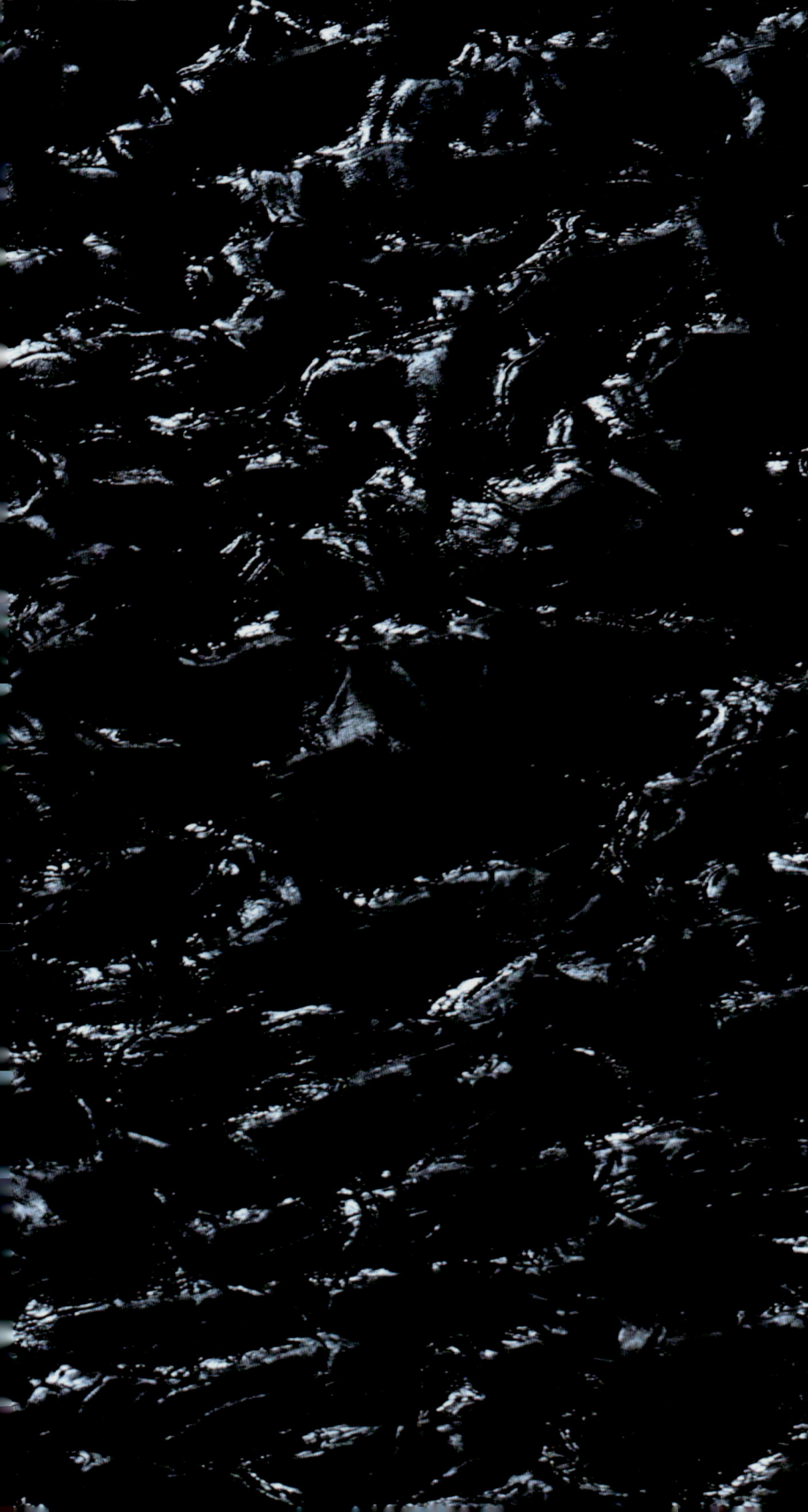

The Brazos

Below the Possum Kingdom Dam,
this stretch, like a housewife
toward a happy anniversary, hurries
certainly, knowing how steadily,
far but sure like an ocean
gussied up with palms and mangroves,
Anhingas patient on cypress knees,
Phalaropes anxious for circles,
in circles, fate waits.

She has encircled me
with her bare arms, and her eyes
don't worry like a canoe
tied to a river island. Her eyes
are wet and quick like a swallow
skimming the river with a little splash.

In shadow the wind on water
over white rocks moves light to delight,
and just downstream high-tension wires
hold above the scene. They travel
to a hospital and to houses,
one house where a woman,
irons a shirtsleeve smooth
as the arms of God.

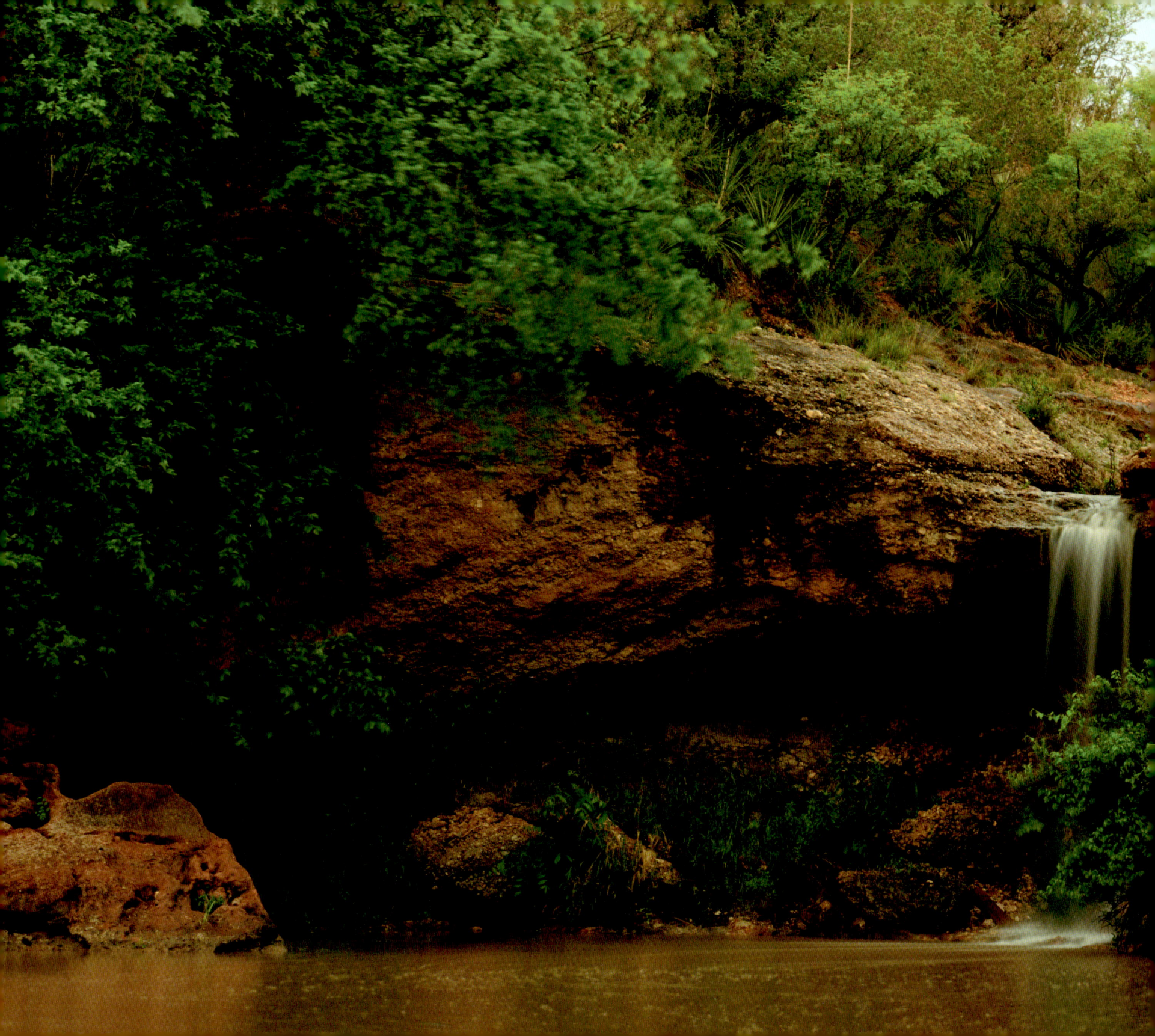

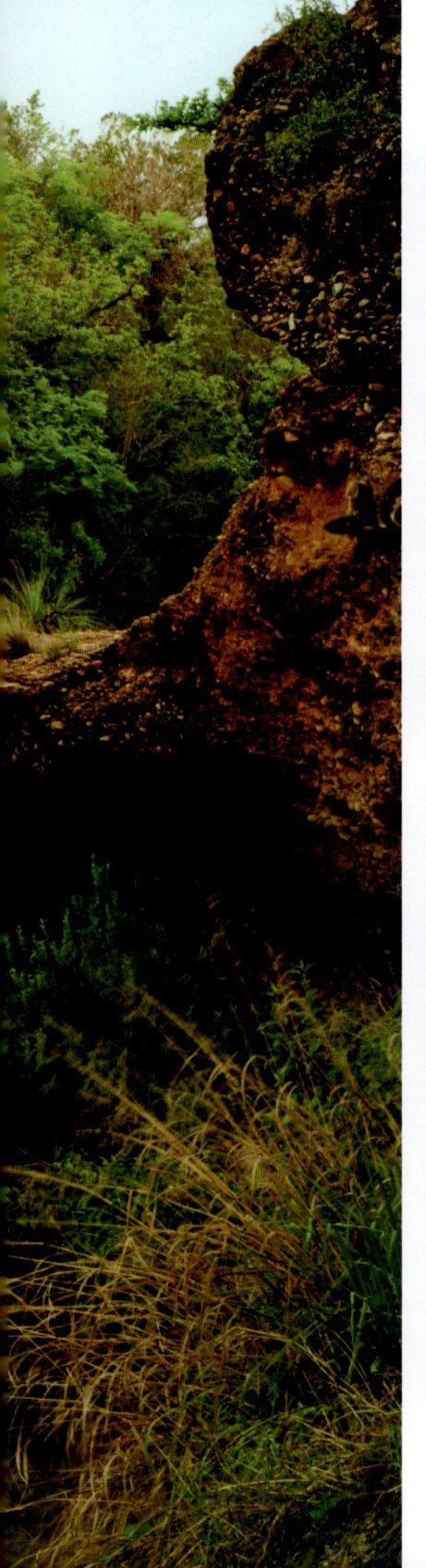

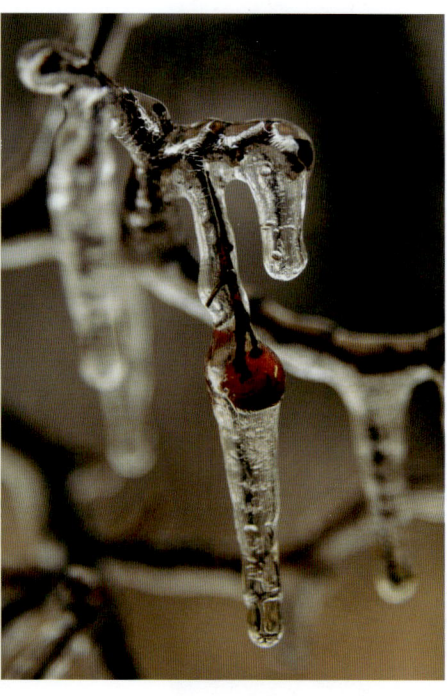

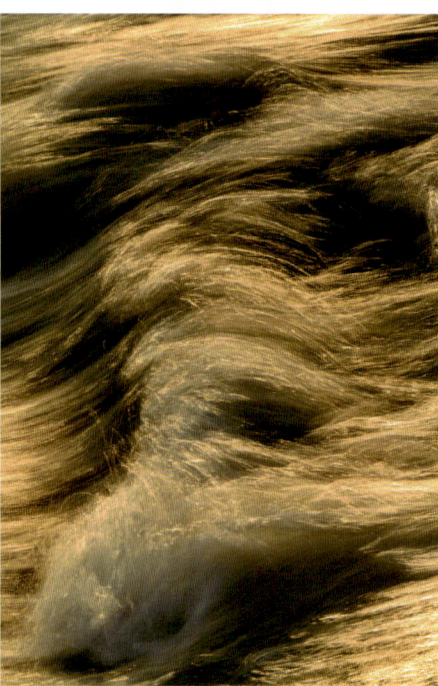

Sonnet on Time

You recognize what weight the river carries,
imagining your body swims to learn
the current. Then, but what below would bury
your errors, even troubles? What lusts burn
and might be baptized, raised surprised to the height
of love, floating? Earth the rivers shoulder
is imperceptibly removed like night
believing in its wisdom, as grows older
each star awakening to know its wrecked
and fixed position in a myth. Higher,
we ask how time exists beyond effect:
marrow in bone, electrons on a wire.
The river rises to meet the falling rain.
Whose strokes make Time sway on its gold watch chain?

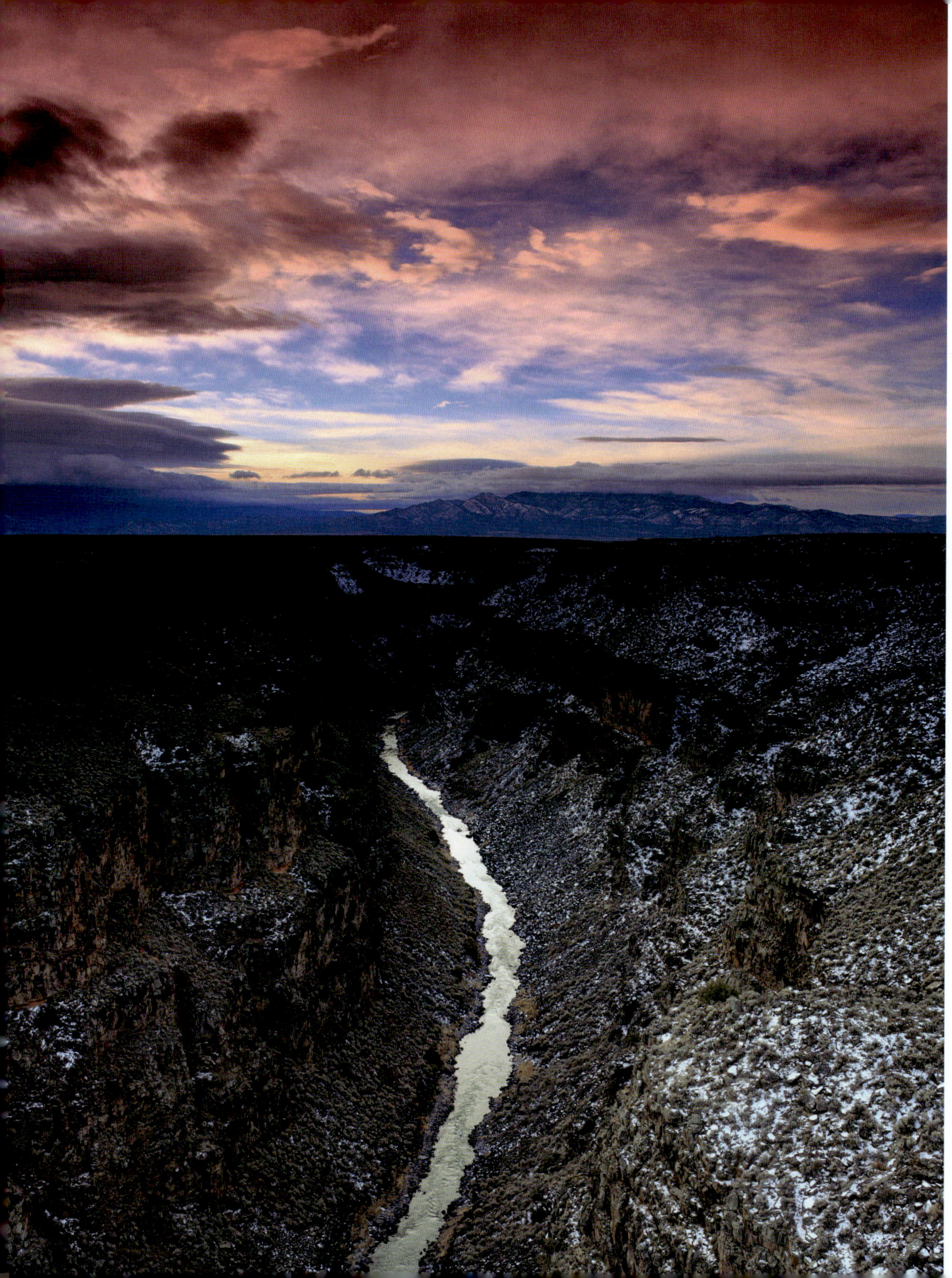

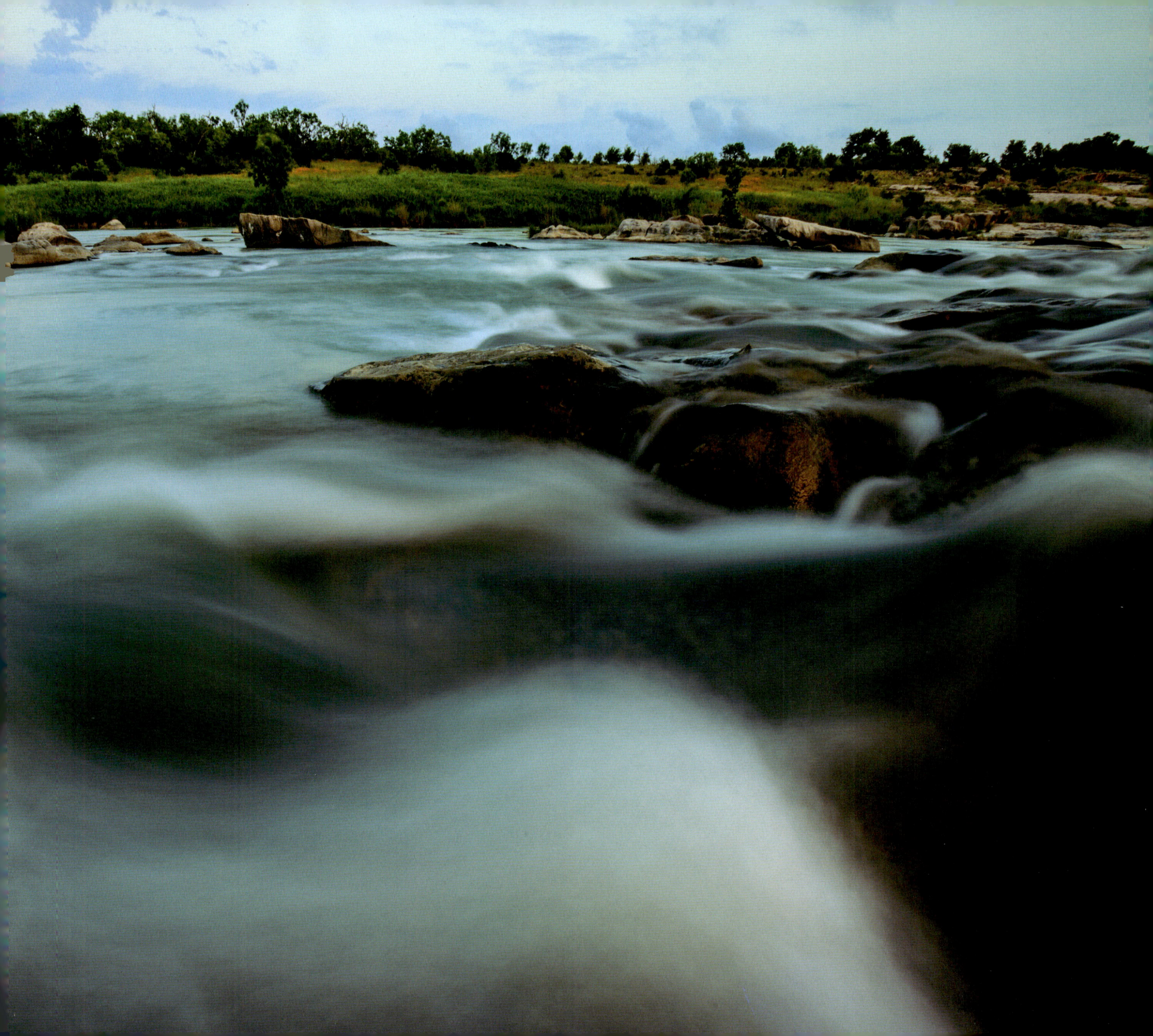

Entre Dos Aguas

Among the perfection of the Biblical seven
and Dante's nine, you lie there in the sheets,
the lithest sepia late-eighteenth century eight
in the Archive of the Indies, the hand curved
on laid cotton in some fertile praise of the Mississippi
from one honorable servant of the governor.
You govern color, the fuschia bougainvillea,
the pink, the orange of dying fire all hung over
my Sevilla morning walk like new dresses teasing
the ravishing girls to give up their studies and run.

Your figure is classic as the study of a pedestal,
as the anchor rung into song by its own chain,
brown skeins of seaweed waiting in the wind
like the hair of the saddest waitress in Andalucía,
drowsy among the shadows of the orange trees
in the shadow of the abandoned castle
in the shadow of the cathedral and her tower,
tipping her cigarette into siesta's oblivion.
Her infinite motto: *No me ha dejado.*

Your hair is the color of the buff rust swallows'
bellies banking above after four days of rain
filling the air and lit from below by the sun
setting on a gentle water, that color, chattering
and scissoring the light into confettied money, banking.

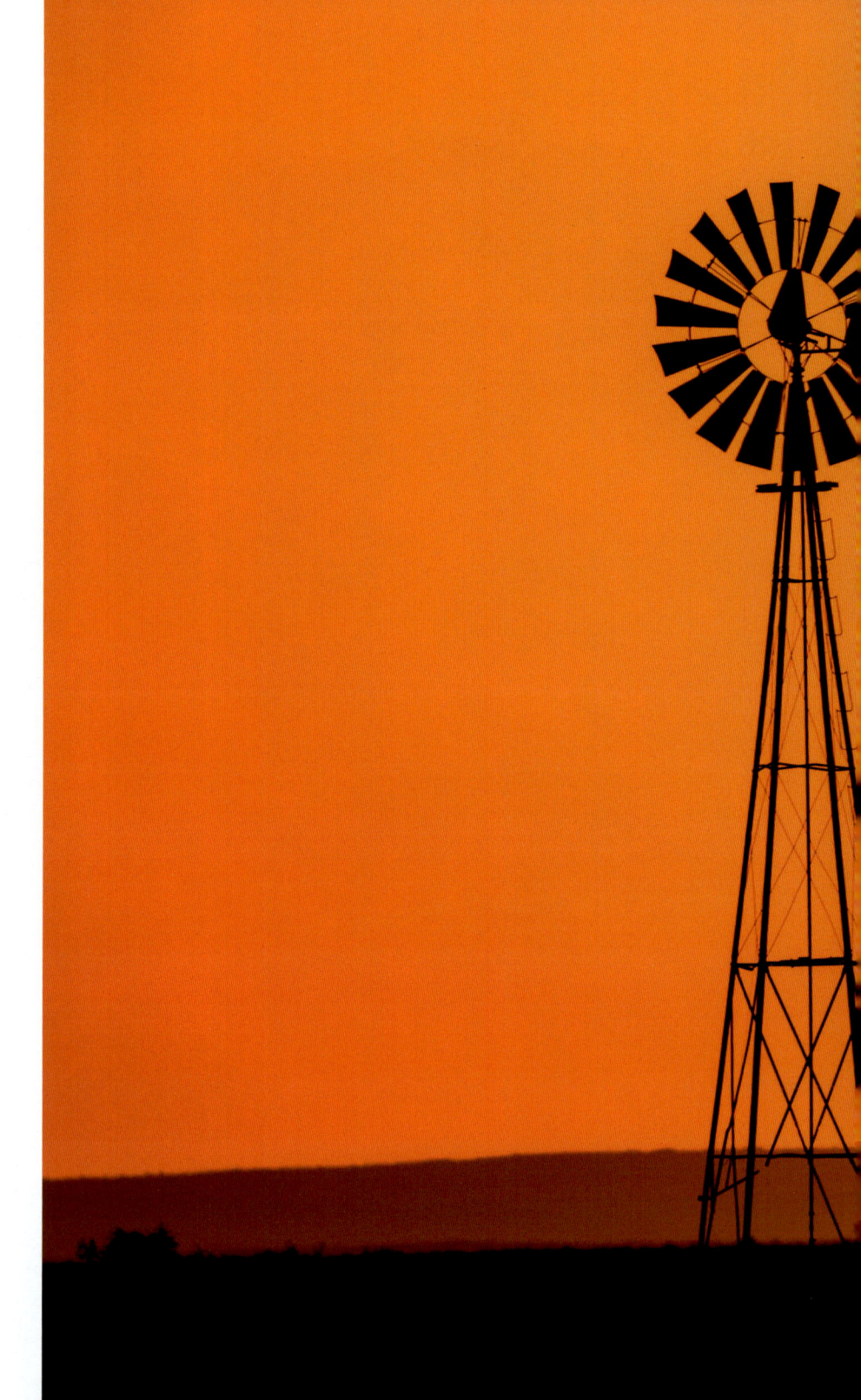

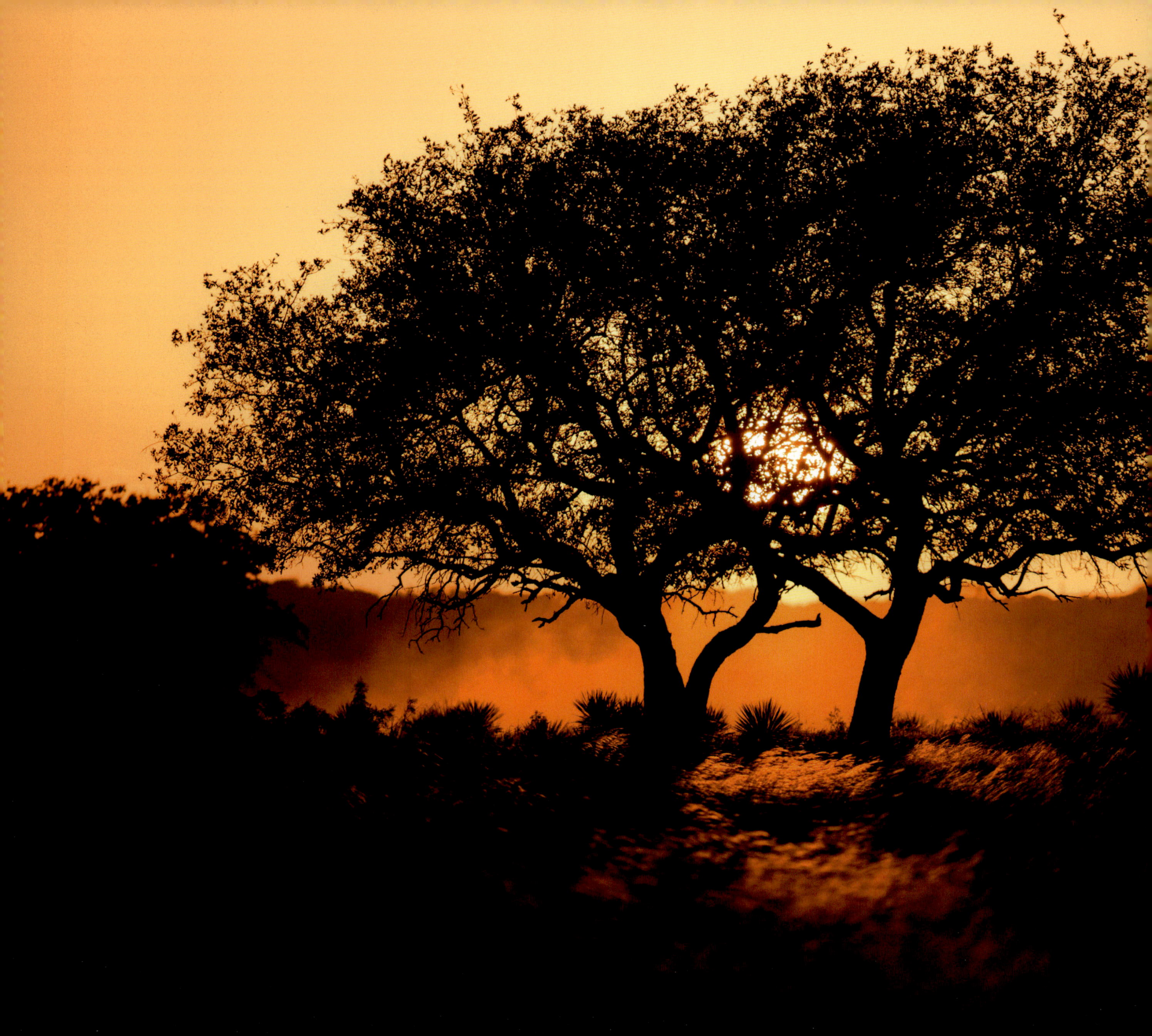

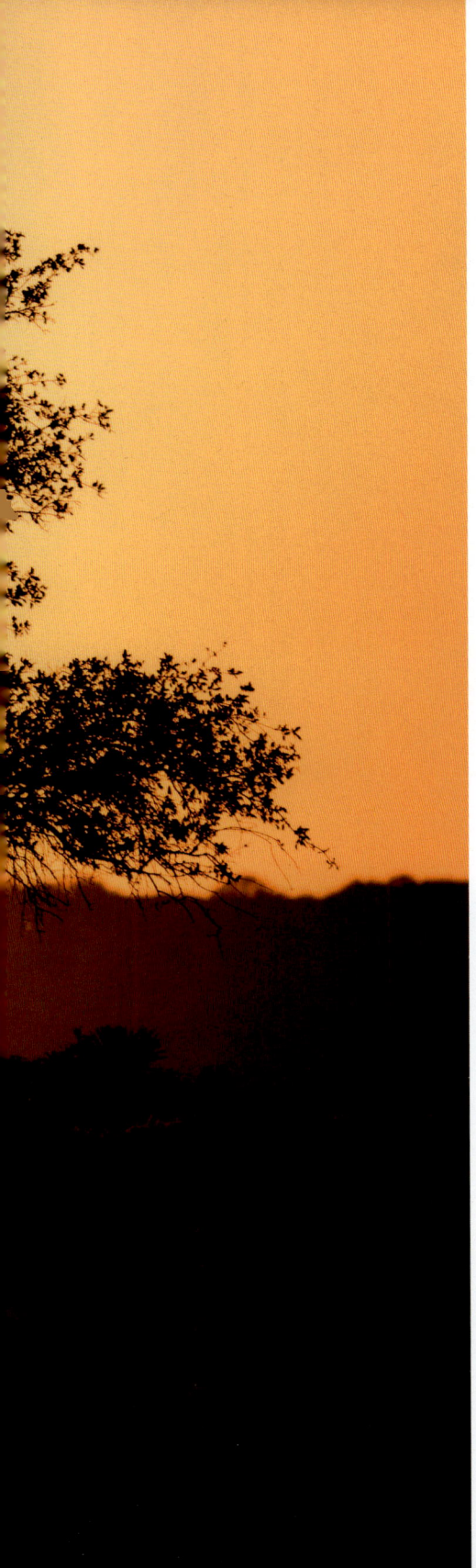

If you are the book I imagine photographers read
to understand the shadow and whet the line,
I am less than a chunk of broken concrete, and you
with all our married years of river waves lapping
might still like a pretty green pebble in me. You free
also the wind inside the water, the aching pulse
that moves the crest, how a song lifts forward
words, waking, making an imaginary wave
pulse like a true fiction's friction and the verse
of that invisible river between the ocean and the sea.

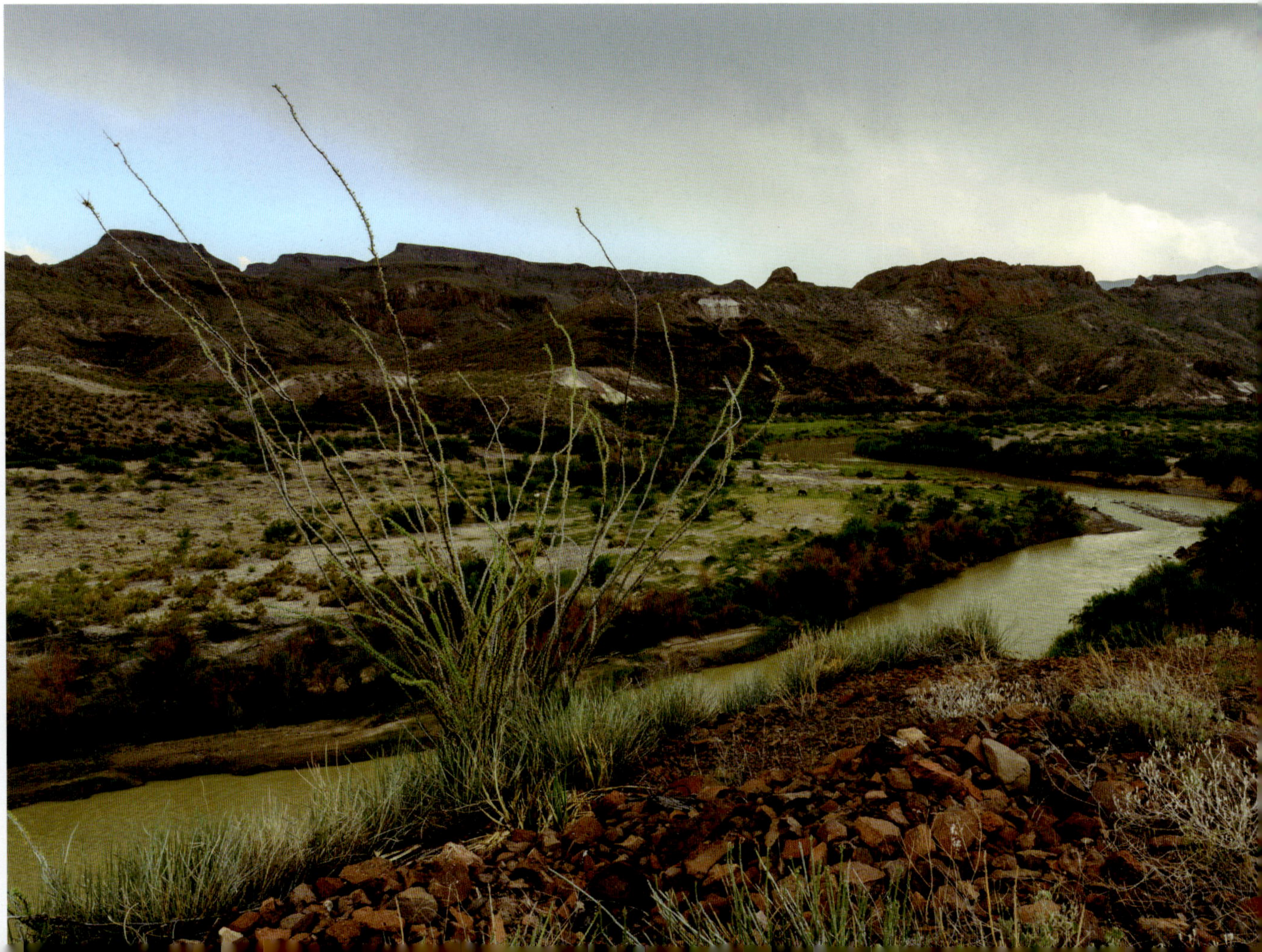

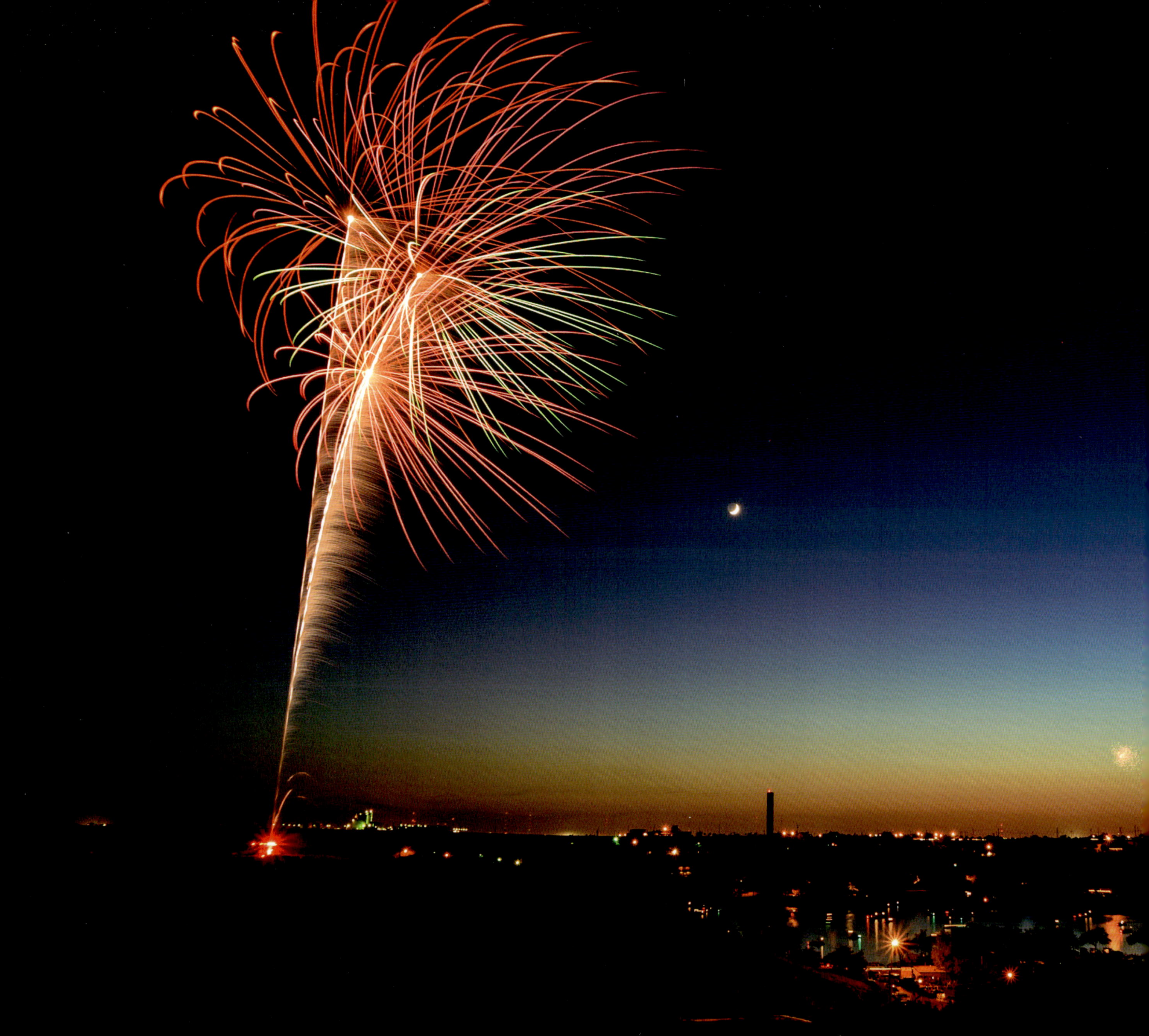

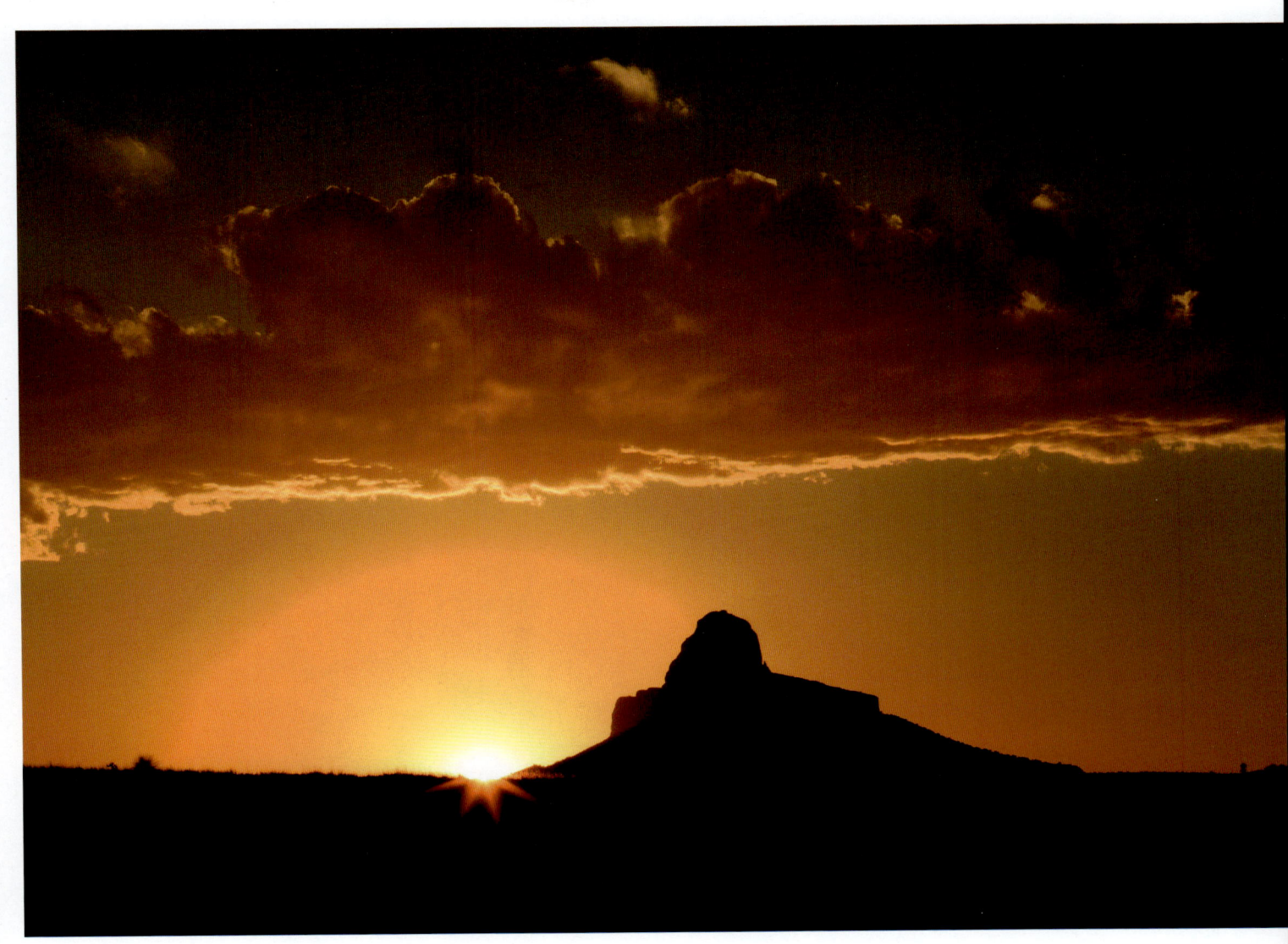

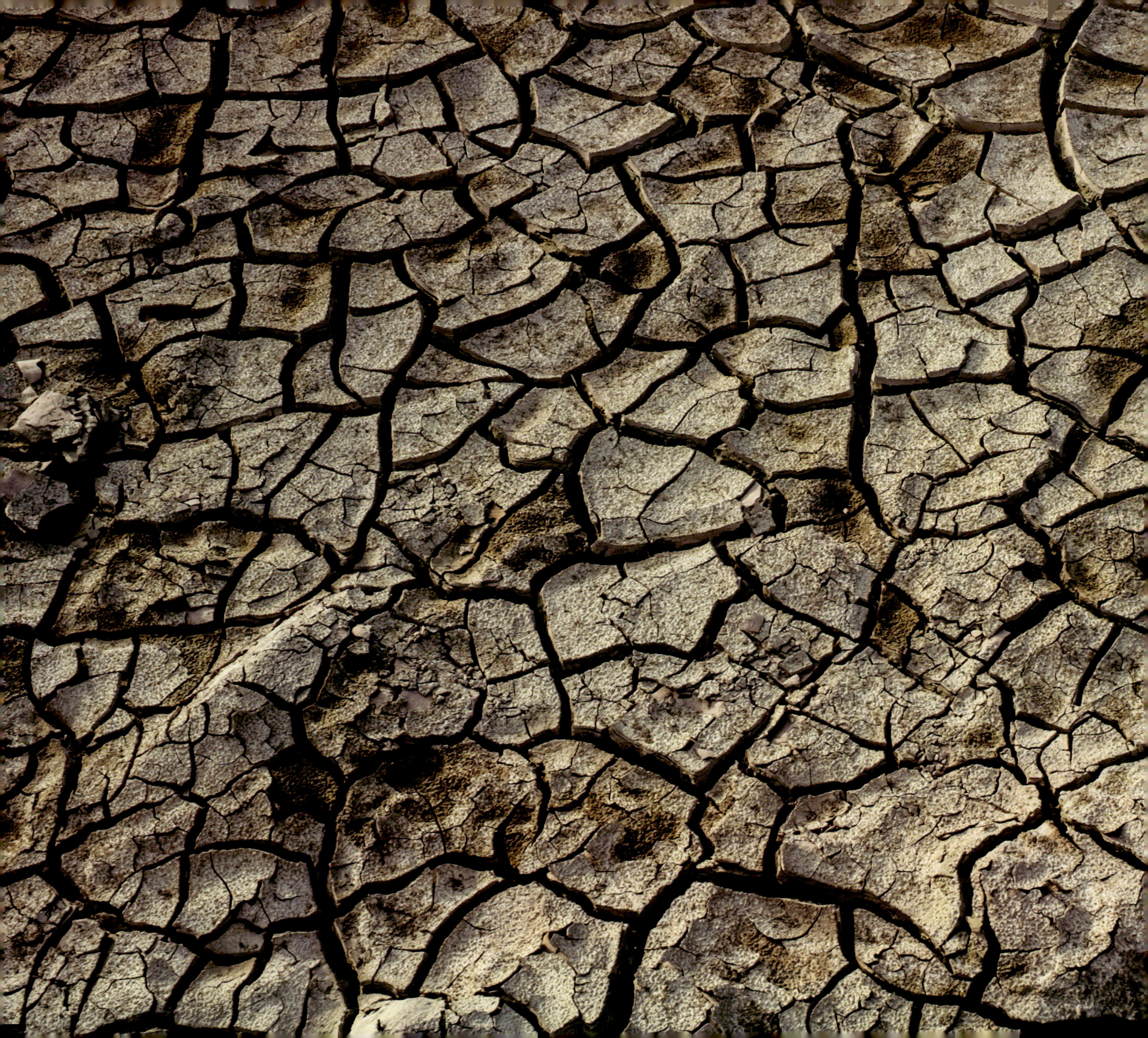

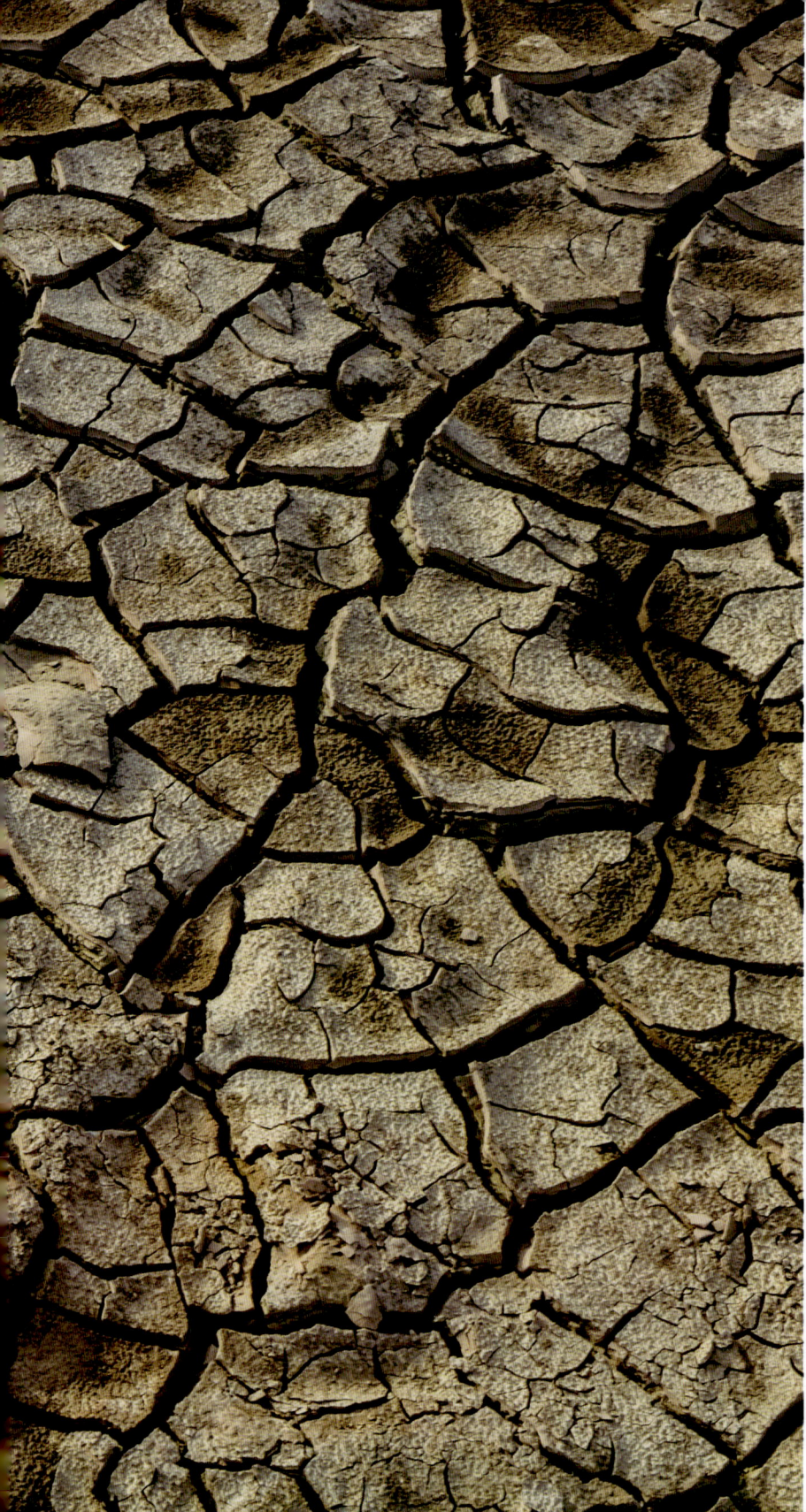

The Wash

Lie down with me in this dry riverbed.
Imagine water spanned these banks instead.

The Moon

On a calm river, only a temporary
architect of water, old, exiled
from some cold nation, in
white-gown, gothic, she
draws with her knife
the slowest sparks
of herself toward
an imagined fire,
hardly believing
in failure, failing.
Apt tomb haunted
by wasps, last year's
wasp nest, this old skull
of an owl is a bleak future,
delicate, a mere meaningless-
ness of last month's newspapers.

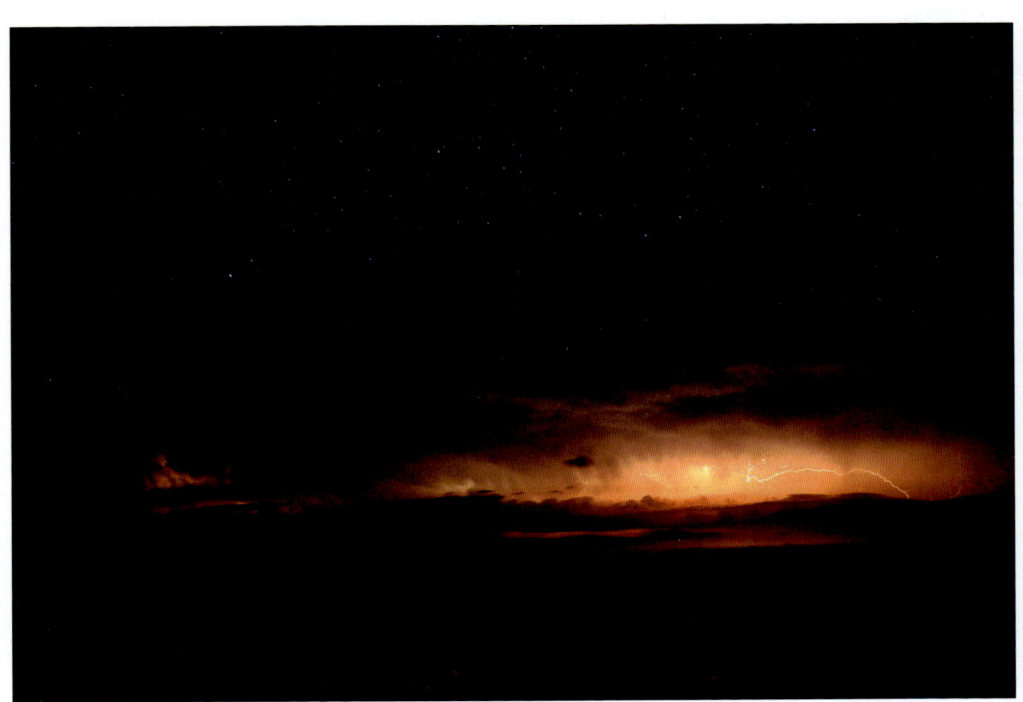

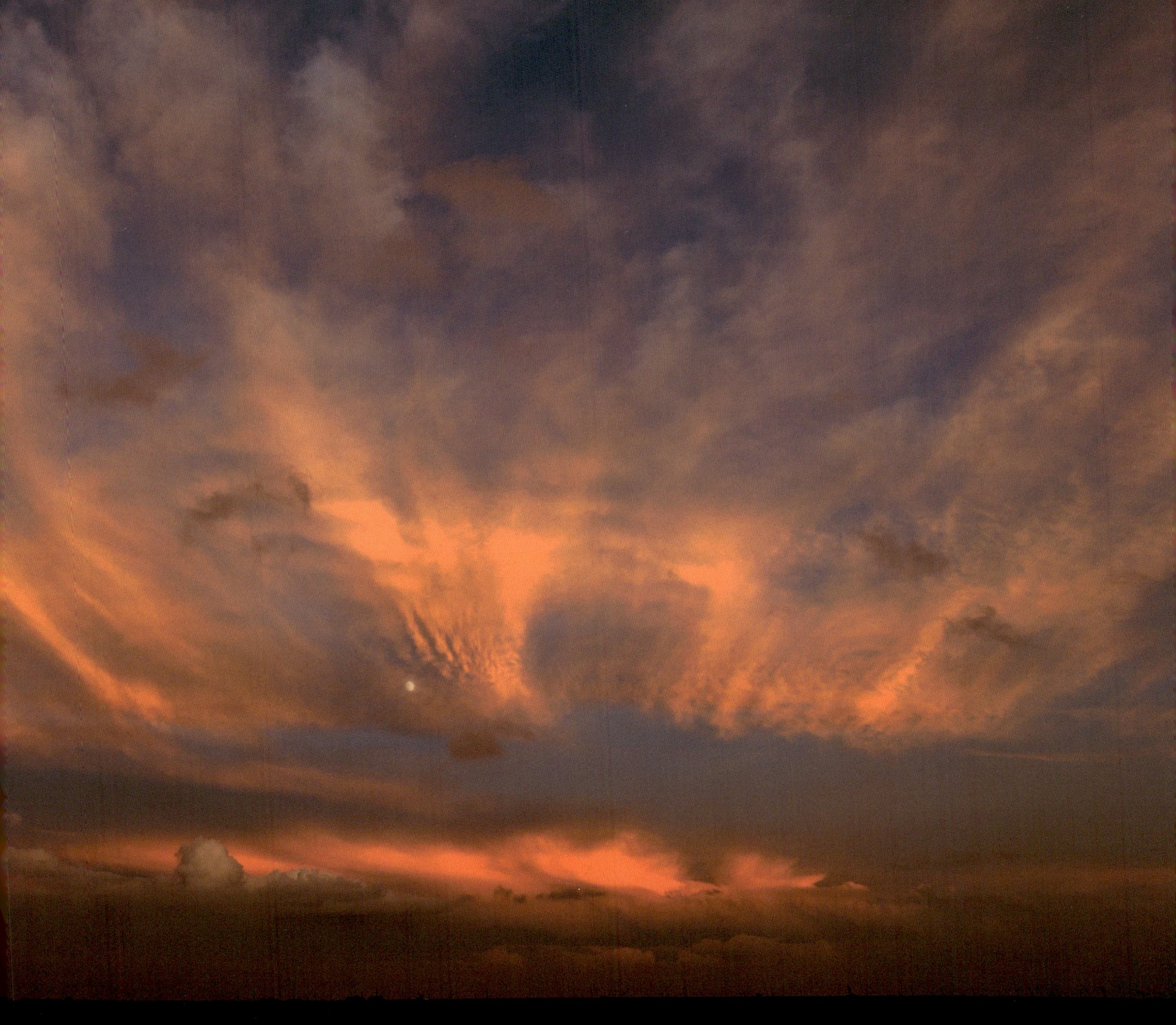

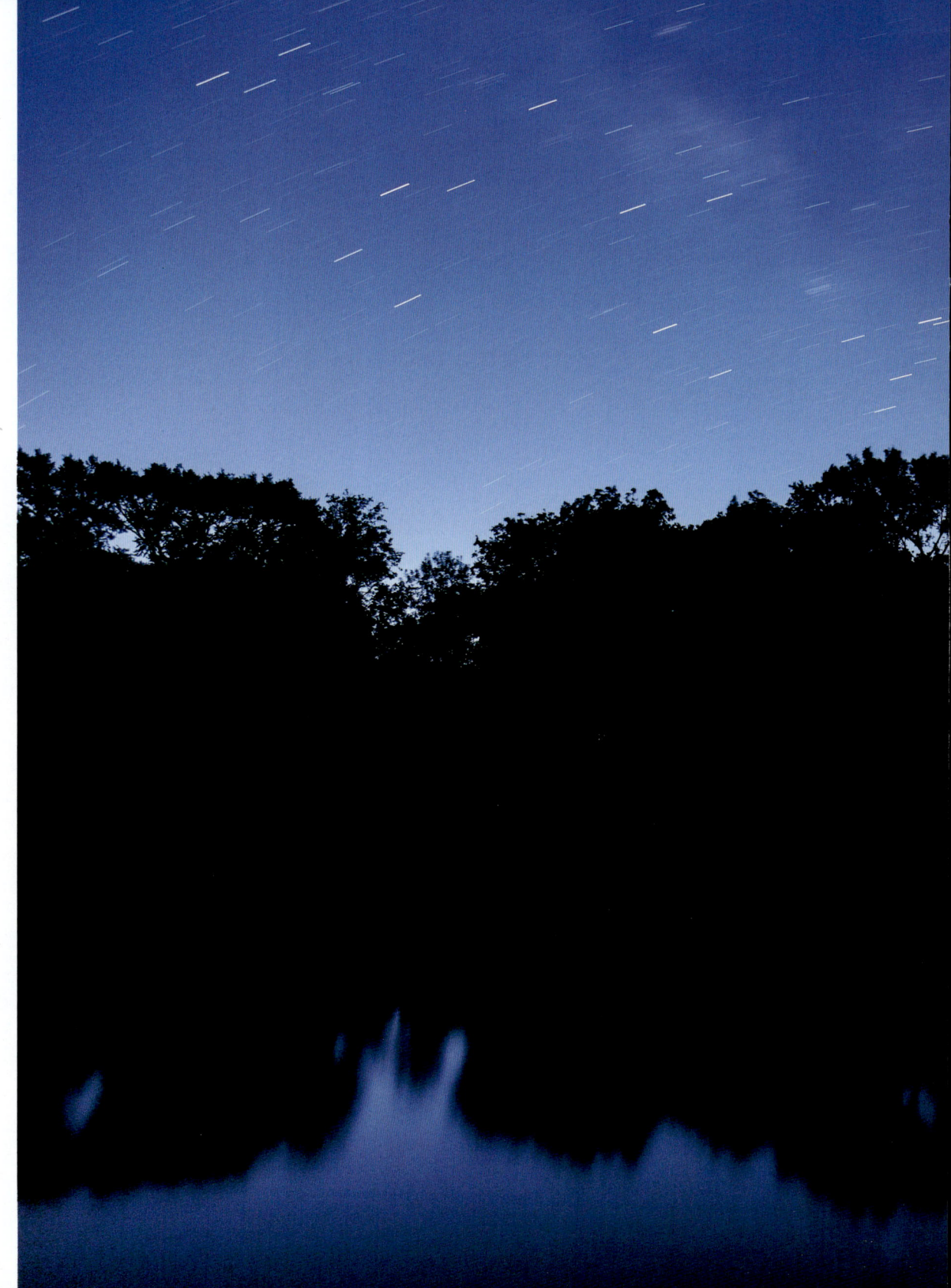

The Vapor on Rivers

Tonight, why don't you unfold a chair
beside the deep river and let your hair
down to change the country air?

We can sit and whisper loss. Strip
off your clothes, wade in, don't trip.
Faux-dramatically, maybe I'll rip

mine off, too, and swim to you, grate-
ful for your wilderness, your first-rate
love of simple things. In Eden, we ate

the fruit, regretted much. Torn apart,
we know how wounds heal. Part
of God, we swim against the river, art

of the voyage thought of. Still
we drift uncondemned, till
death do us divide, healthy, ill,

clothed, naked, and who will scold
us here fighting the heat with cold
and moving water until we're old?

No one wants to swim or die alone.
I want you swimming out here, a lone
soul, and I will be, as well, one.

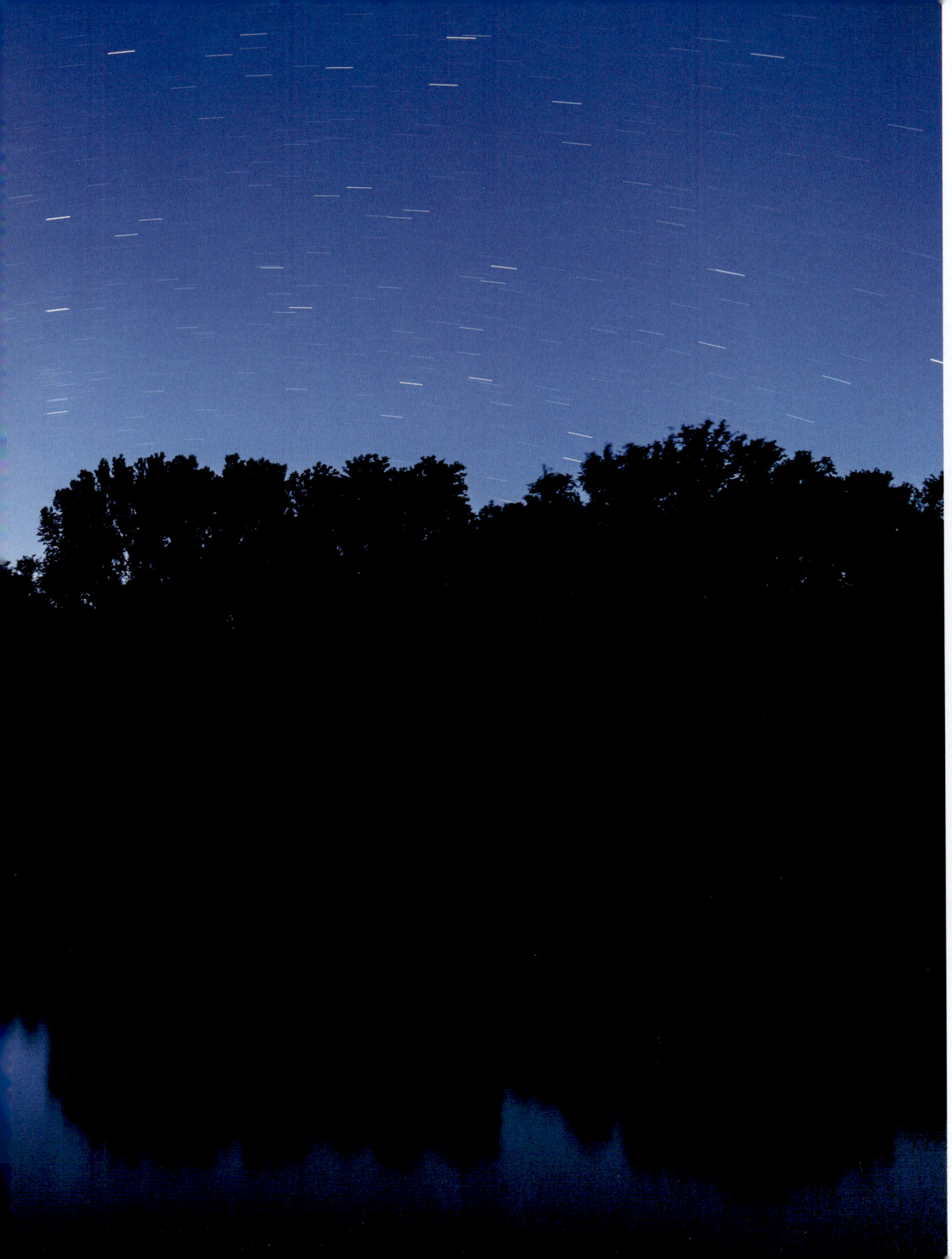

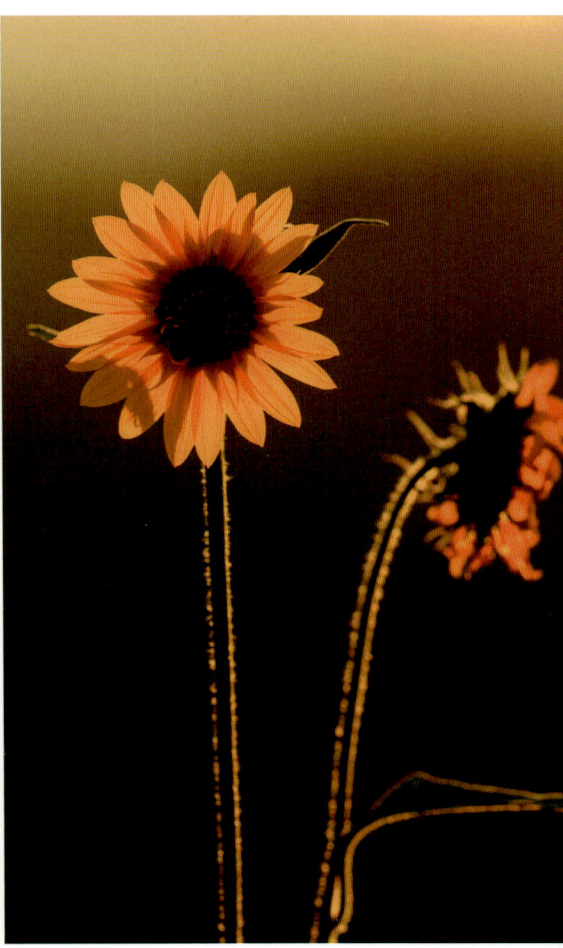

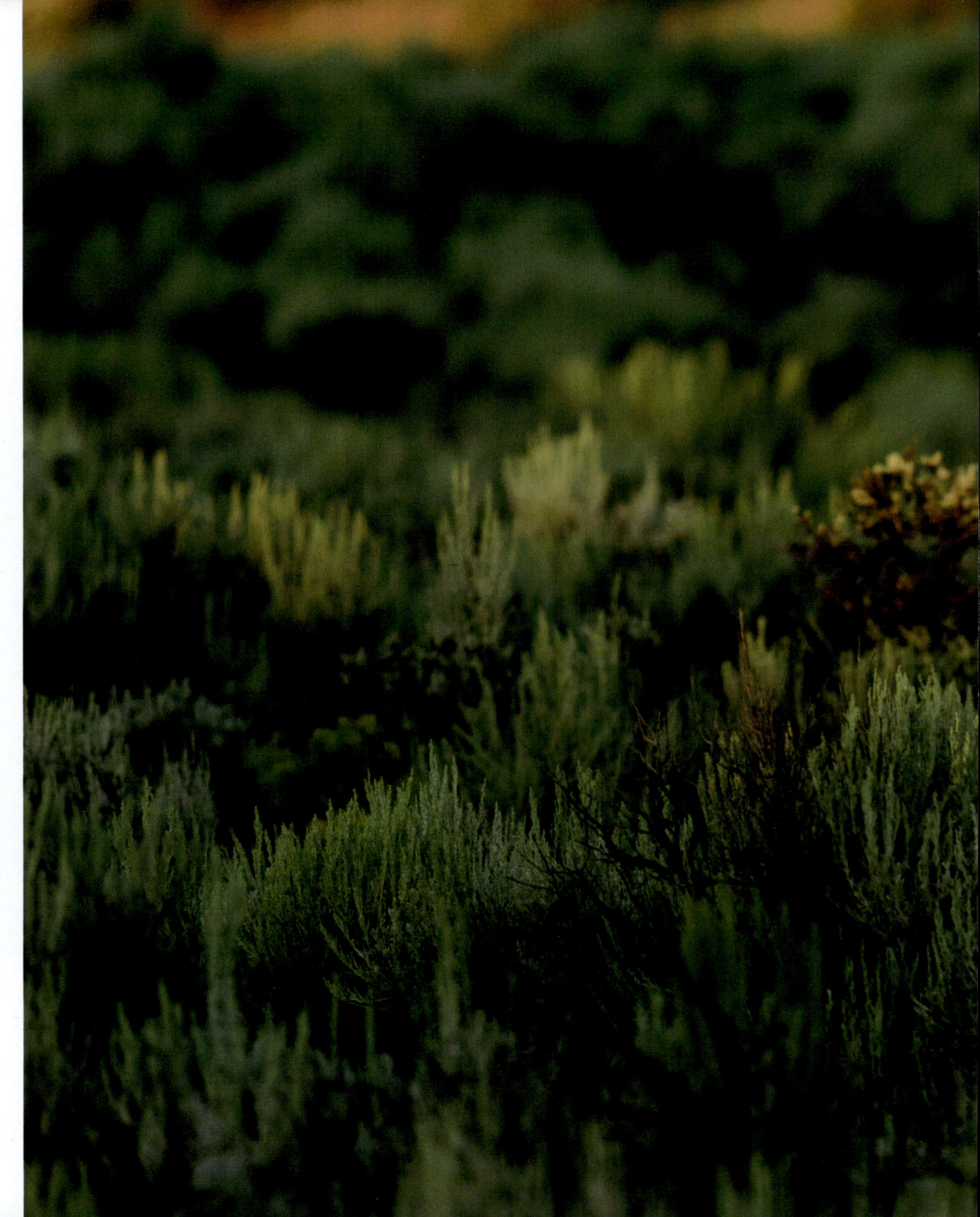

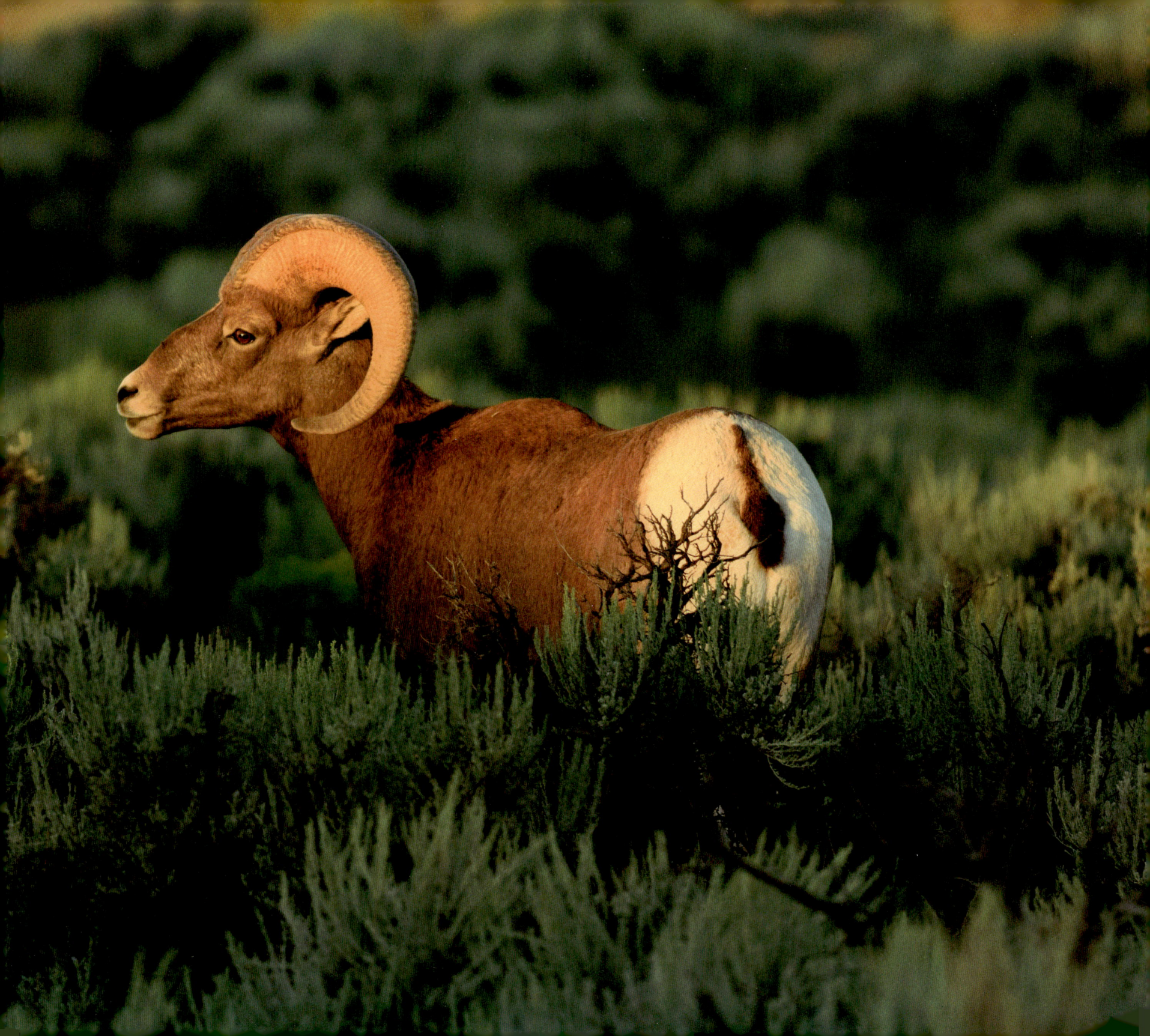

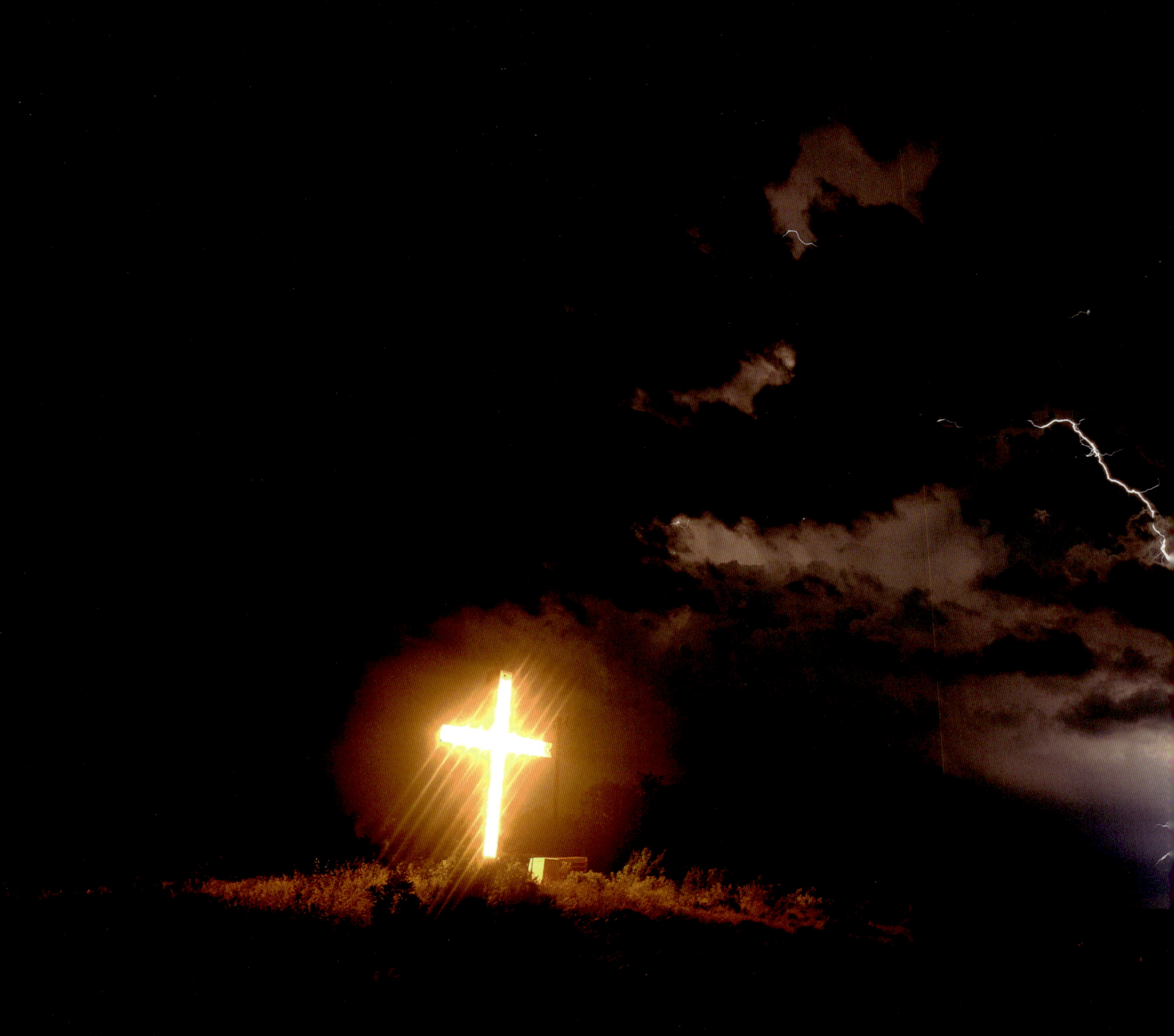

For the Christian Angler

If God is angler, Christ the fly, and we
the trout that He by gentle cast befriend,
then how to justify this thorny gift?

Mere hunger seems to ravage liberty.
Over the sins of falling Time, His mend
across the current, boulders, and wind will lift

our eyes to a beautiful illusion, achieve
in us the faith we choose our heaven's end.
We rise to an immaculate dead drift.

Catch and release me. Make, if I believe,
short shrift.

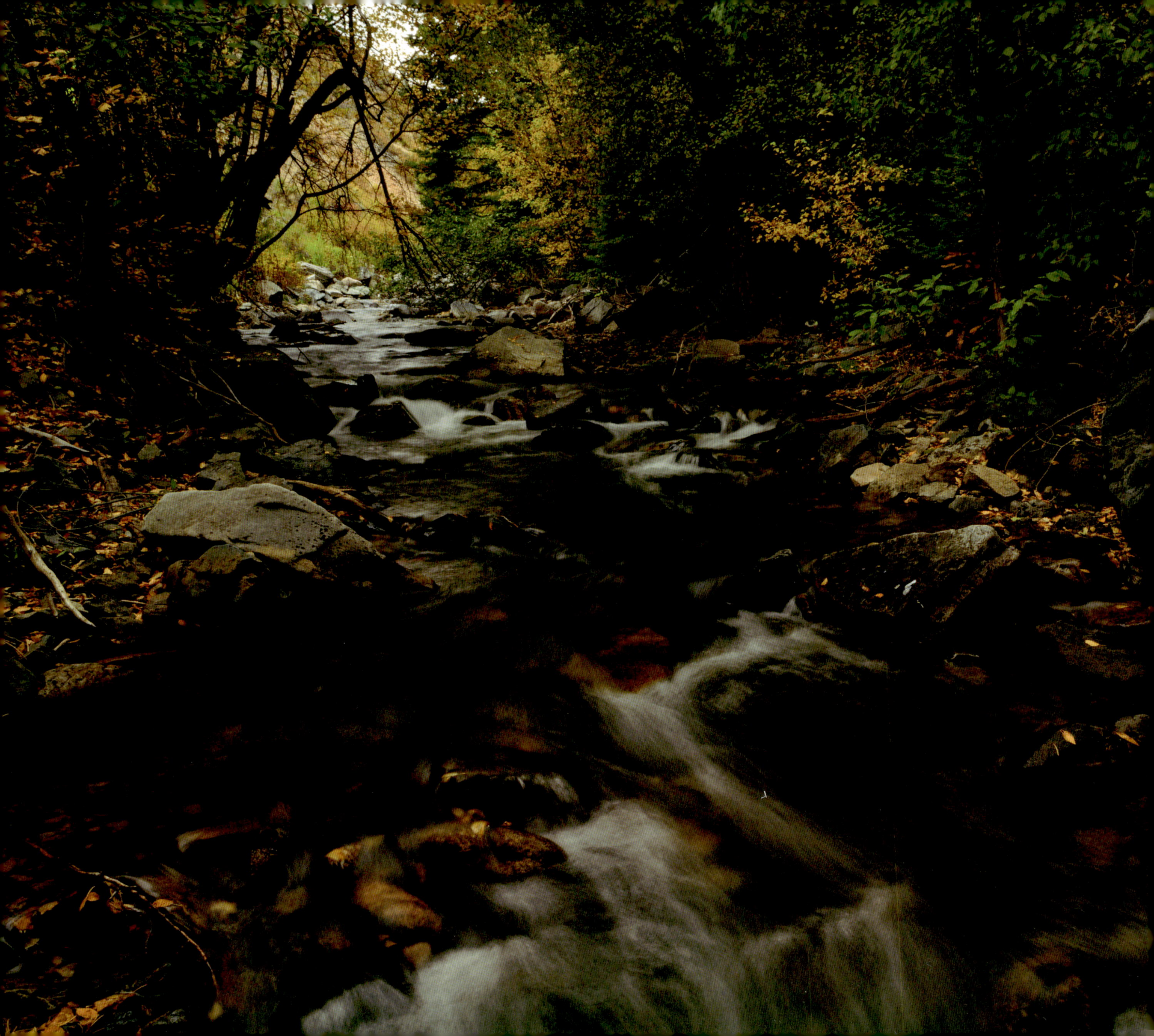

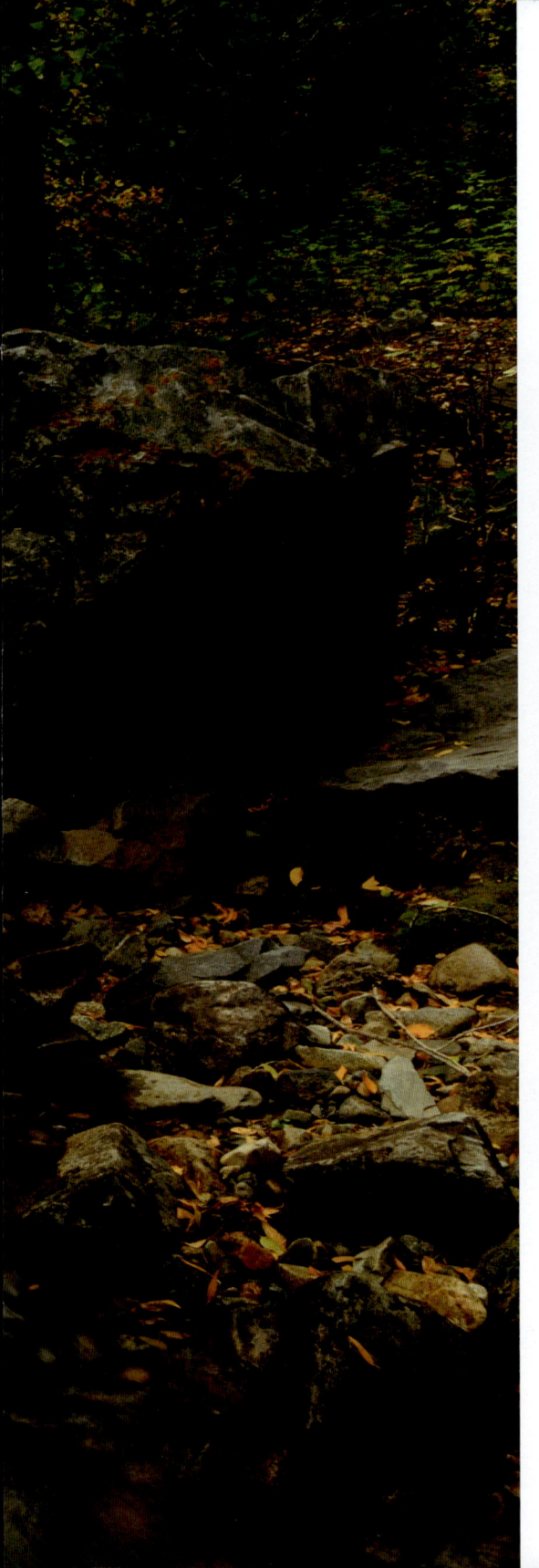

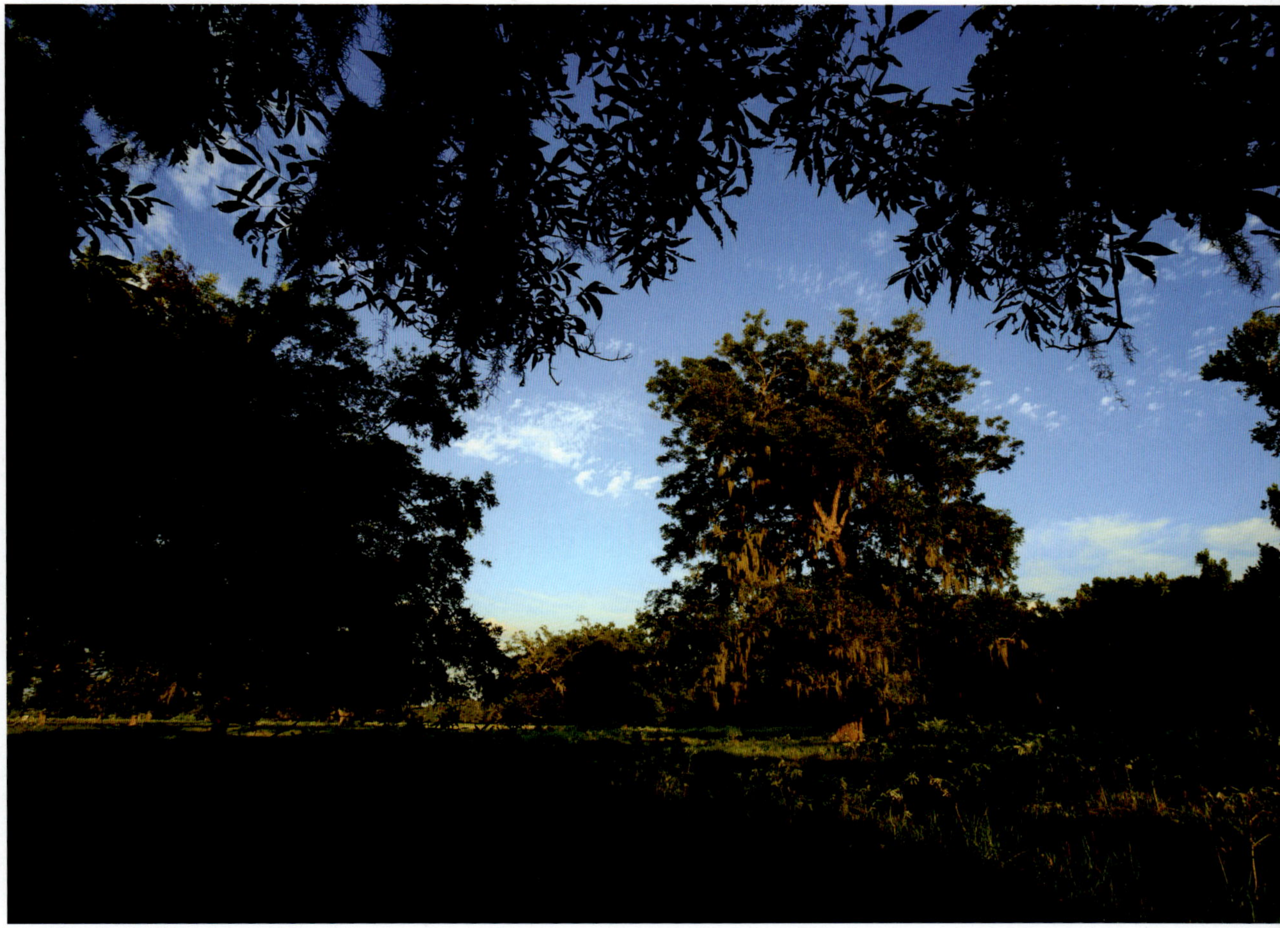

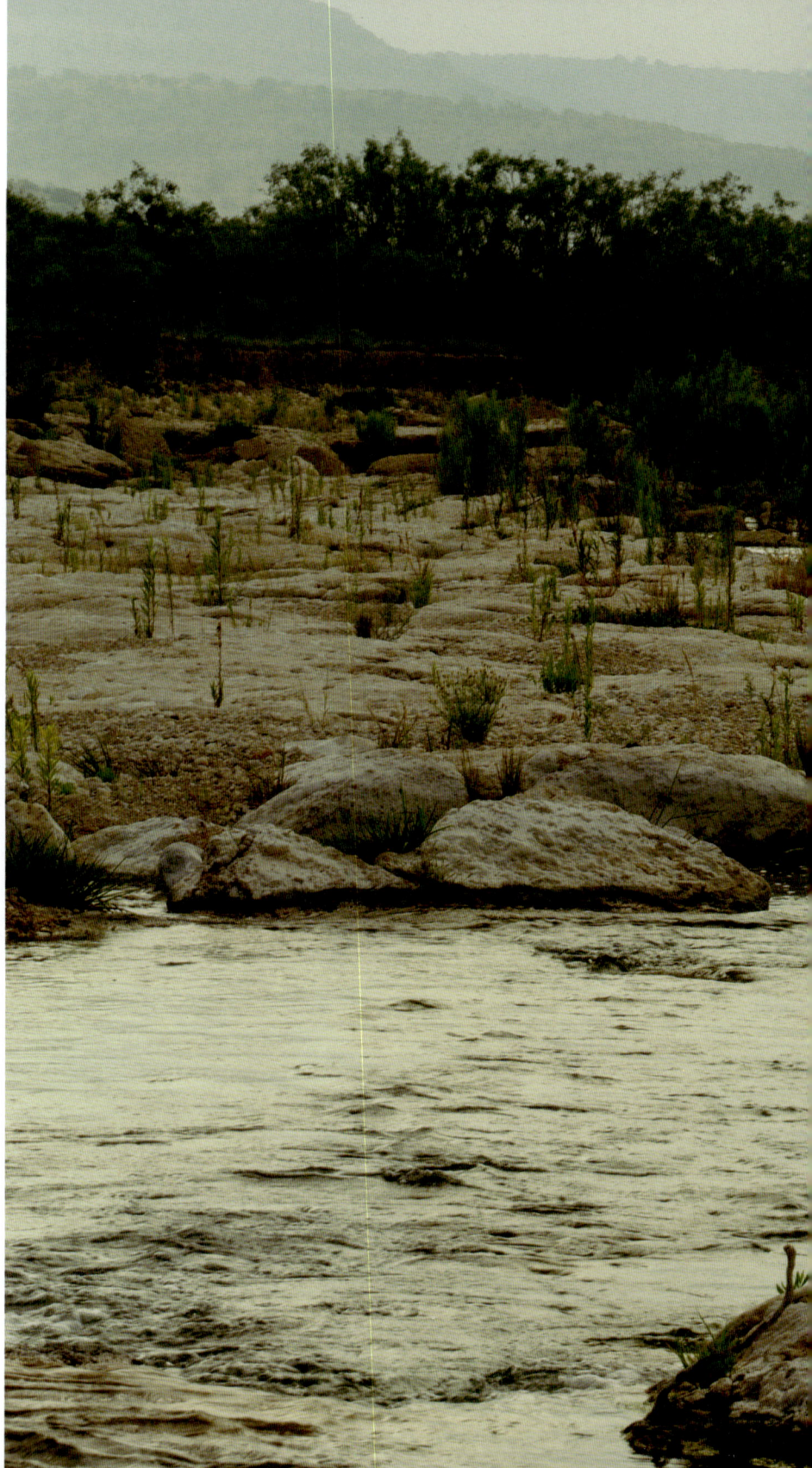

River

The river past, and God forgotten.
George Herbert

I.

If you like, like the ample morning
behind blinds, or no. Outside, laugh at
these woodpeckers flying from cottonwood
to elm and back, their breasts shining pink
as erasers, wings graphite, making
whole their fates in the given morning.
Only a month ago, the cottonwood cotton
filled the ditches and every doorway,
a summer blindness now swept away.
In time, how order does seem to lower
on the world and clarify like a river.

II.

Dull and unrewarding as a halo shadow,
thick as old ship rope, a sacral pain
screws in, taking its good Time. What
broken thing of a broken thing unworks
you older, reduces the mind to argument?
Repetition tedious as a simile of a simile,
you could almost laugh at the monotony,
that sunrise rising in fog. It could be
in your head, a ground clutter nothing.
Gone, the sensuality of numbers, the stars.
Not one to refuse a star, last night

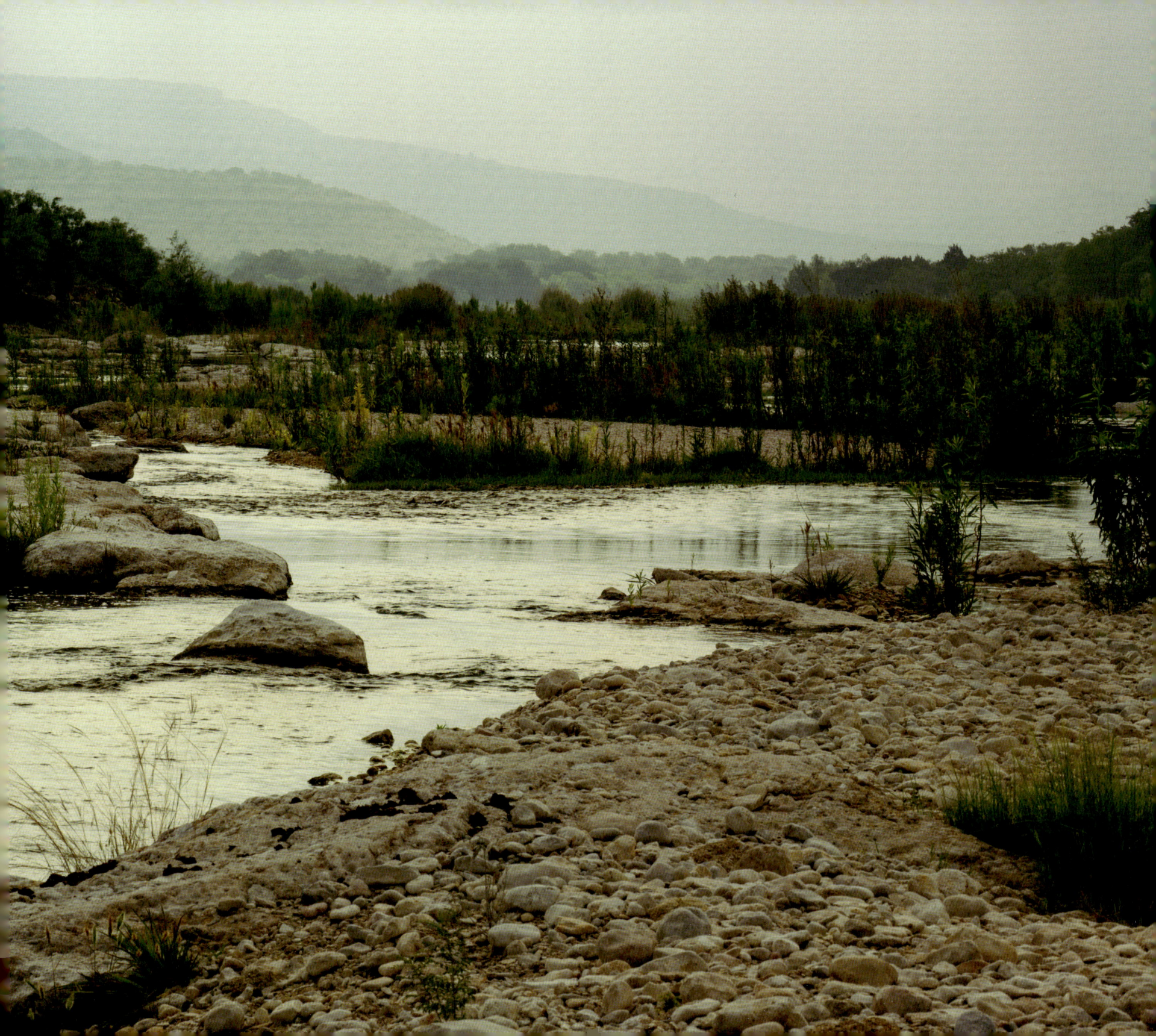

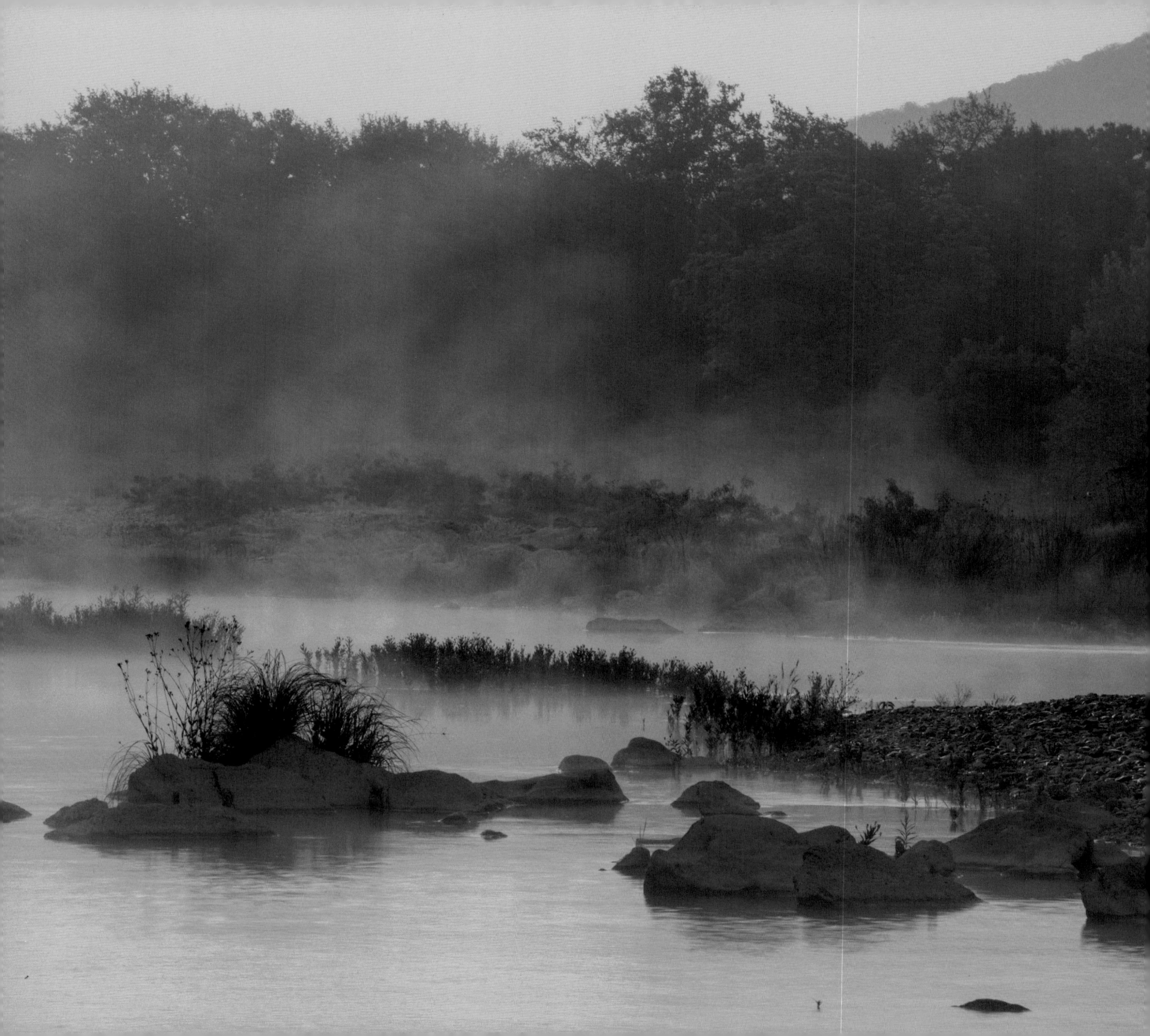

you refused stars when your eyes
glazed over like beach-glass sugar-coat.
If to suffer could truly polish the soul…
but this mist, this blind indoors, the haze
of a morning for an afternoon of storms,
but storms refusing here and moving east
to water another. Go ahead with your petition,
but can you make it steady as a saxophone
to a piano in a dimly lit blue 2 a.m.?
Each distraction holds thick as an iron bike
lock rattling rack and frame.

I know your name.
I have trusted you with this pain.
Quantify it with a whole number.
A number, a word, a line, a sympathy:
your talk would be a prayer if you could find
one grain to do your pain diary justice.
In a drawer, buried in the dark of the wax,
there is a wick. I know how you refuse stars
for a weak sleep in good cotton. By morning,
husband to a column, full of arrows, beyond flight,
patient with affliction, come, ecstasy.

III.

Afternoon, an anvil cloud mounts
only to be sheared off by a country wind,
subtle as an oven rack.
The missing feathers of an old crow
fly over with the crow. Shotguns
of yesterday forgotten but for the nothing.
Mean afternoons deep in the arroyo,

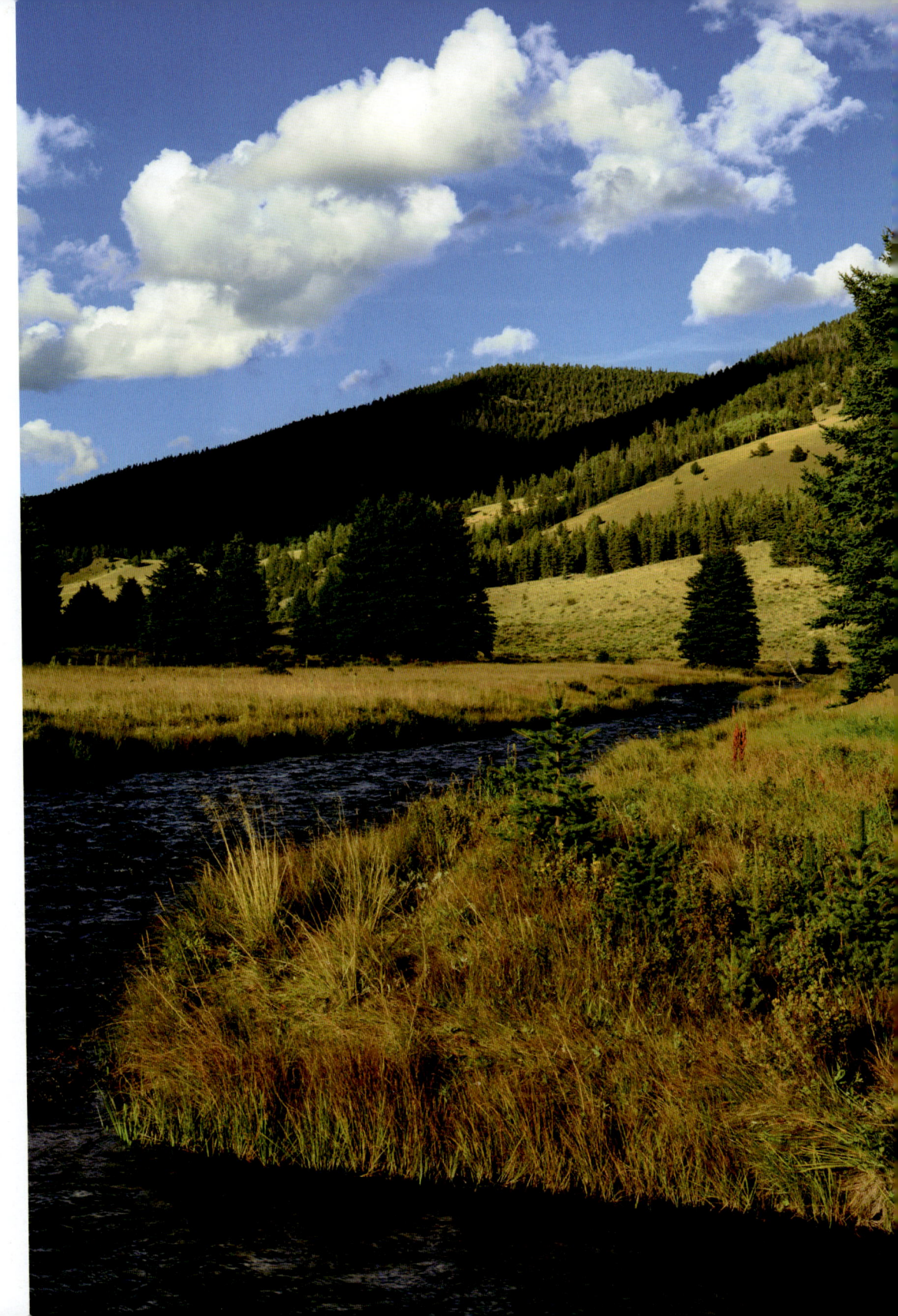

to cover distance might be enough.
Meaning, to witness the river in the river.
Birds whisper in the cedars till they don't.
The river is all God and love
writing its long name. The wind
picks up, and you forget the pain of will,
the exhaust and repetition. Weight forward,
you taper yourself to the point of a hook,
a lovely *lonely* in a handsome hand.

IV.

The last week, the one
that comes after seven others slip by
like a lowering, un-clouding river
revealing its small boulders,
the less-than-a-week week,
clouds, but no rain,
maybe a late-night rain
that swallows the stars and spits
them out like teeth shining and dull,
the hurt week, the one of sun
you swear to make the most of,
to eat a toasted marshmallow,
to wind sage sticks with red thread,
to find a potsherd or an ancient point
you might identify as your law of life,
the days flashing like car windows
passing, but nothing fits into both
your hand and eye, nothing holds except
the shadow's gravity and a bright blue,

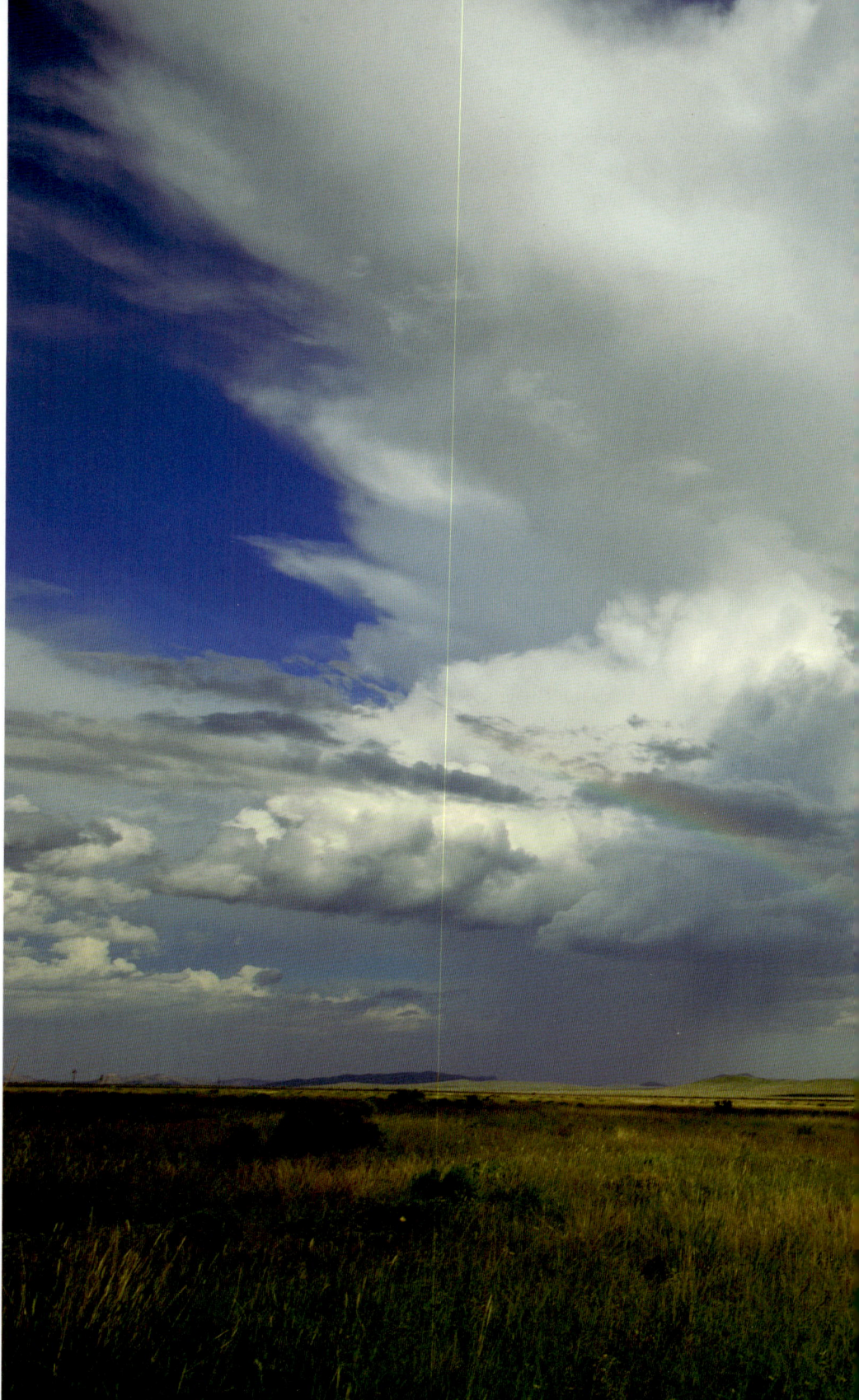

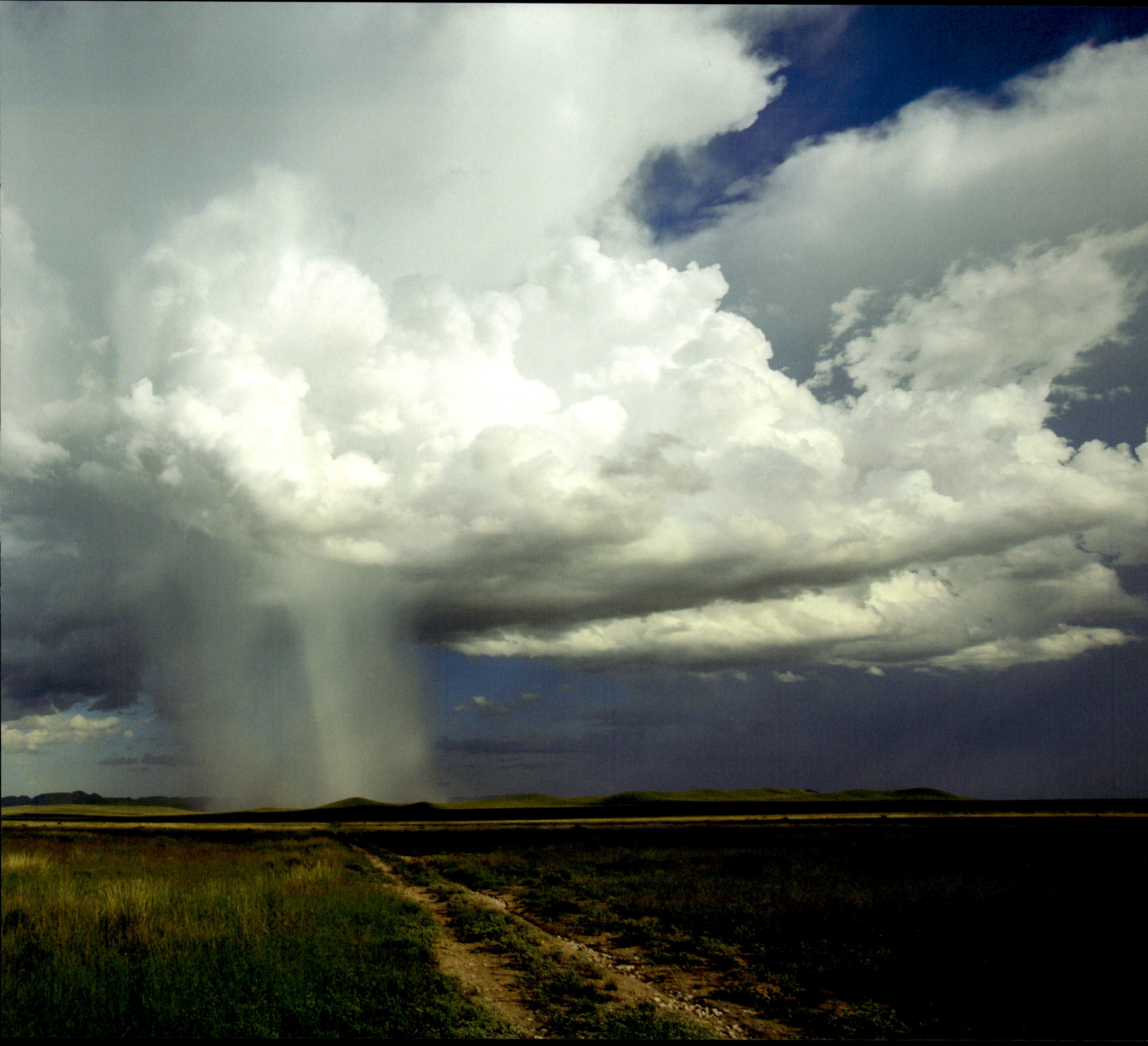

the arrival of others who take your place
in the river, in the week a heap
of casting into wind your petitions,
fragmented, knotted, unanswered,
knots, failure to pray, lost journey,
look at her.

V.

God knows the law of life is death
and you can feel it in your warbler neck,
your river-quick high-stick wrist
at the end of day. But the trophies:
a goldfinch tearing up a pink thistle,
a magpie dipping her wingtips
in a white cloud, an ouzel barreling
hip-high upstream with a warning.
You wish you had a river. To make
a river, it takes some mountains.
Some rain to watershed. You wish
you had a steady meadow and pink thistles
bobbing at the border for your horizons,
pale robins bouncing their good postures
in the spruce shadows. Instead, the law
of life comes for you like three men
and a car. In your dreams, you win them over
with your dreams: a goldfinch tearing up
a pink thistle, a magpie so slow
she knows how to keep death at bay.
She takes her time with argument
and hides her royal blue in black.
Shy as a blue grouse, nevertheless God
doesn't forget his green mountains.
You wish you had a river.

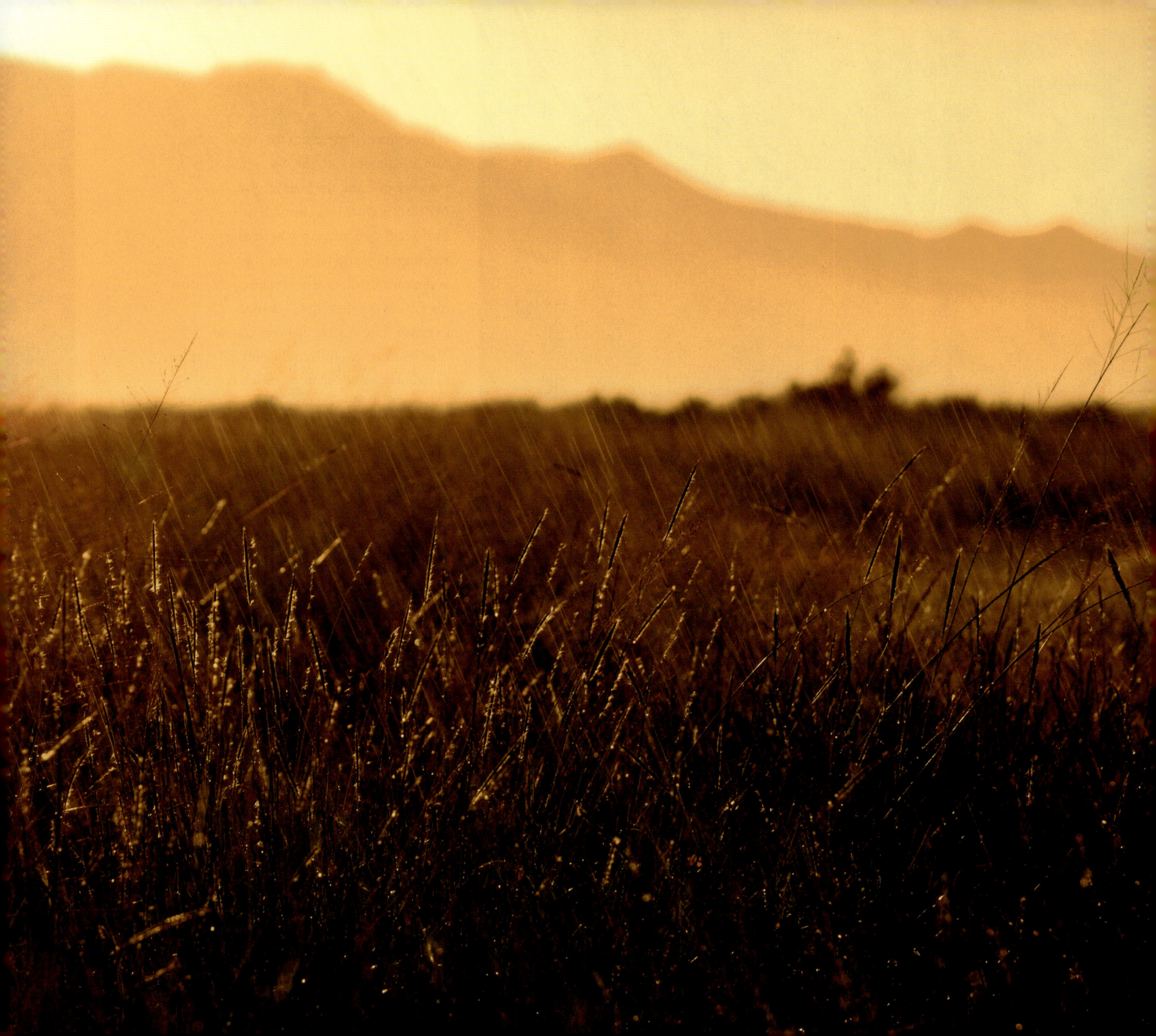

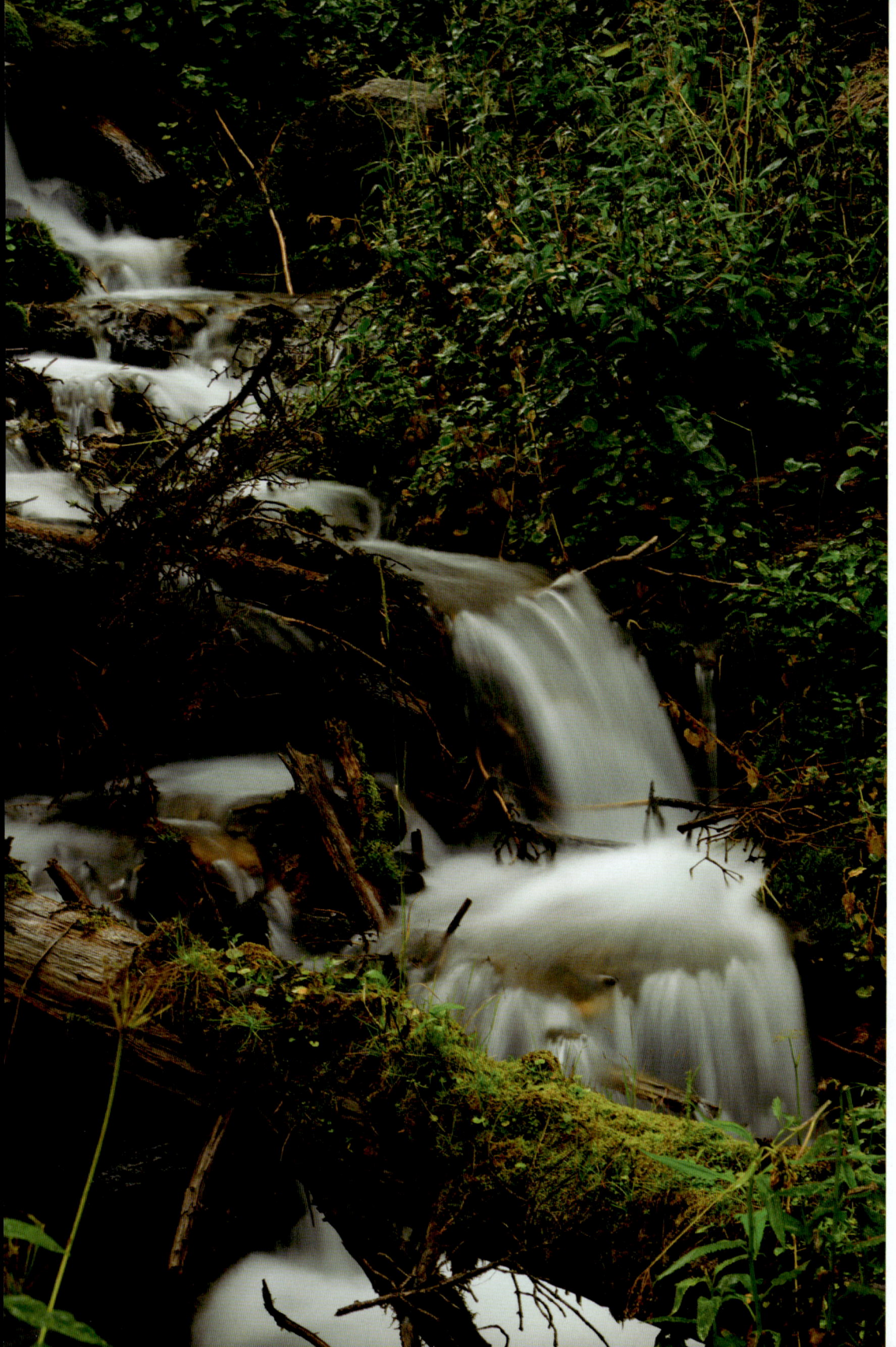

VI.

If I had opened myself to the hooks of sky,
hungered more with the discriminate
patience of trout, the lazy survival
of drawing close to a clear current,
or if I had recognized my need as a feel
for migration and taken it as my own
coping with will, no sweet tune could satisfy
my ears as no filtering gill denies
the river flow. A river changes course.
This boulder fallen from the cliff face makes
a stream, a bank collapses, a clutch
of willows thickens, and pretty stones
mix with muck and a driftwood pile-up
till an oxbow simplifies into a falls
scouring silt from bedrock below.

Terrestrials dangle from the grass blades
and crawl the osha stalks arcing over
the undercut bank. The heavens now
and then bless and let something slip.

VII.

The river being dead, yet speaks.
Remember yesterday? Yes. No. In a way,
the way of rivers, a river is remembered.
Remember God? You don't want yourself
to will Him worship. There is a cast one makes
that sets the fly atop the swirling pool.
There is a pool smooth as a mirror
in an evening party living room.

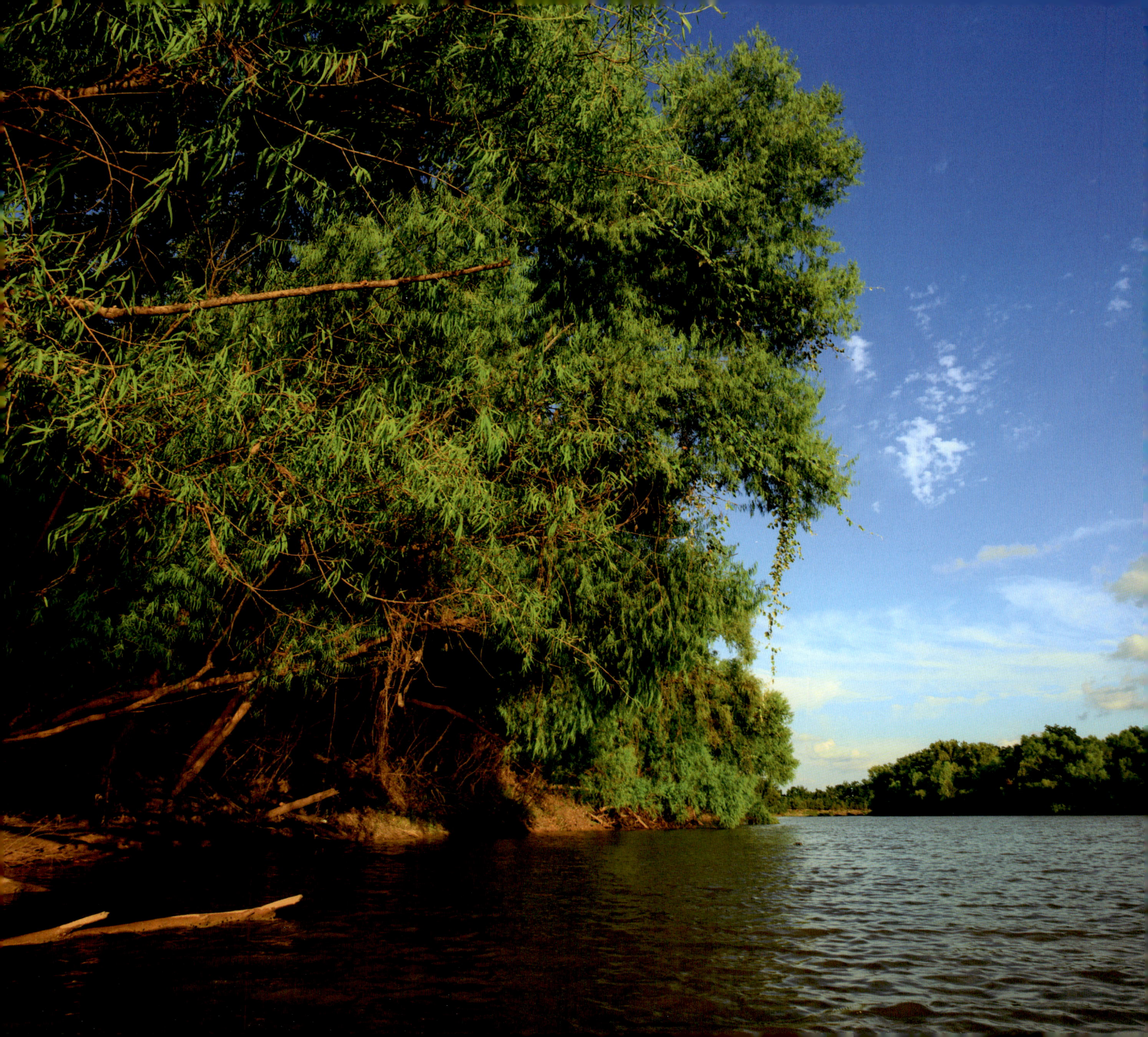

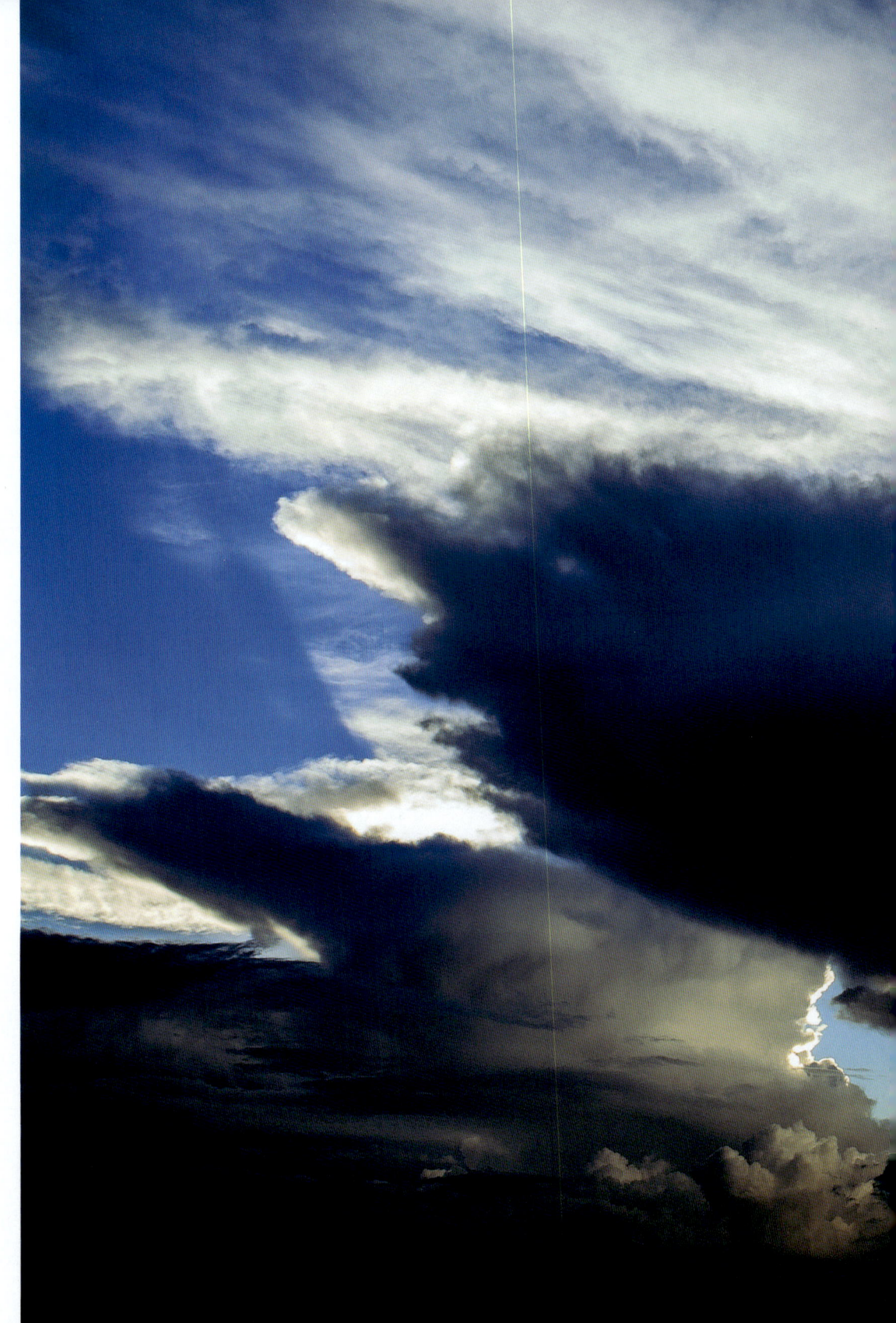

You see yourself in it, you see an aquarium
of bangles and glasses, you see the woman
you want rising to your hand, your offering,
her name. Now we are left with the perfect.
There is dancing, river willow thickets
of feminine arms and dresses, green blouses
moved by a music. God says choose her as if
you had a choice and let her choose you
if she will, and worship me for what will happen.

VIII.

Riparian eyes follow me. I follow riparian eyes.
One can find a vision in a tree. River trees
abide. In my pain, I have tried abiding.
Wanderings strangely abide. Home waits.
I know a man who lived his life farming
at a river's mouth. He bought property
at the trickling headwaters states away.
You cannot be a child again. You can try.
What is music to a child but an ear and mouth
and hands. In seven months a child is clapping.
The water claps against the boulders. It claps
little waves over a fly trying to stay afloat.
The mayfly knows a stairway to the promise of color.

IX.

With a broad, calm ignorance, the mesas keep
from themselves the secret of the gorge. Sure,
the showers fall like an angel is tripping over
his buckets, and the virga swings sleeves
all over the valley. What I want is no less than

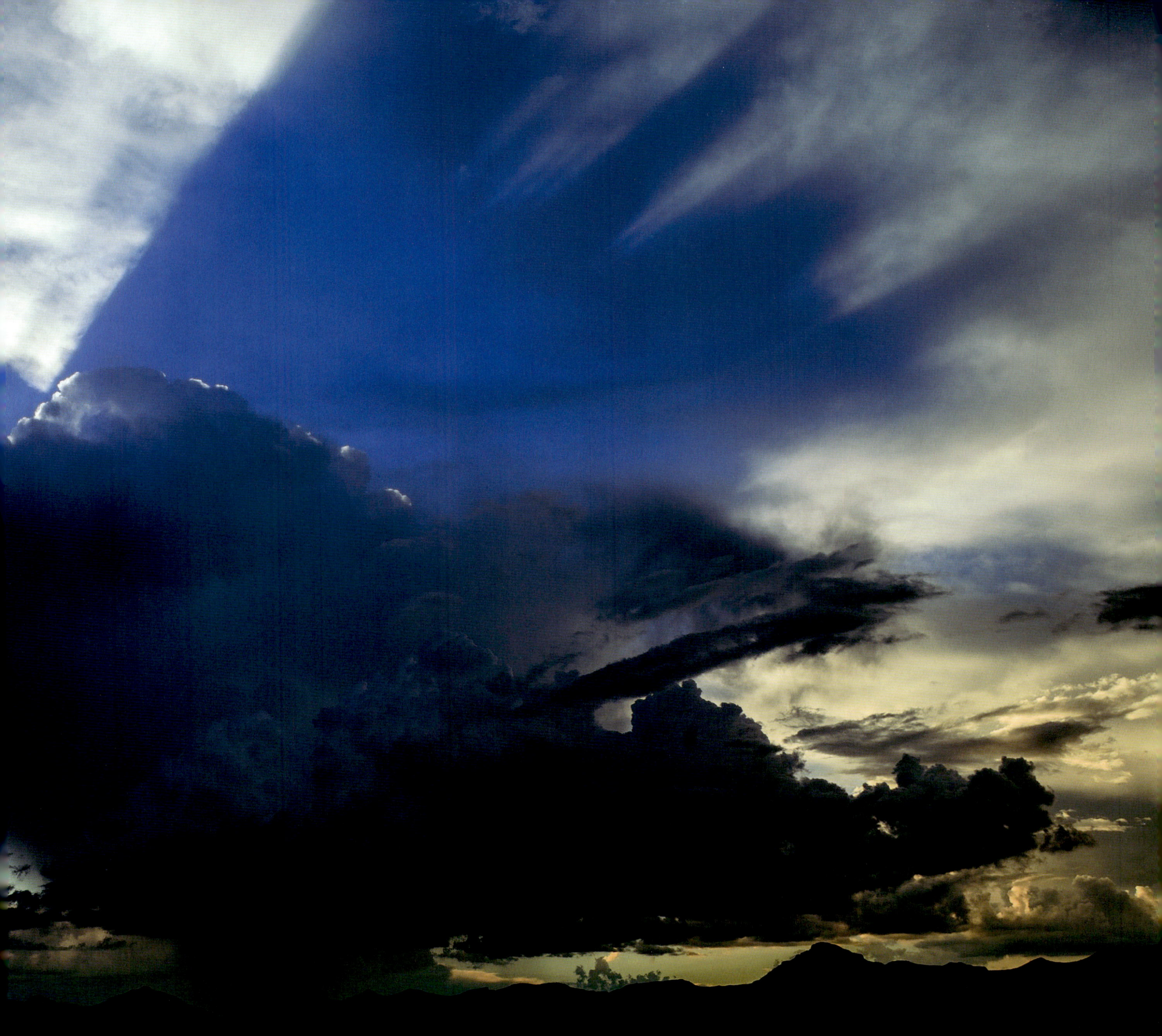

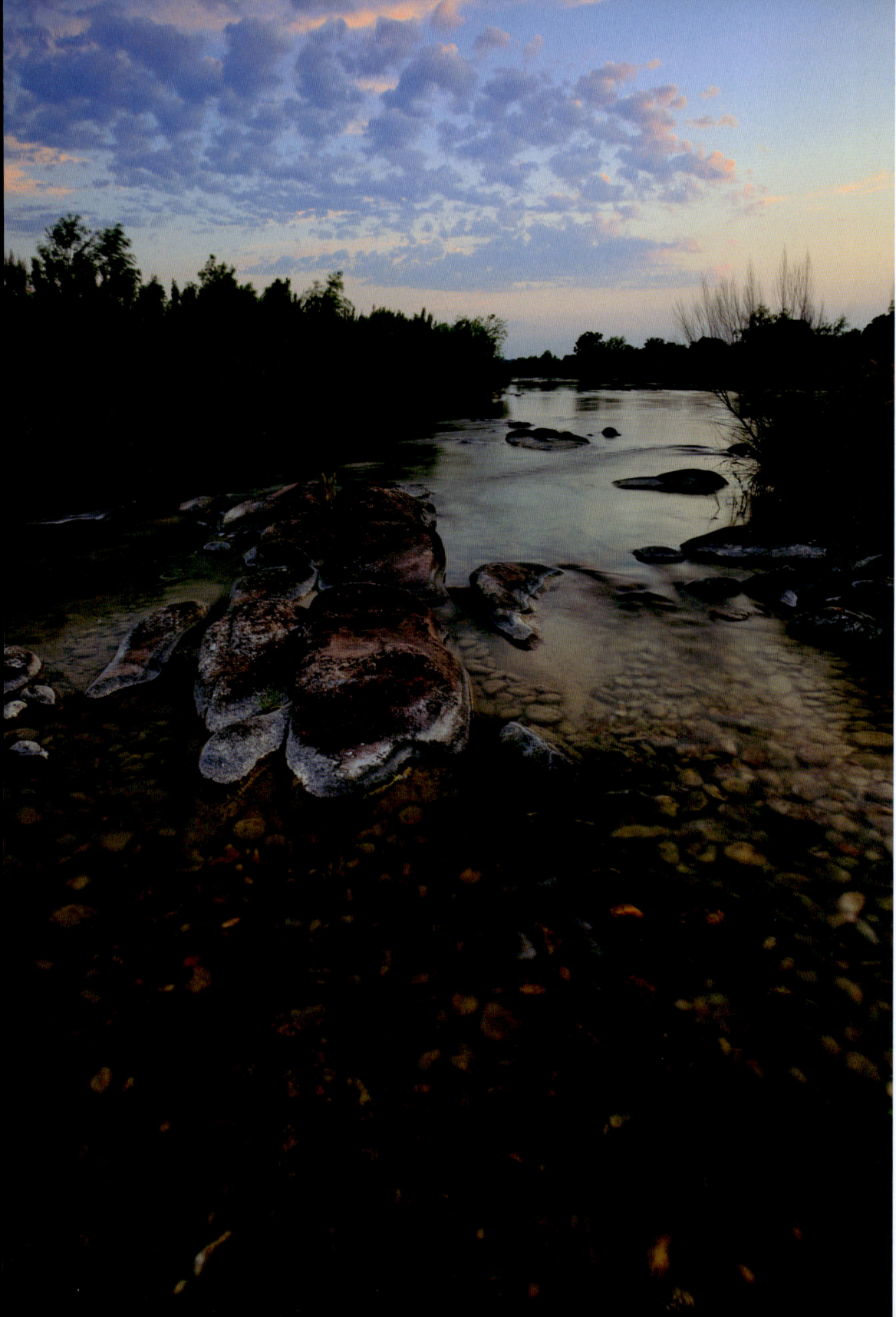

a river and some trout, a God who says,
A river and some trout. Who made this?
Who arranges these orange spots and calls them
brown? Whose thunderhead downdrafts
the valley into leaning silver trees,
acquiescent as a trained ear? I am
trusting you with a light affliction.
Now, with your breath and your dark fist
burnish the surface. My machine made
for motion, stand still and breathe. It's a breeze
when the pressures improvise the summer sun
and a blue haze. I'd call the mountain heaven,
afternoon thunder beyond music. When the clouds
finally peel away like paint, a sunset shines
through, under, warming an orange mesa, a little
chunk of rainbow, a little flesh tone on the cedars
and sagebrush. The world overturned, higher up,
like a shove, the pines baptized in the shadow
of God getting even and the authority of absence.

Tomorrow I will go where the warblers
sip and summer far above the river,
where a spirit in a snow globe worth
of mica silt stirs, like a nest of stars
at the bottom of a pool,
the spring.

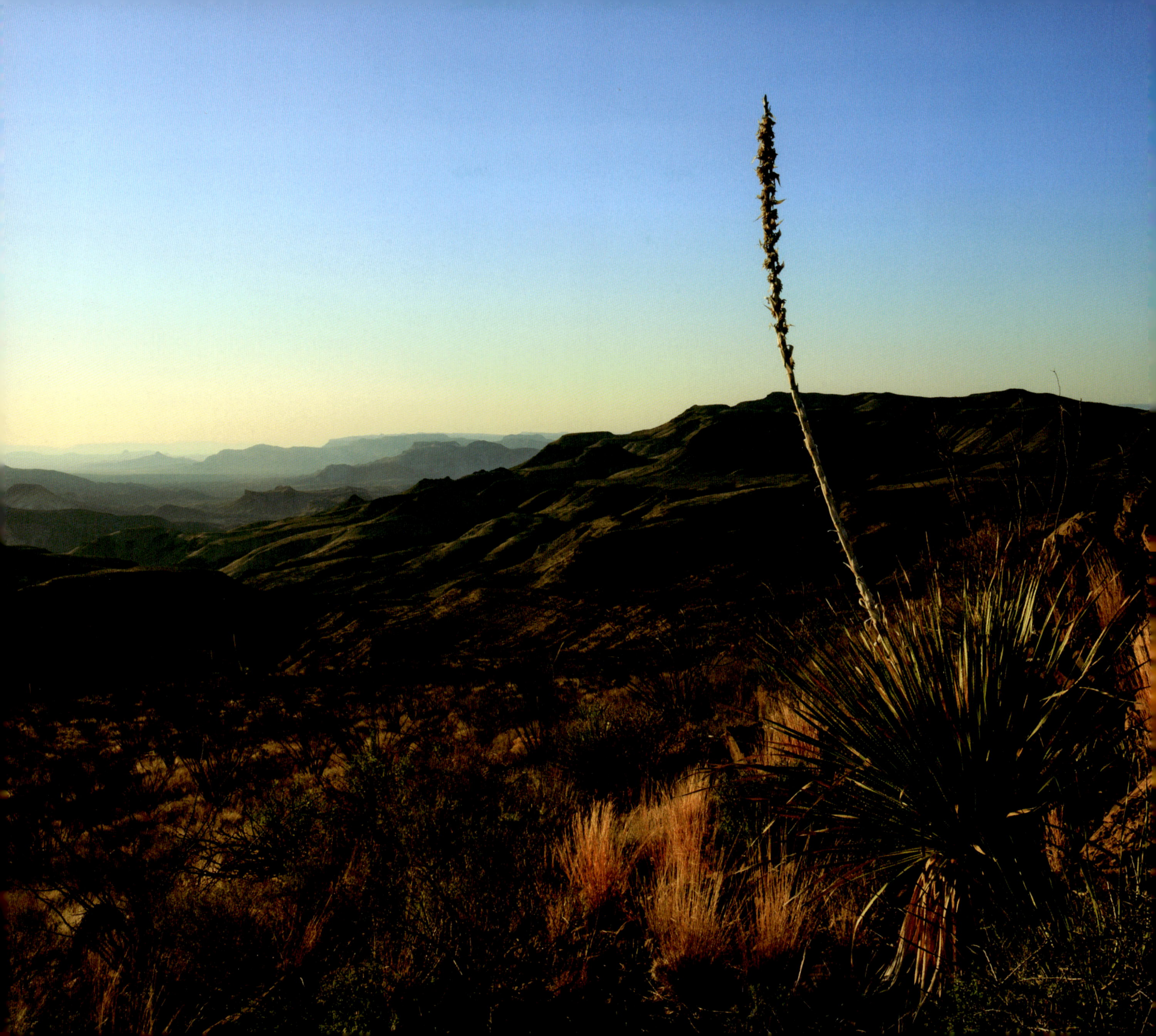

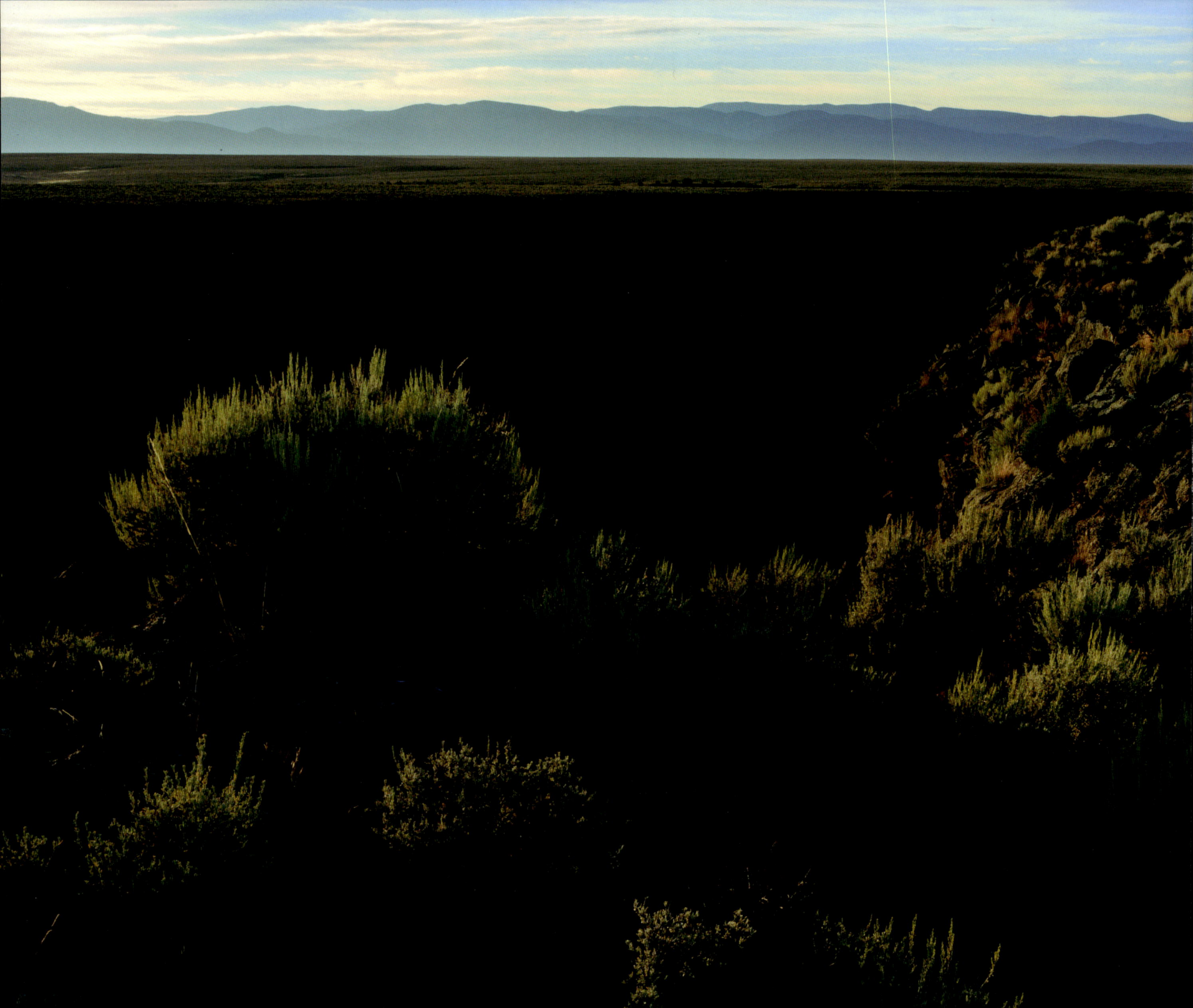

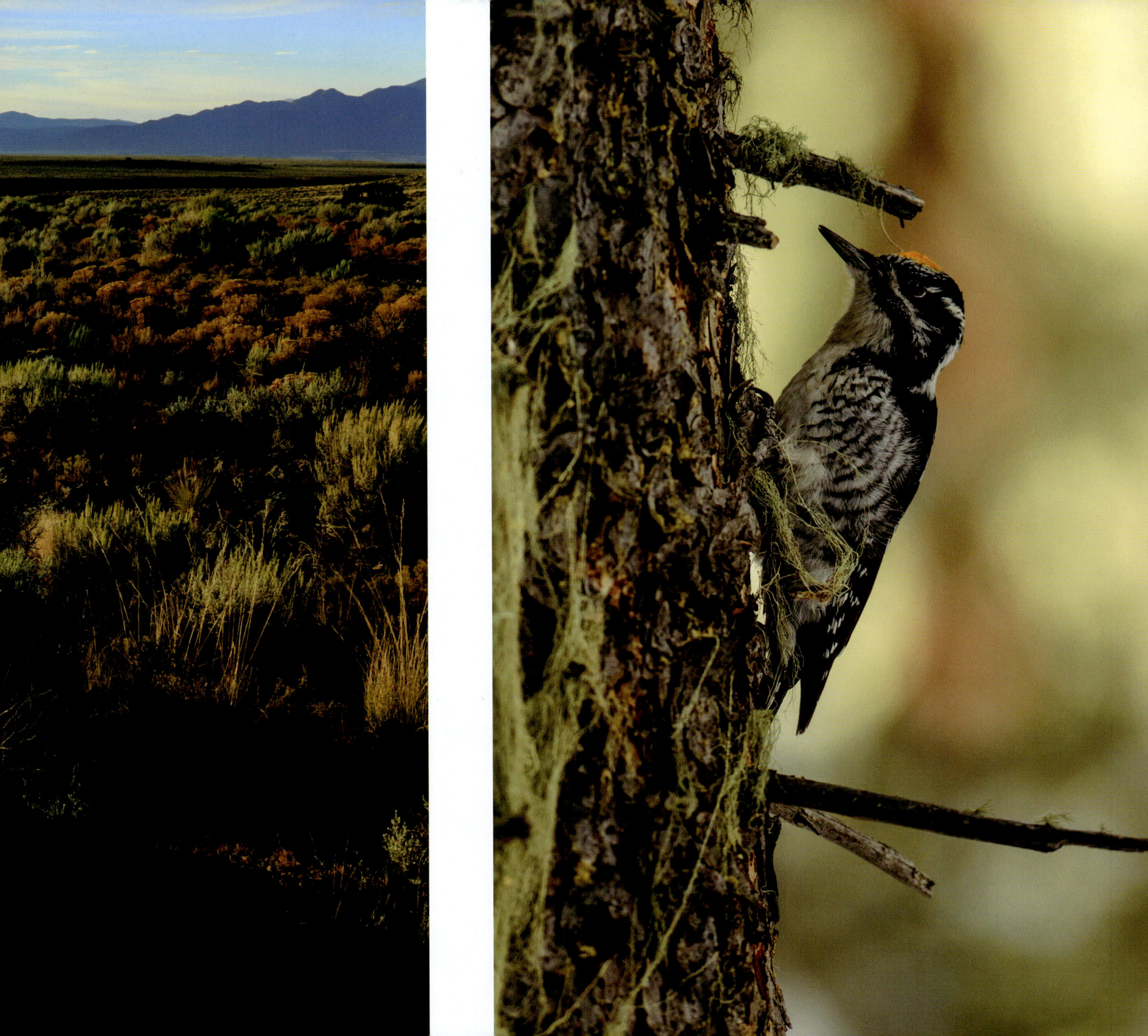

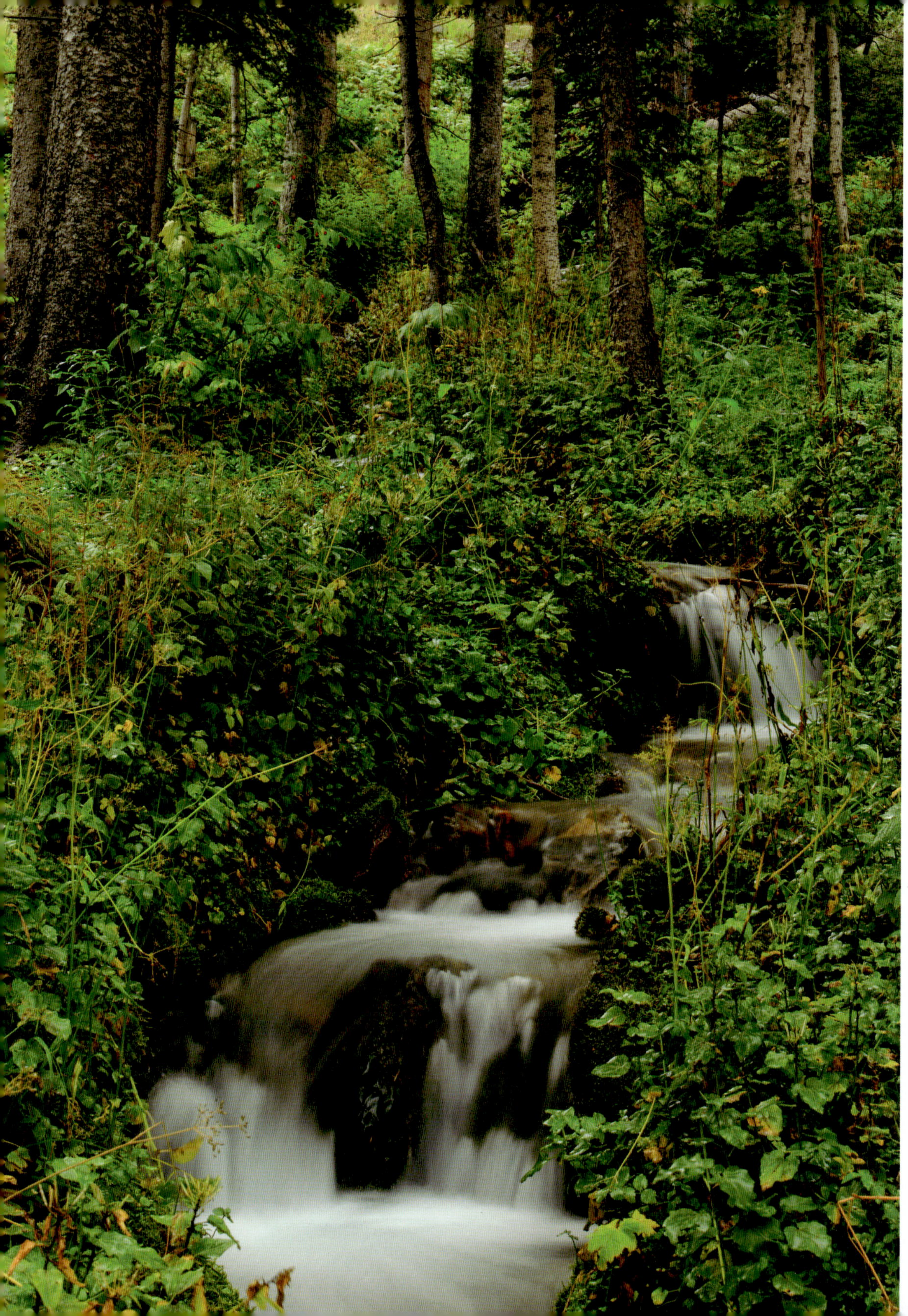

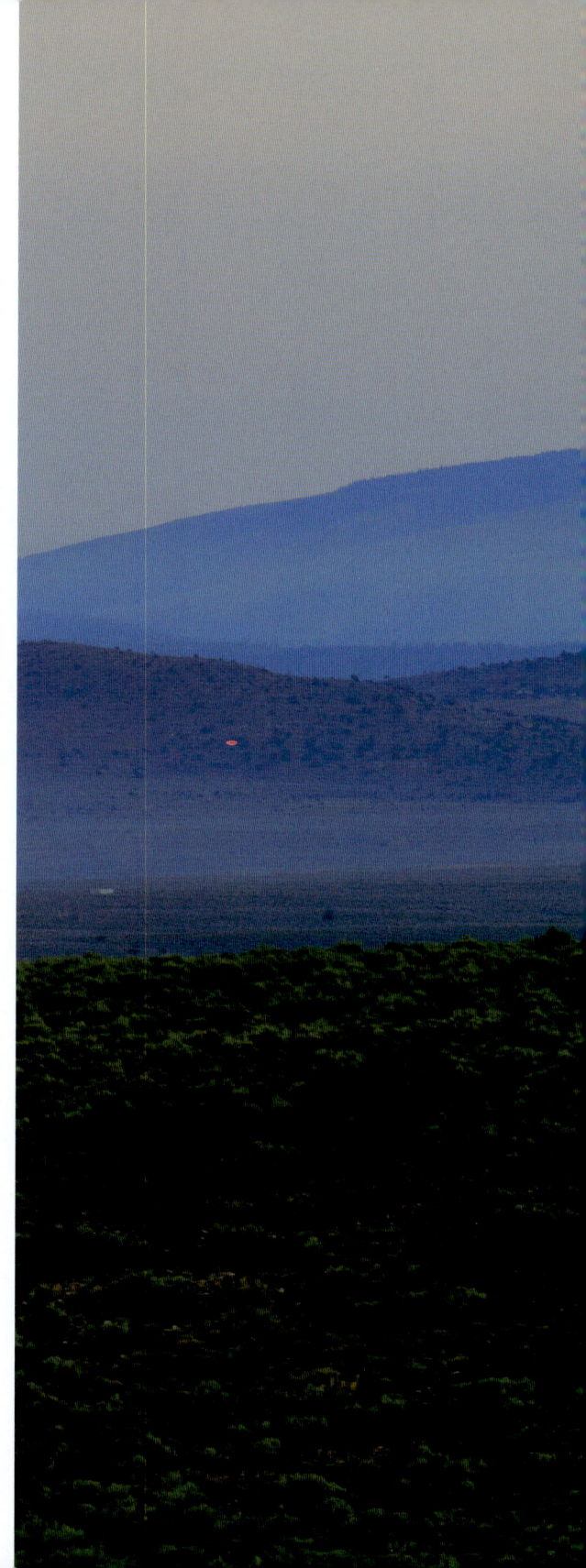

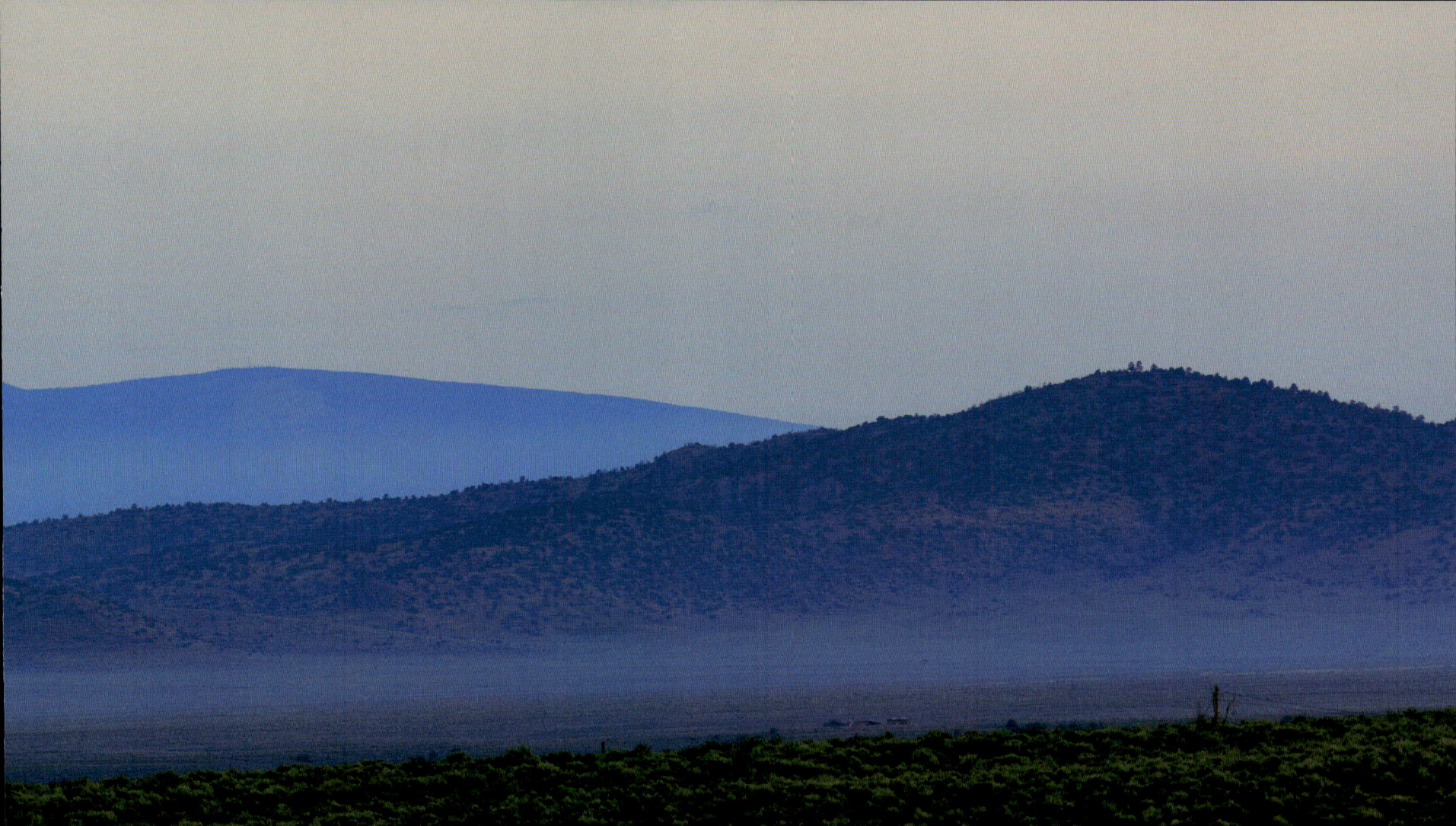

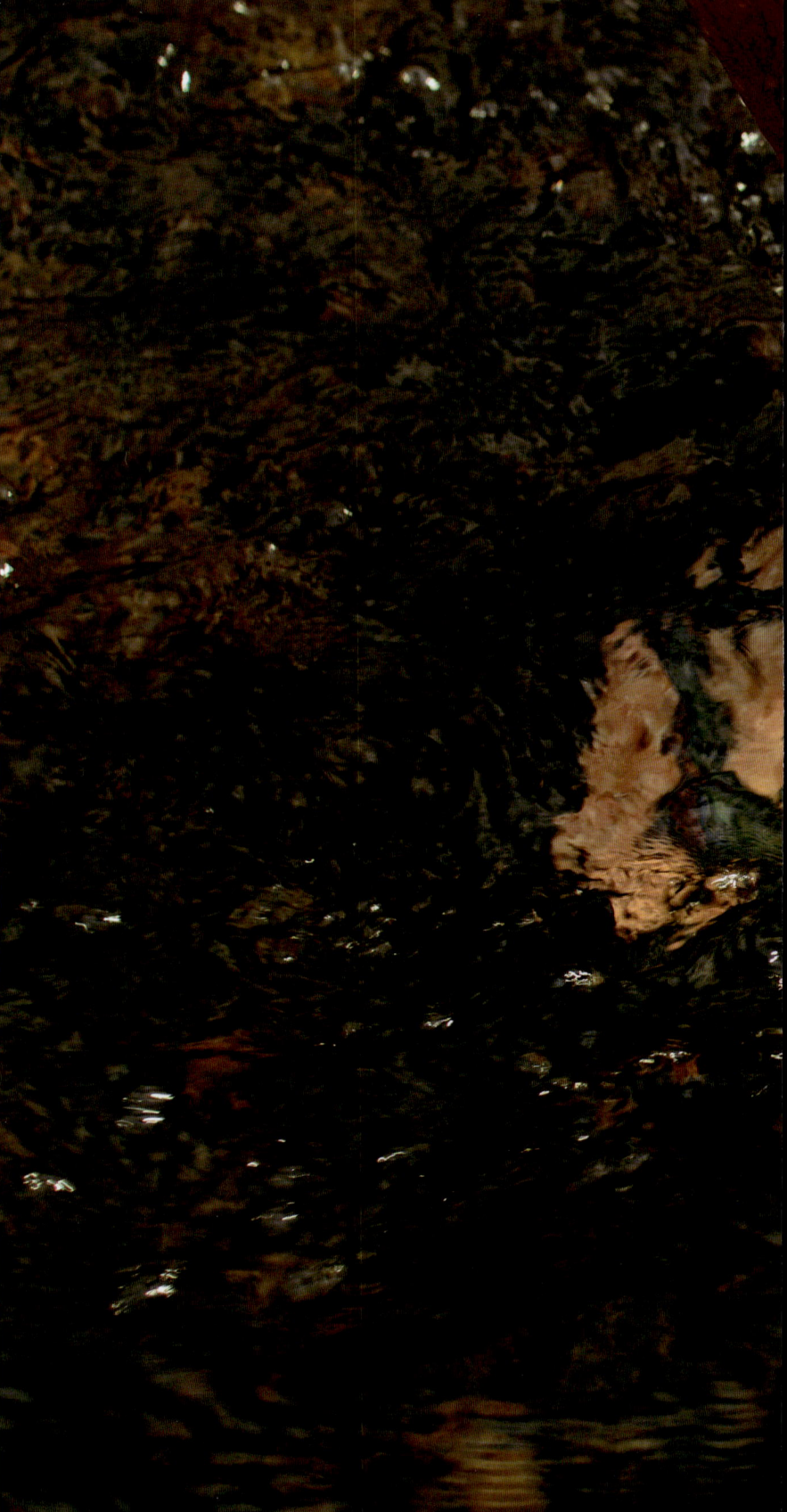

The Cimarron River

The man standing in the shin-deep current between
two head-high piles of red willows fit for foxes, fit for
swaying by a risen river, I hold back the river
in my own way. The dam at Eagle's Nest above me
bored with morning fog lifting holds, but neither
sun nor gravity will stand for standing water.

So now, like some lever, some thin lover leaned on,
an opening, a power cold and blurry has dawned
to touch both banks, loosening fistfuls of algae neon
green as heaven descended. Days farther down
irrigation greens the tidy lines at farms beyond
a gorge's imagination. The dry-fly day is done.

Here hatches rise without trout and, in clockwise vortices,
a different hunger spins. By stepping in a river,
a man does not become the river. But he sees
the man he knows the water will deliver.
As a friend, he sharpens with his eye the surface.
As an enemy, he would spend its gold on purpose.

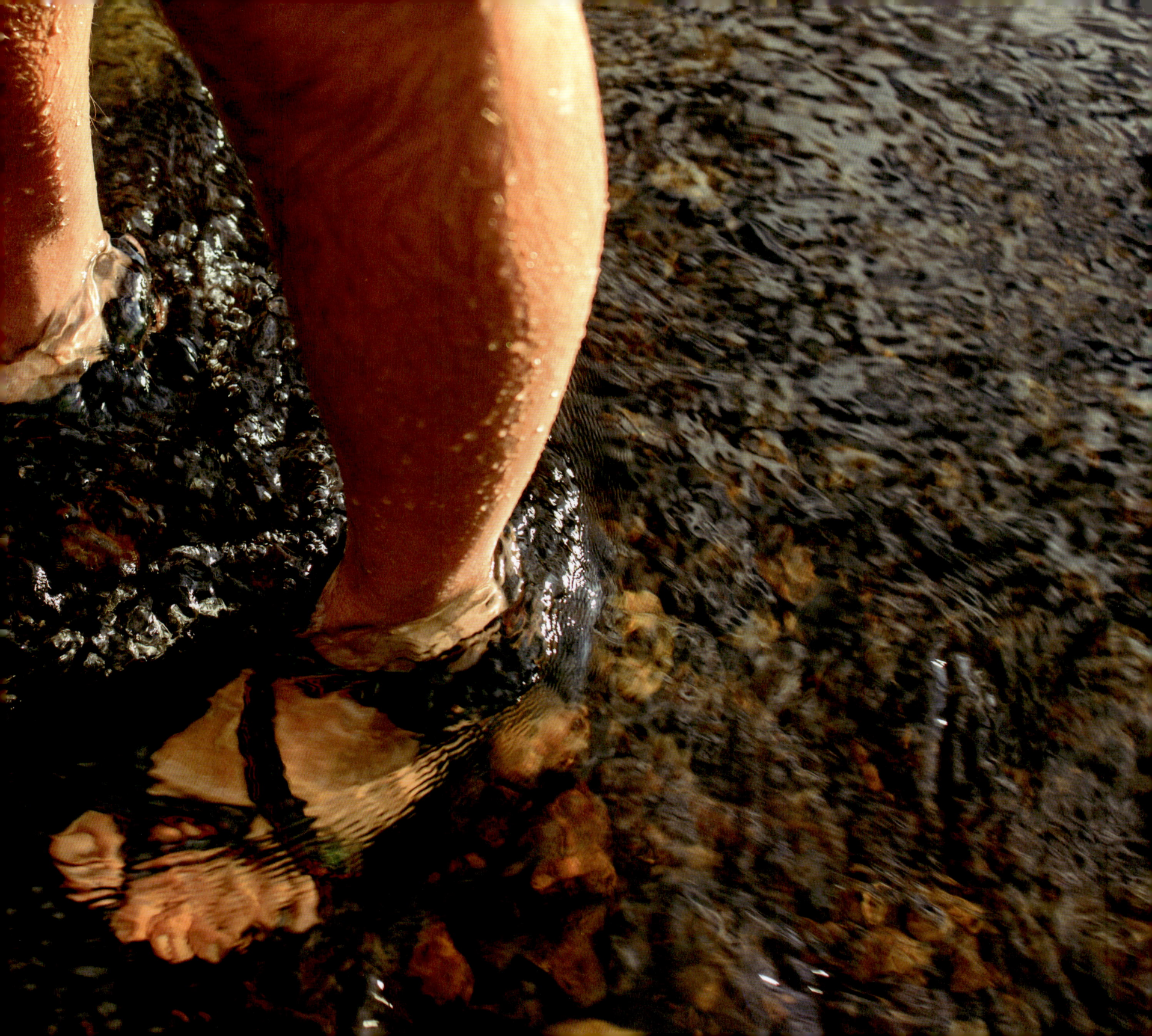

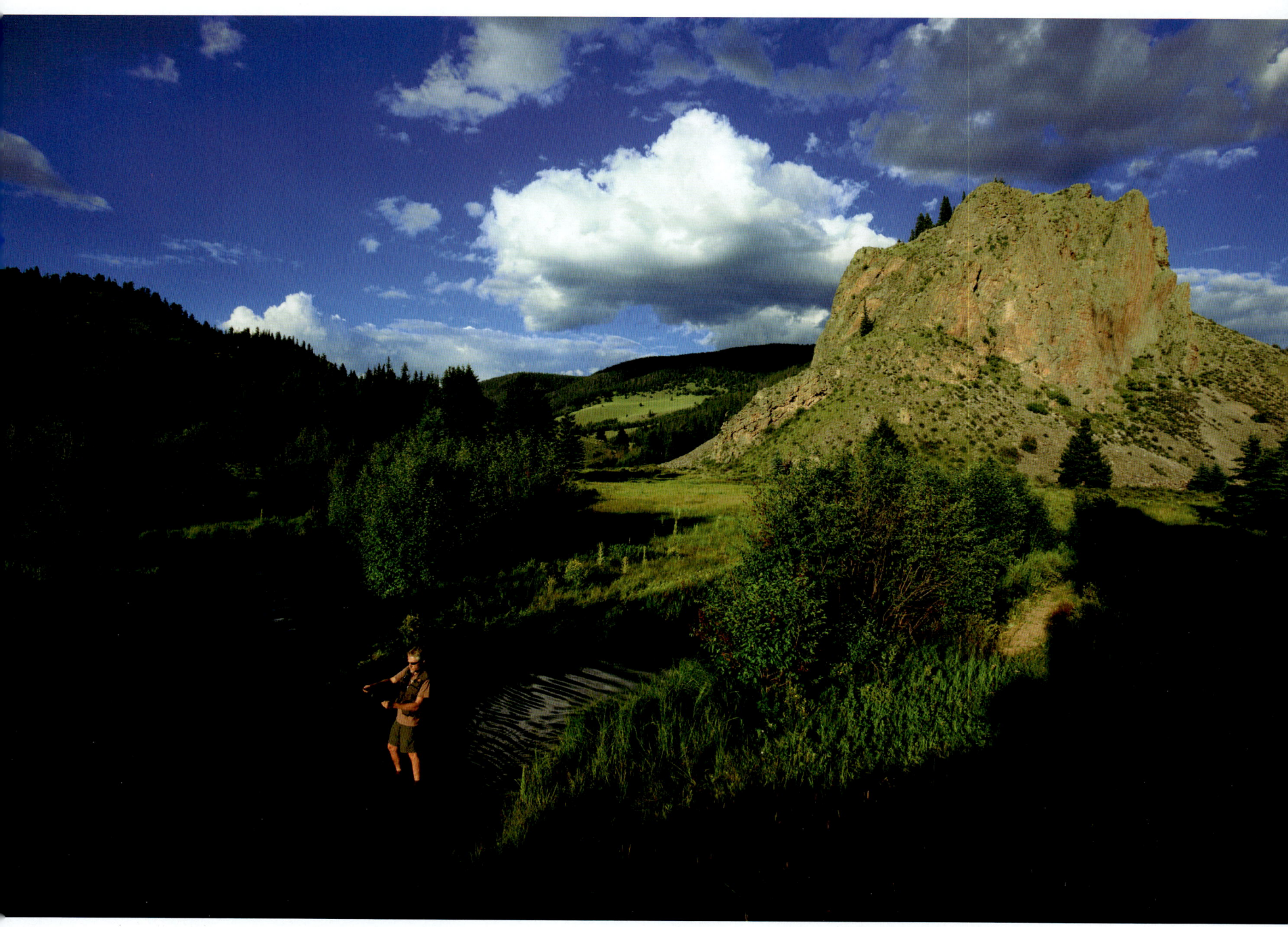

Valle Vidal

Like a cutthroat
in a meadow stream,
I look upstream, through a disturbance.
And I see you,
looking up through a disturbance,
a cutthroat.

The water is like a window with sheets
of rainwater running over it,
and I stand here as one who waits
for someone I need to appear.

Some say the orange gash below your gills
is a repository of a sixth sense.
If you could thirst, this is how you thirst.
Your patience amazes, as you wait
for the stonefly nymph to rise, molt, lift,
and then you fly as if to teach the stonefly
flight. Again, you wait below a boulder
watching the river pass as I wait
below a mountain watching the stream pass.
Your green algae drifts in the current.
My willows stream above the stream
with the wind of a coming storm.
God is watching.
How could I be a fisher of men
if I had never stood in moving water
with an invisible line between my hands

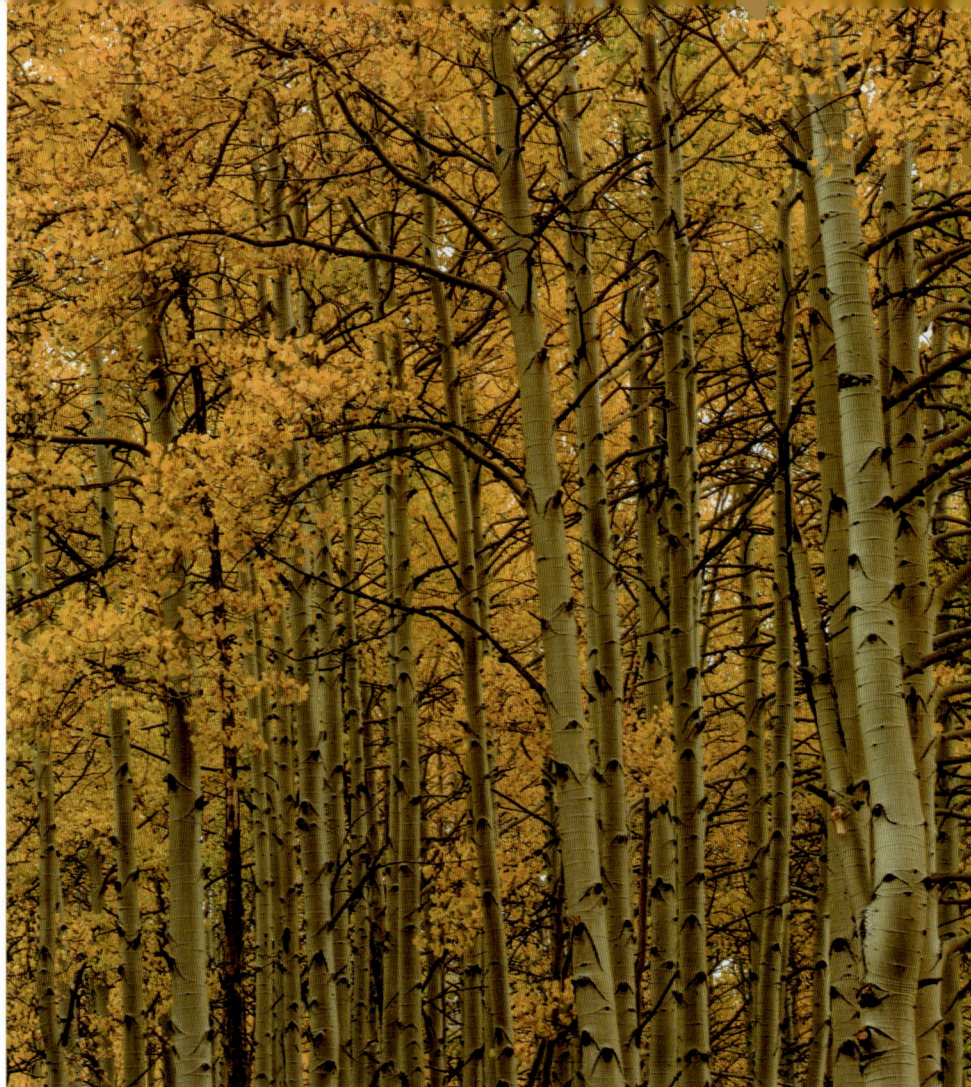

and a multitude of choosing and mending,
if I had not turned over the most unremarkable
of rocks and apprenticed to an insect,
if I had not witnessed the orange prisms of dew
dropping from the tips of spearmint leaves
touched by the small breeze cleansing this place?

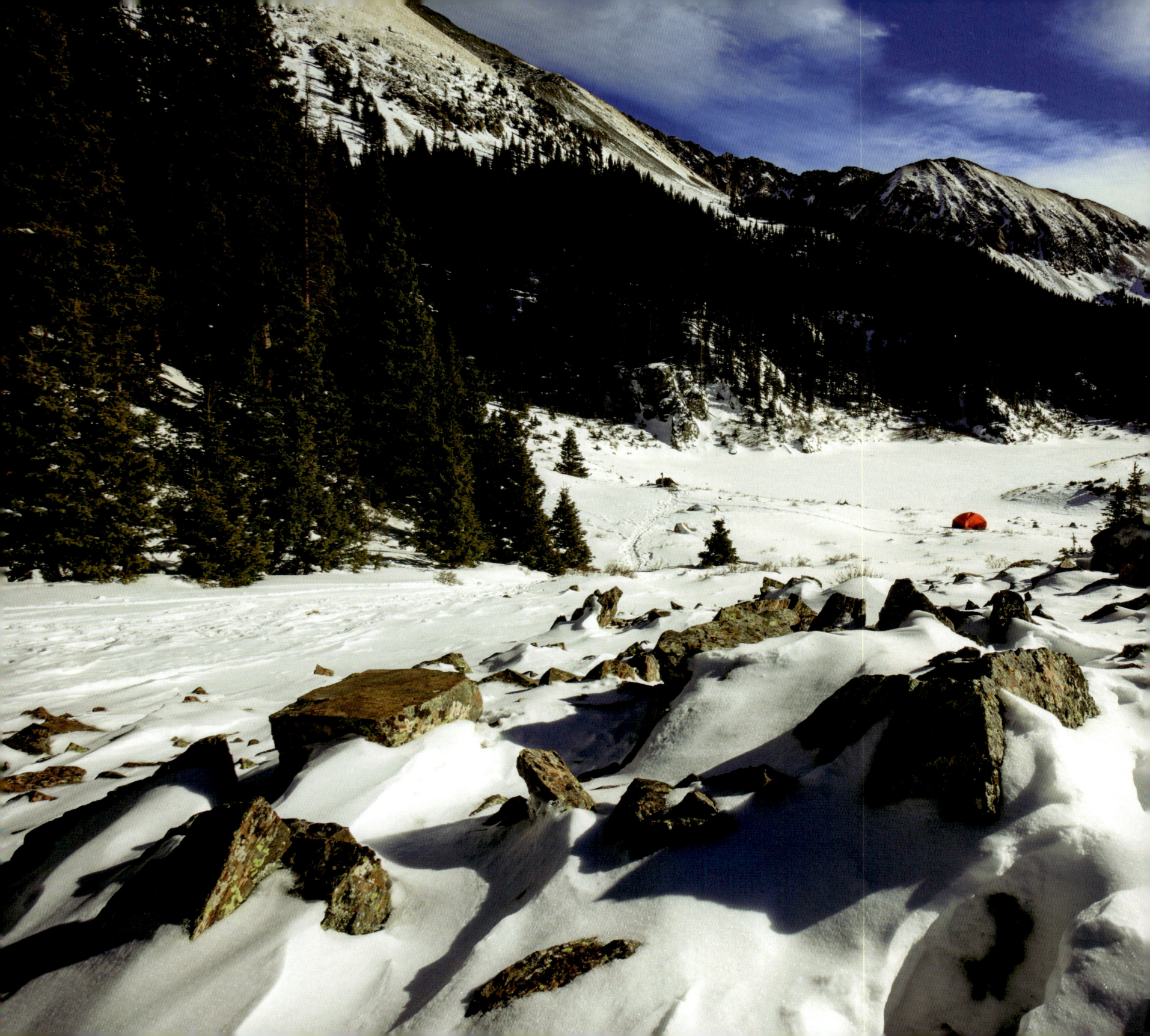

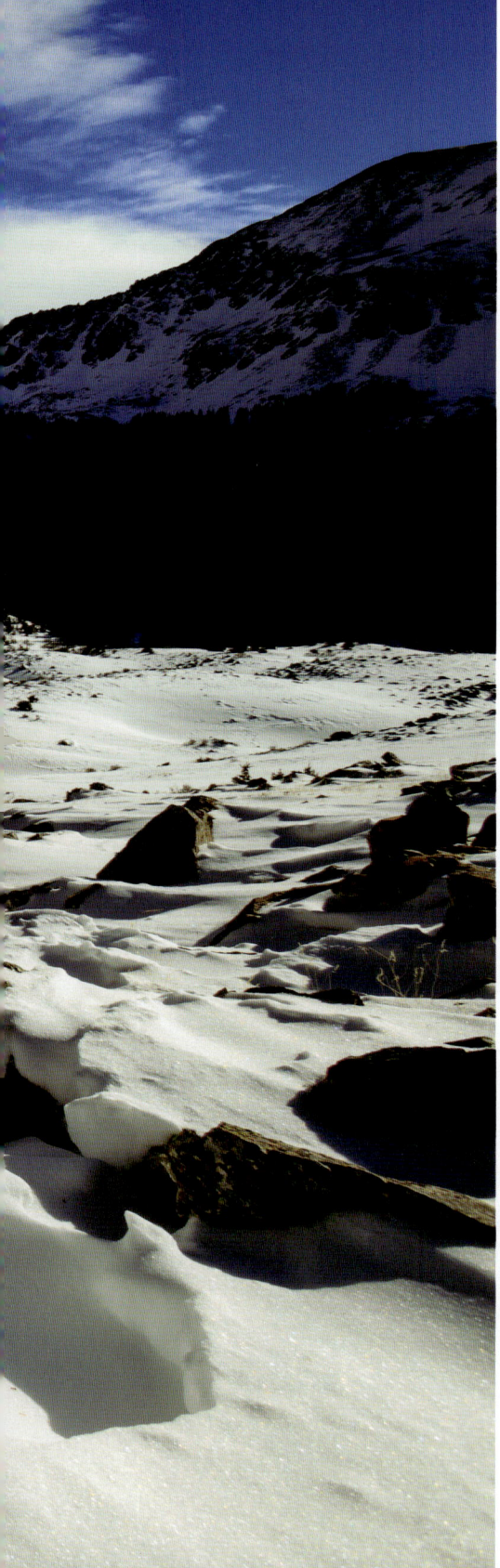

The Rio Hondo

Upper

By June the record snows released a cold
torrent of water bulging over each falls
like the molten glass contemporary art

the Taos galleries gush over. We're sold
on twisted color trapped in shaped globules:
a tropical bird or jellyfish, a heart.

What little blue the river holds must come
by open sky through green and canyon walls
contributing their igneous colorchart.

Up at the Ski Valley source I drink, both dumb
and smart.

Lower

This stretch, too fast, brown, casts a dry-fly curse
with summer runoff at a decade-high.
My favorite local fishing spot. No worry

that anyone will find it: who reads verse?
On the crumbling bank, think what to do, fret, sigh,
despair on wishing (a river's never sorry)

for nature's sympathy. This muddy knowing
threads almost nothing through my empty eye.
From the car, I take my lunch two hours early,

a pen, a notebook. I watch the river going.
No hurry.

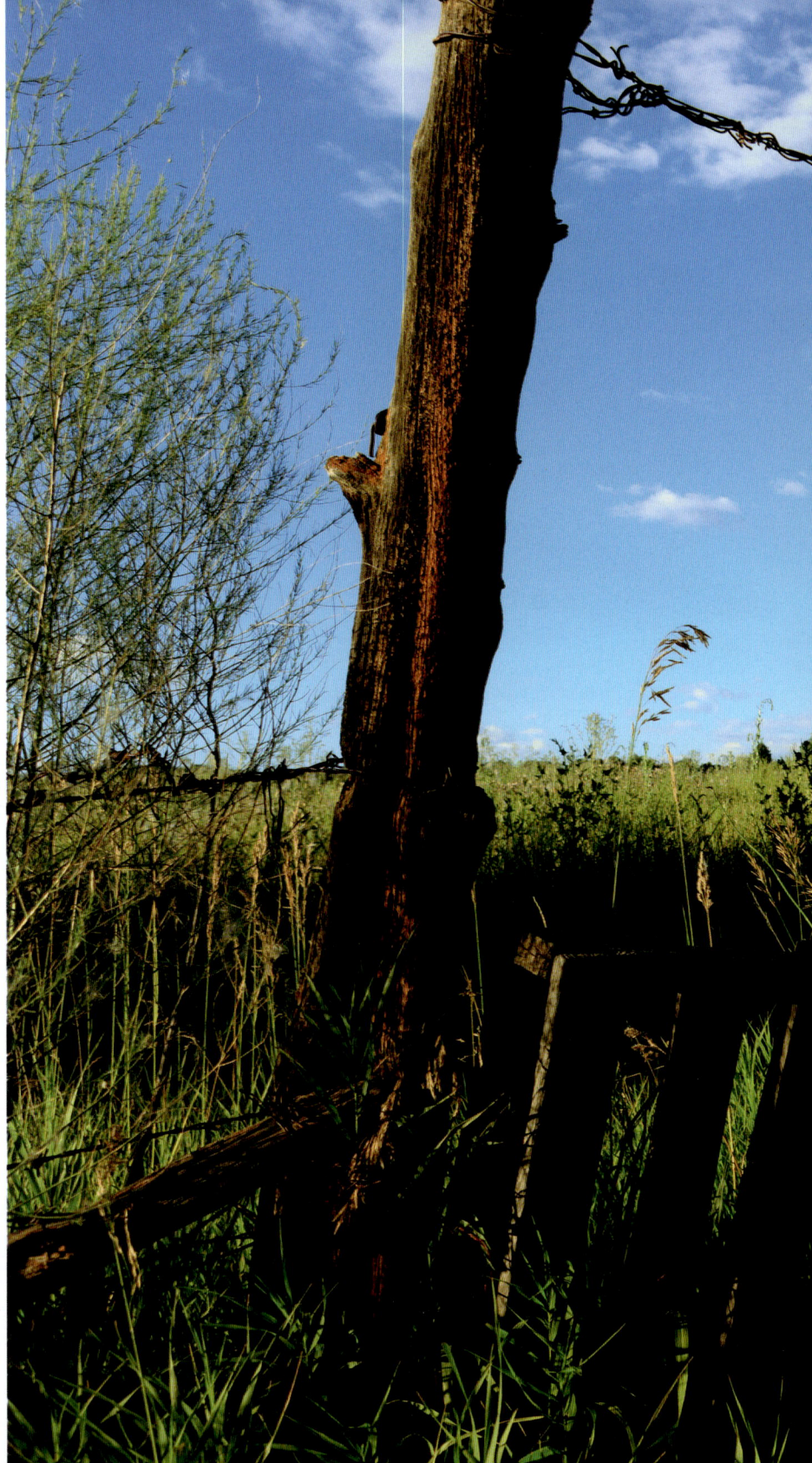

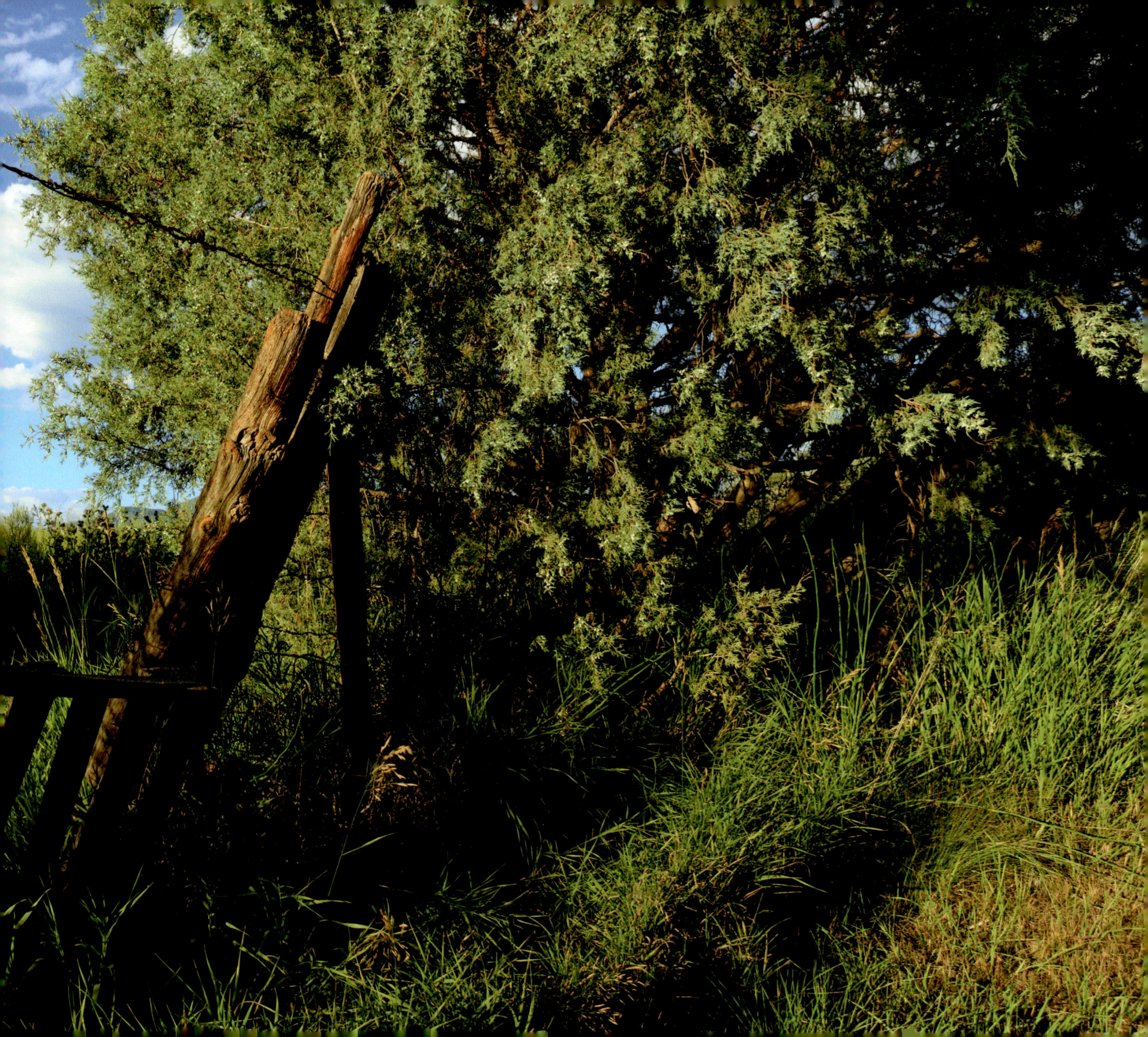

Rio Fernando

Child of a river, mere stream, for hours
you play with your sticks and stones, no words.
You try falling into quiet green stretches
but cannot lie still. Before Taos flowers,
you turn to the left and veer, fleeing
the profile of a magpie wired above
a sagebrush hillside. How fast you scrub
your worries, and laughter hops and scratches
at your ribs like a slew of thirsty wrens.
You wear like a long necklace aluminum cans
and bottles strung for miles, and the wind
sometimes sings across them. Light and time can
make jewels from little sins and the dead.
On a clear night you understand
by hoping the milky way is your mother.
With his own hands the wind, your father,
you firmly believe, dug this watershed.
Steep power from above and well below
give even the light respite in the willow
and ponderosa shadow where you turn dust
to sparkles. After all, there is no now.
Release and catch, dear, swift, small water,
two sweet dreams to this supreme trust:
in your lowest let seven winter elk bow
only to carry you to a meadow and aspens,
and in your highest reaches let happen
clearly the second dream as you wake like notes
ascending pool by pool proud cutthroats.

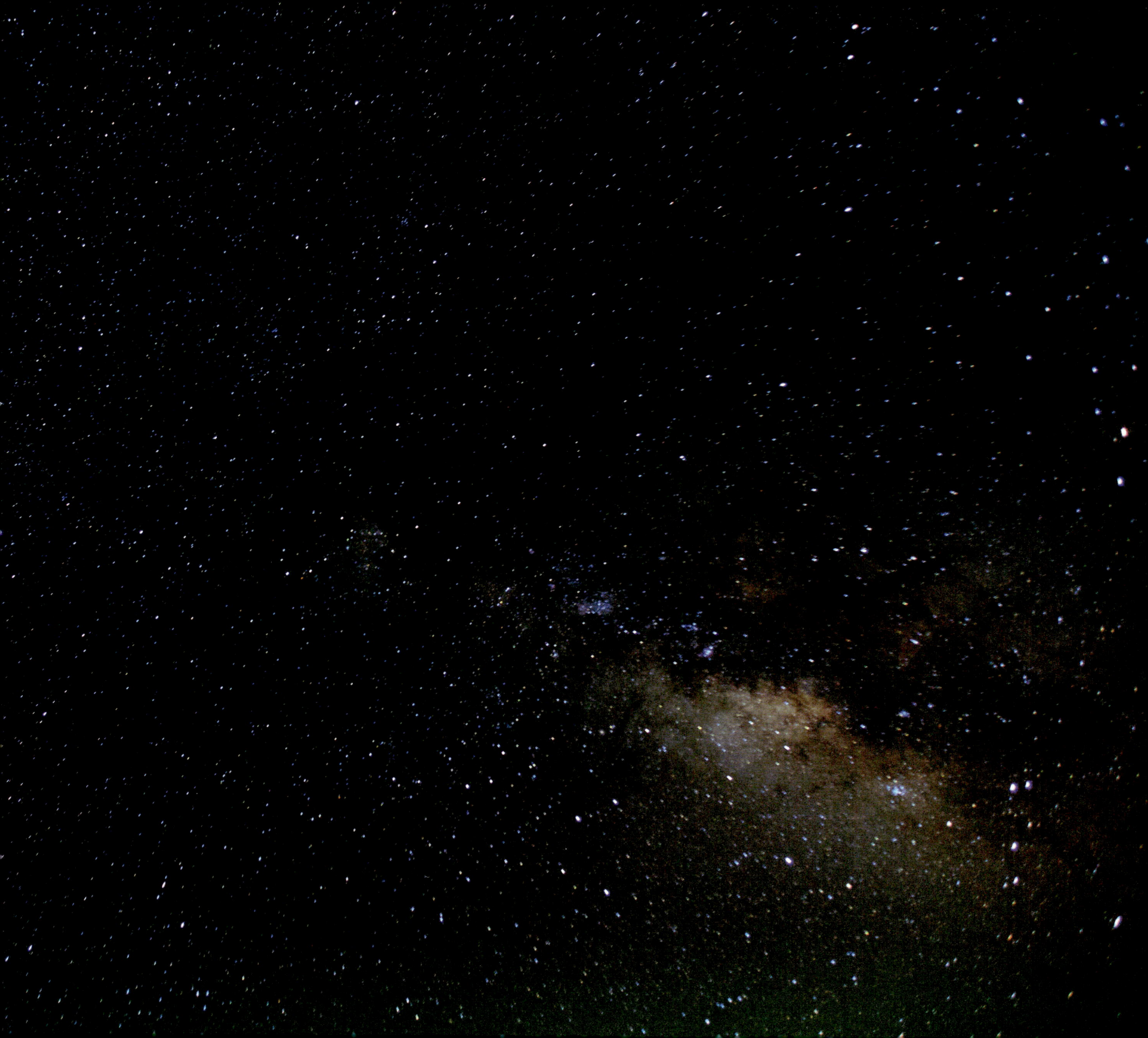

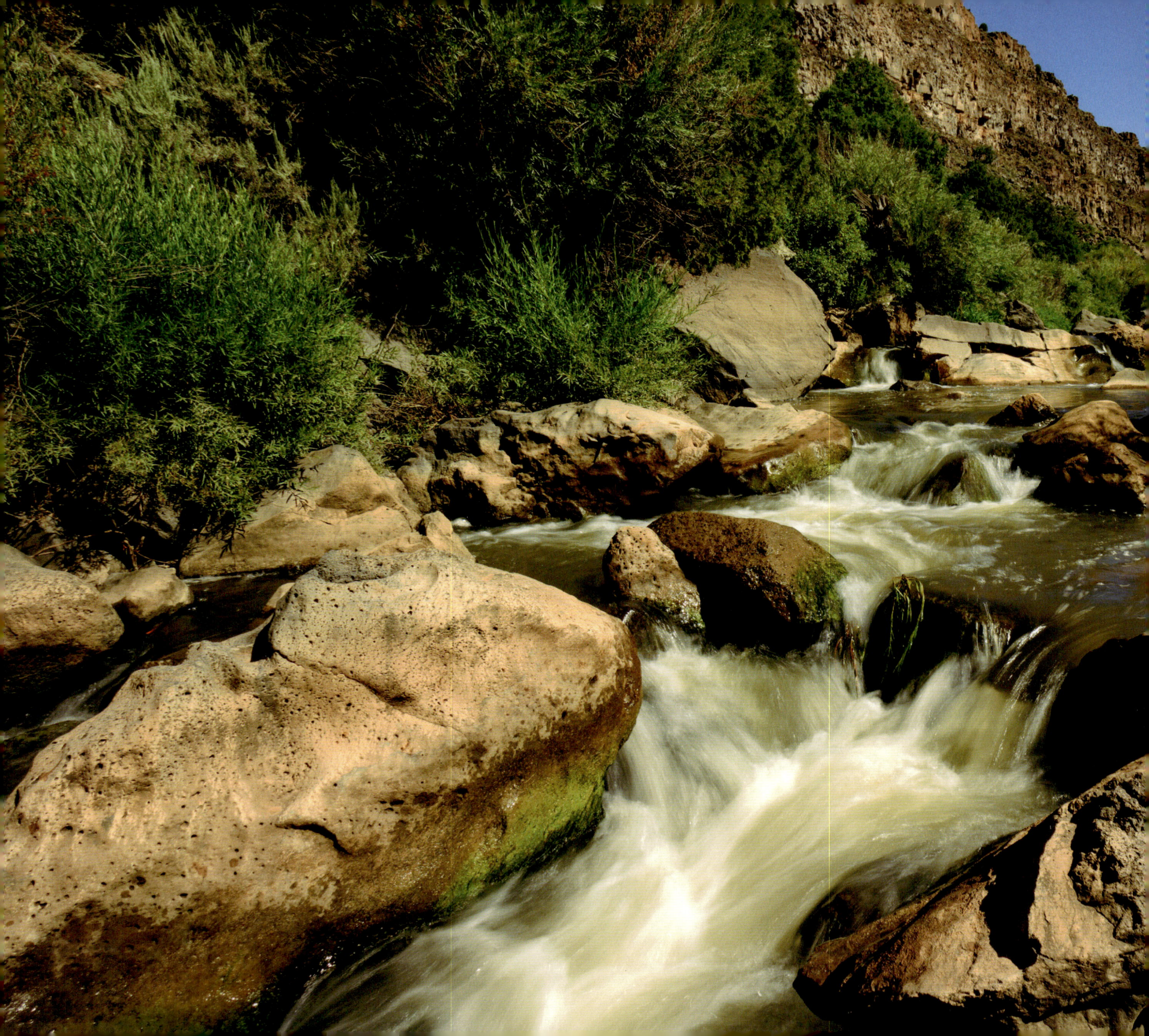

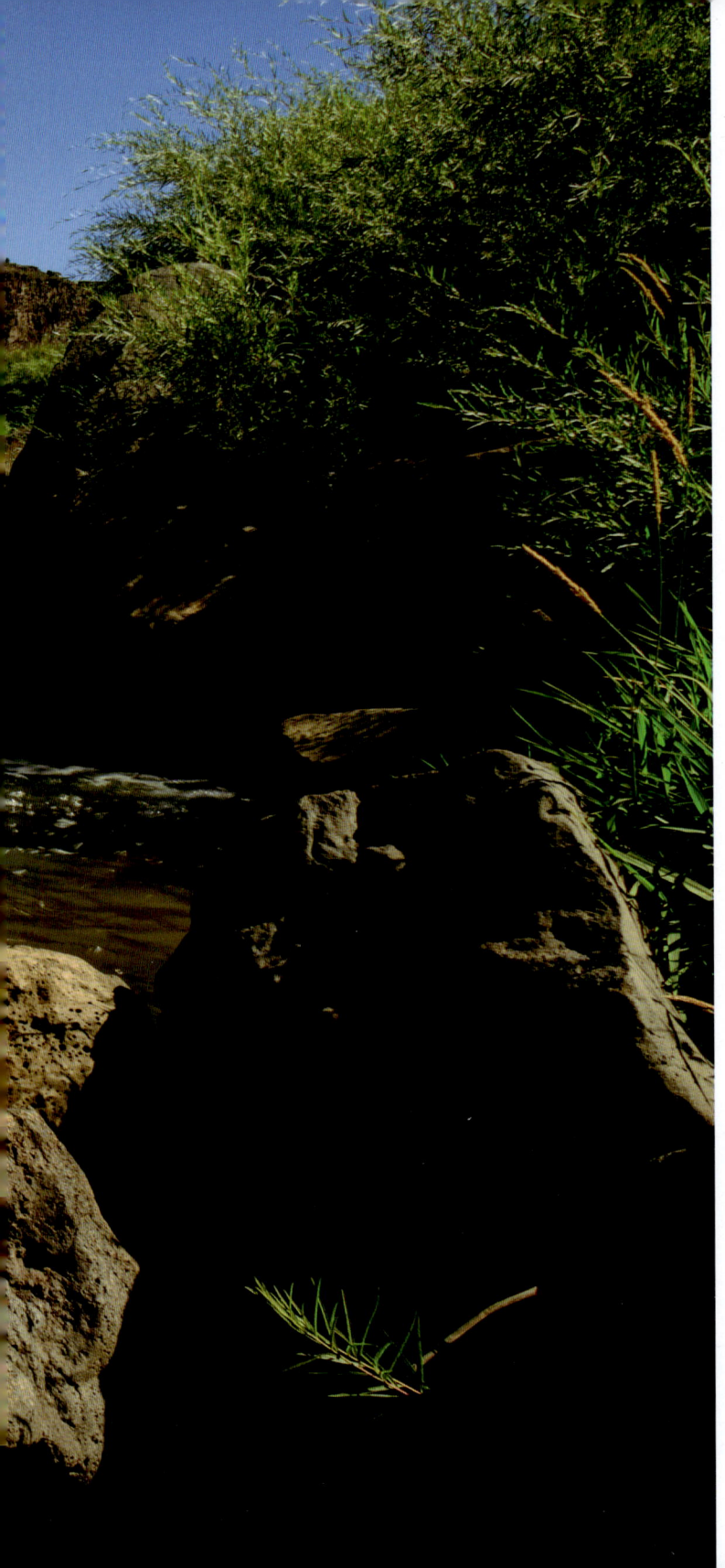

The Little Rio Grande

Past spruce, down meadows, and I'm trickling up
a storm of cottonwoods. I run beside
the road the redneck rides his 4X4 on,

then along Route 518 until I drop
into trout-filled acequias, the pride
of Rancho. Except that every other moron

tosses his beer cans here. I join big water
at the gorge and watch these lowlife rafters (and guide)
get back to nature. Who's the oxymoron?

All this leisure, hard to believe we've got a
war on.

Pot Creek

I took a dozen Anasazi shards
and left a hundred more behind because
I'm not the only one who likes an antique,

a bit of history that no one guards
(the funding for the site expired). And laws?
Abandoned land, the posted stream, the meek

remains of art, once kingdom to a few
abstract expressionists: these gave me pause.
But then I walked back to the car to sneak

my rod. The brown trout leapt from, at my cue,
pot creek.

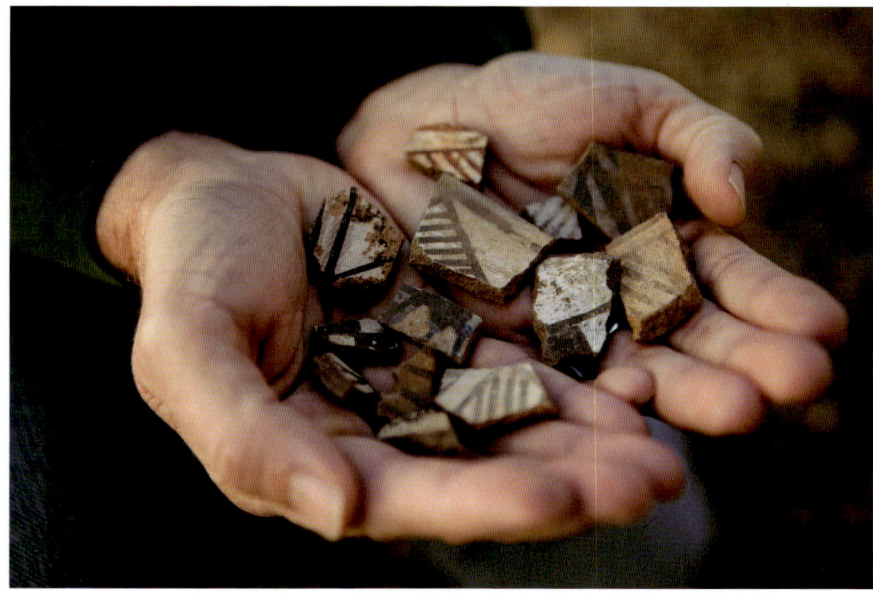

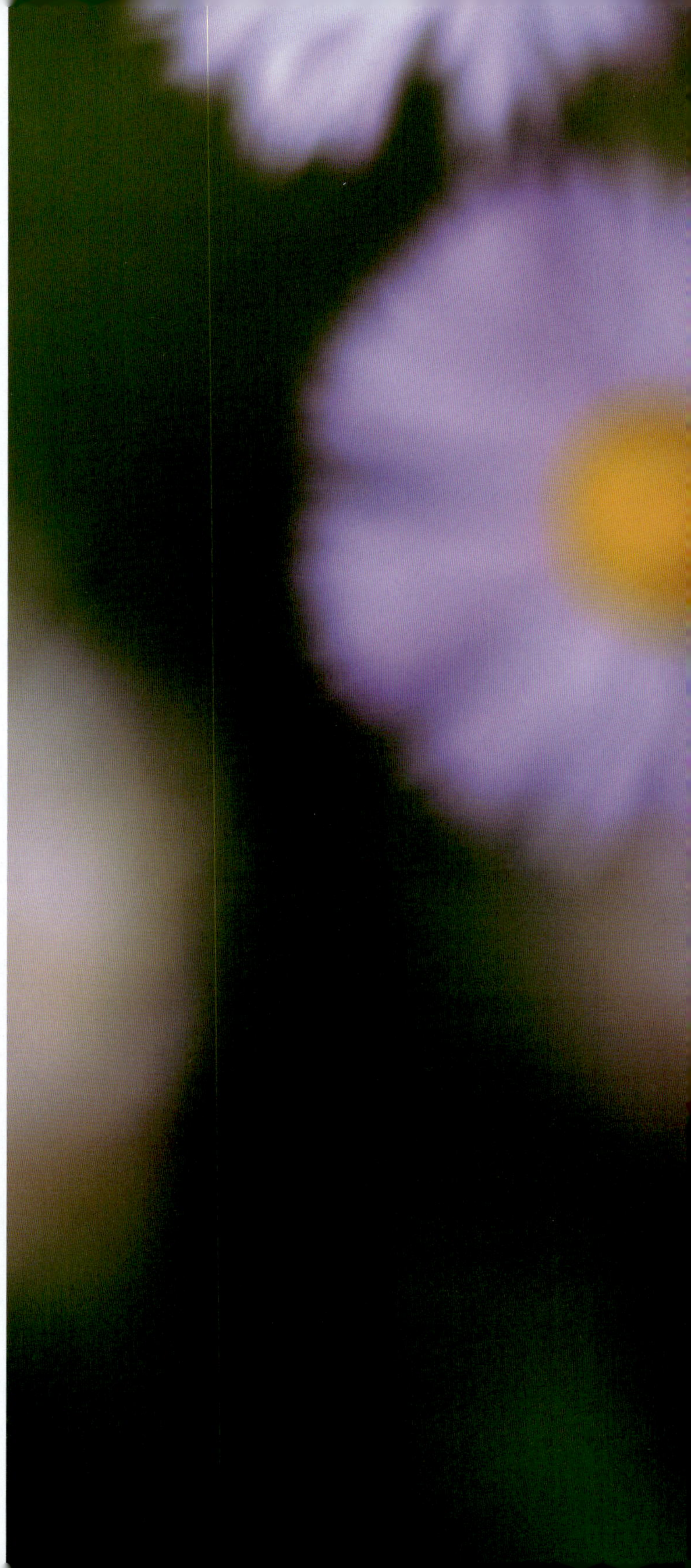

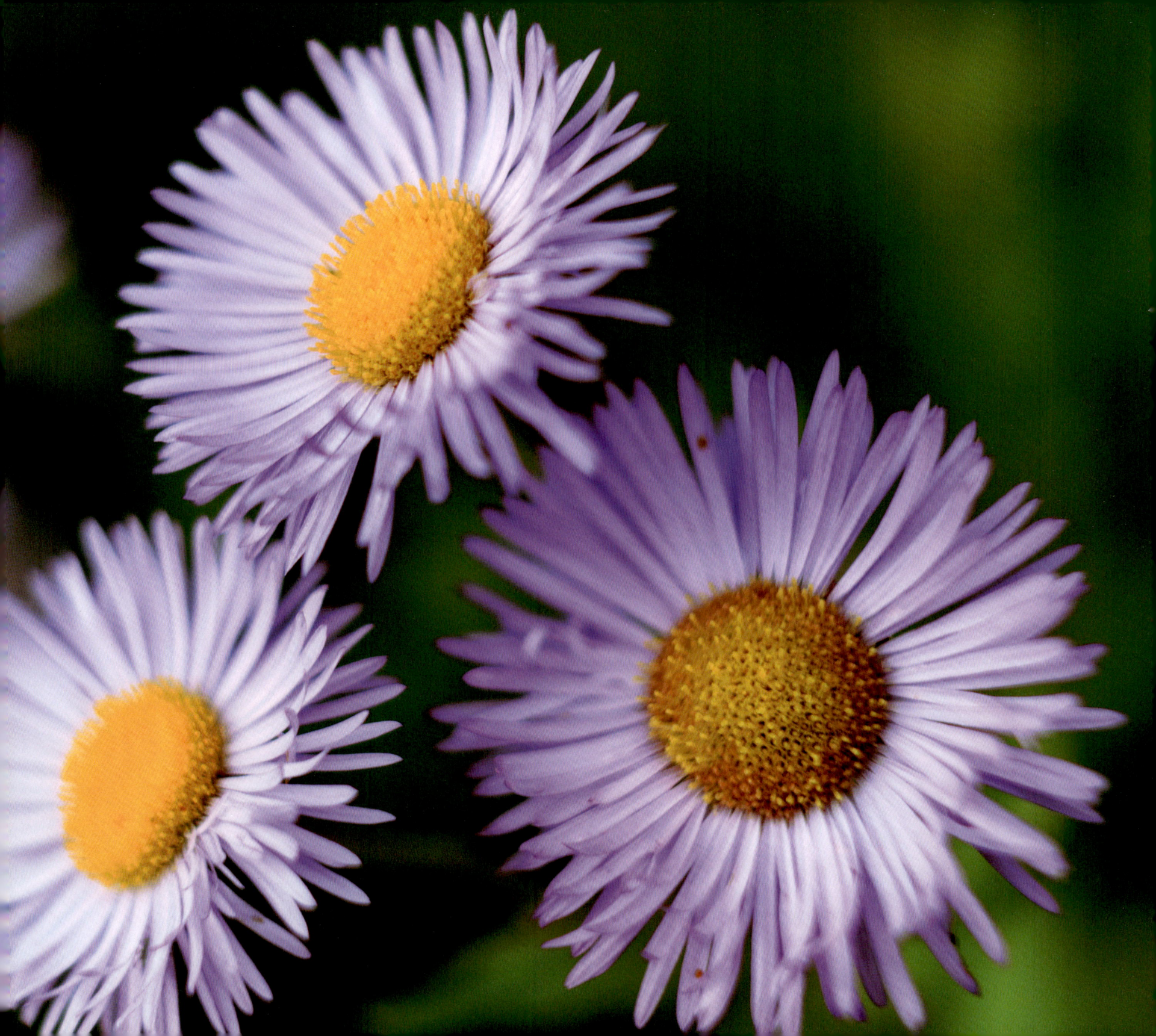

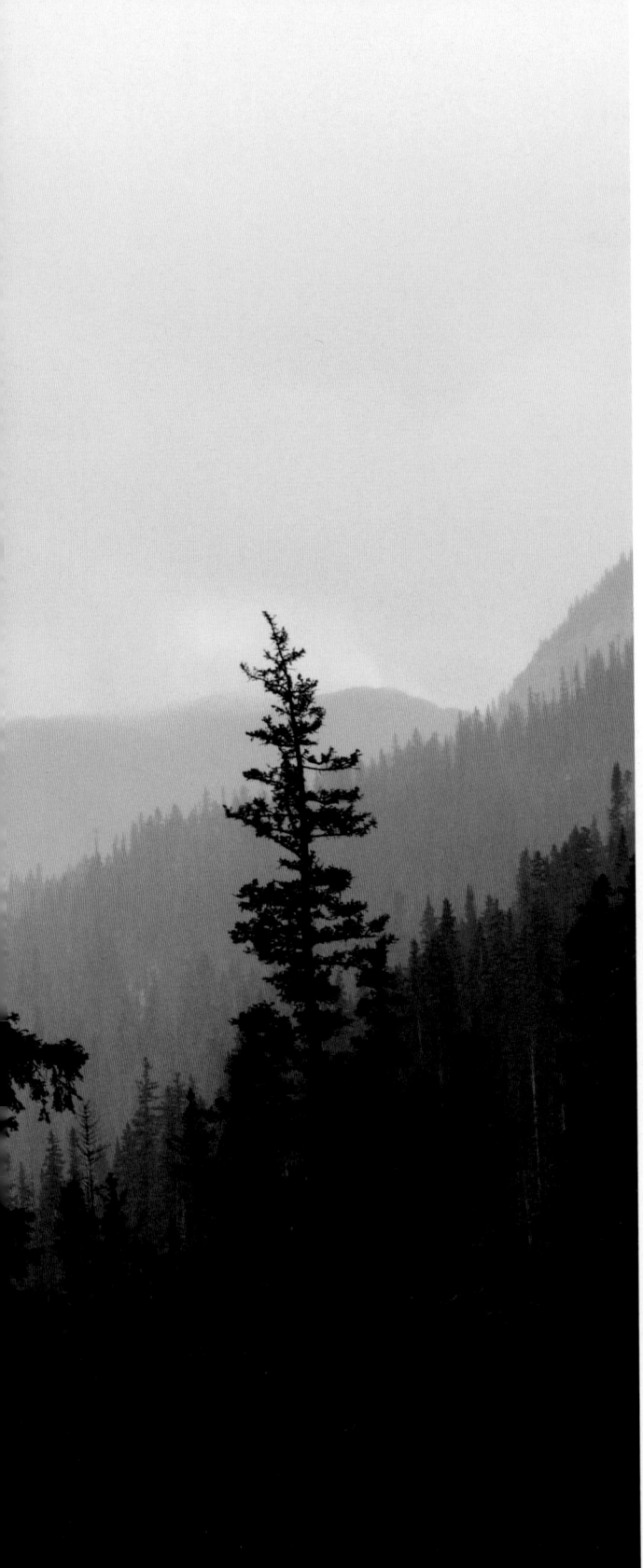

Rio Lucero

A stream can form when a river overflows
and splits in two around a freestone island.
Taos, this year, greened in a good monsoon.

This stream's native browns, some stocked rainbows
this little paradise, will vanish some dry and
quiet night, and the island's wildflower swoon

will lay aside her blues and purples, dumber
than still water. If tomorrow seems a dry land,
know that the autumn river runs, trout-strewn

enough. Our prayer: snowmelt next summer
come soon.

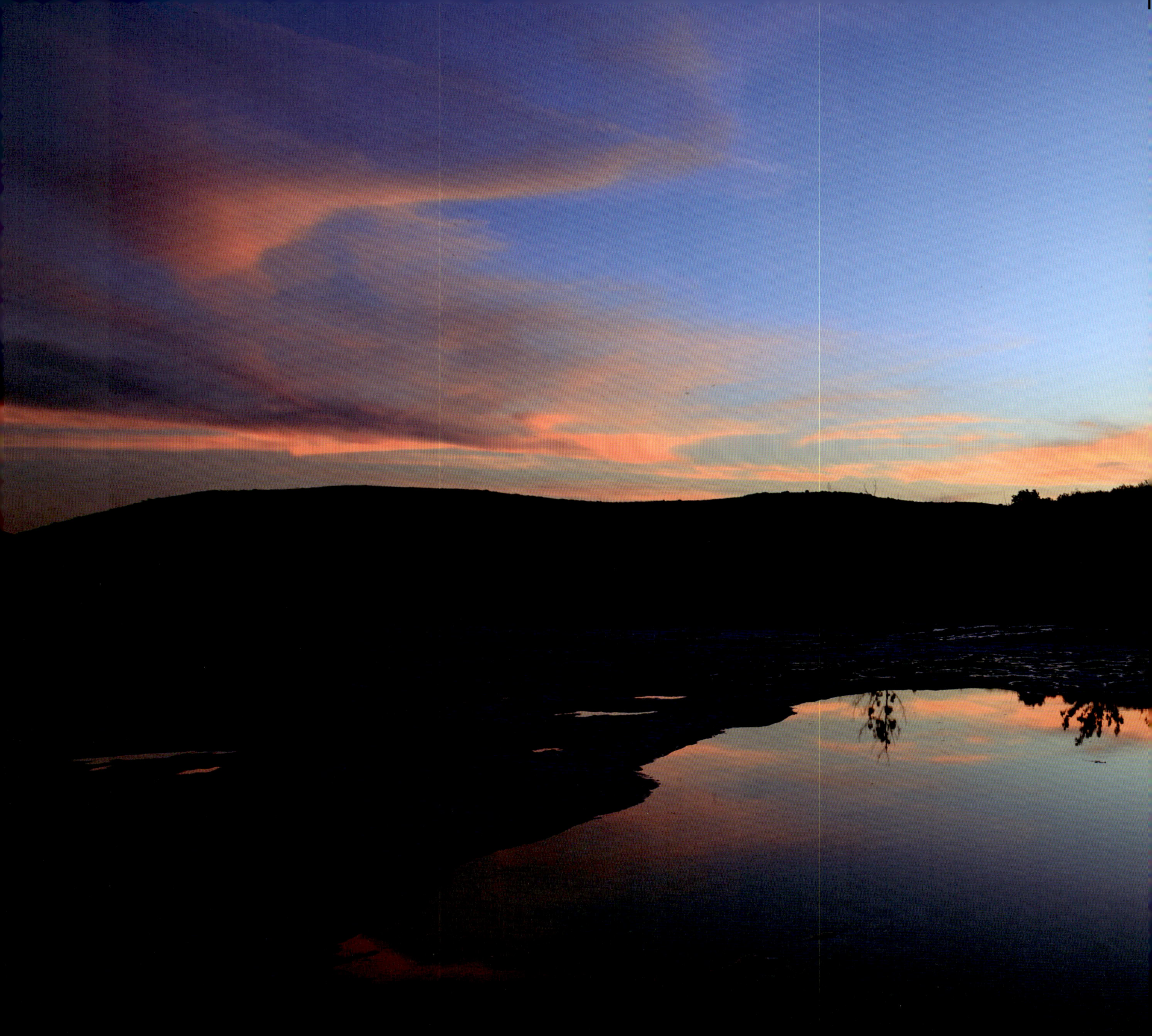

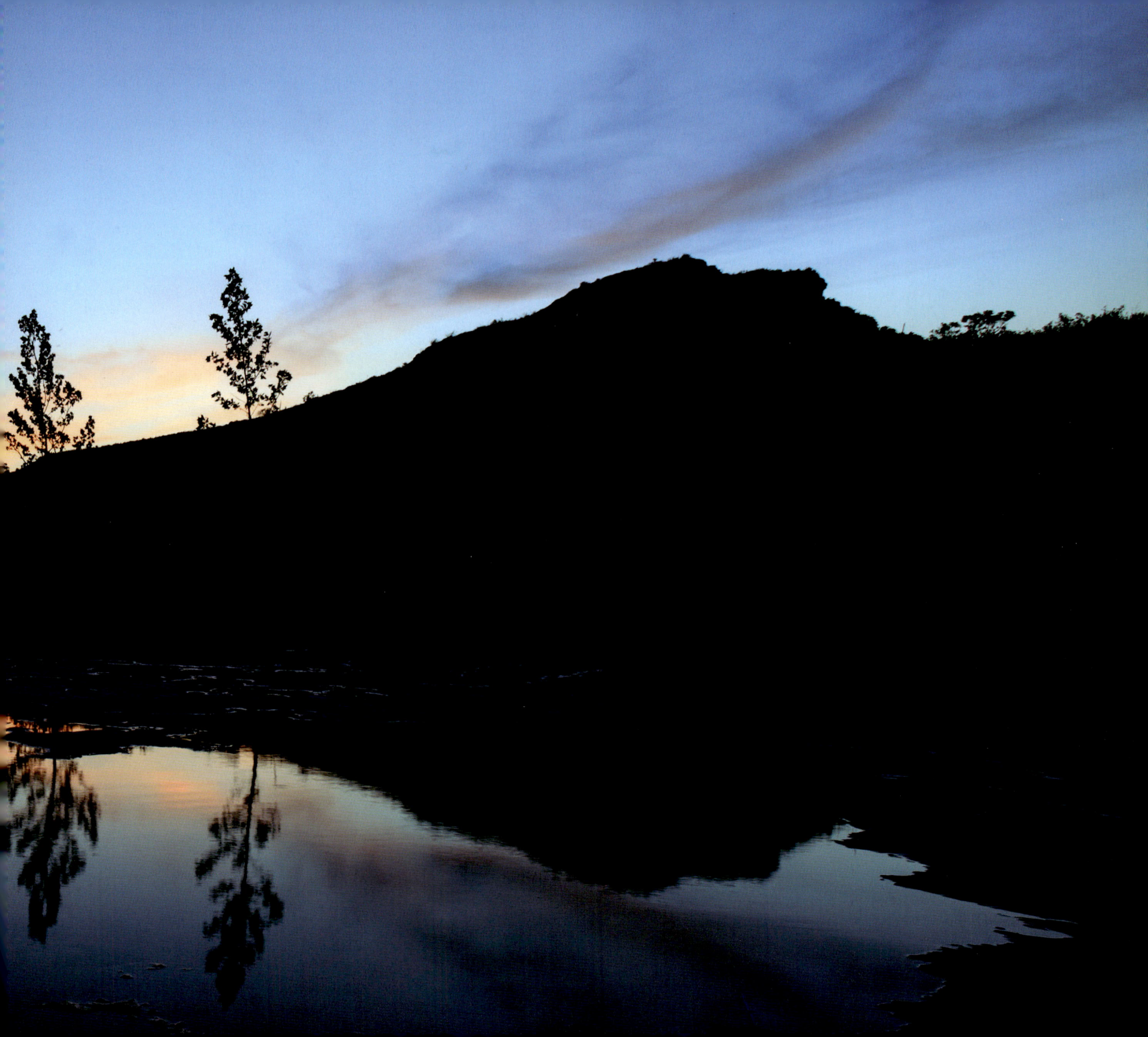

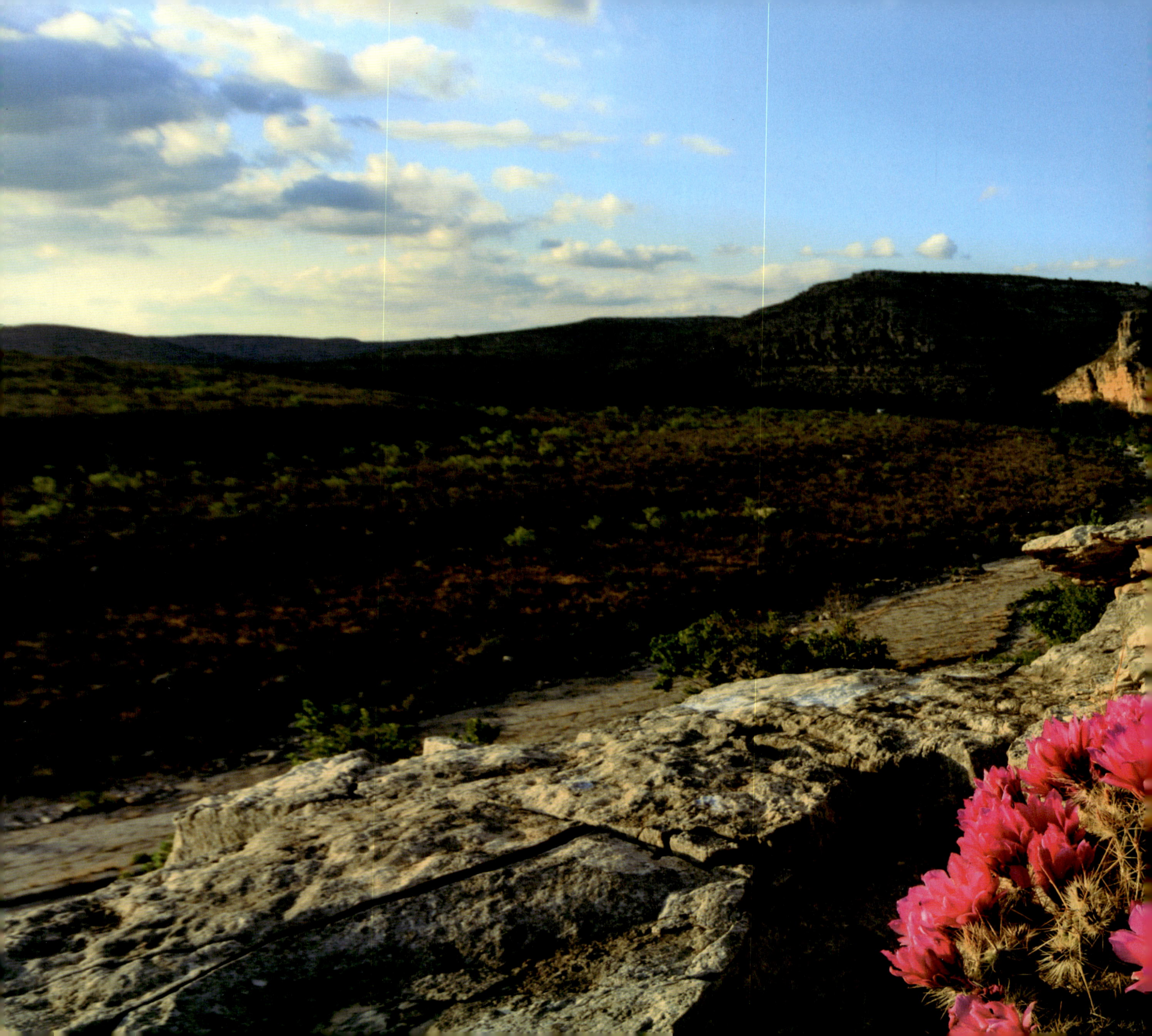

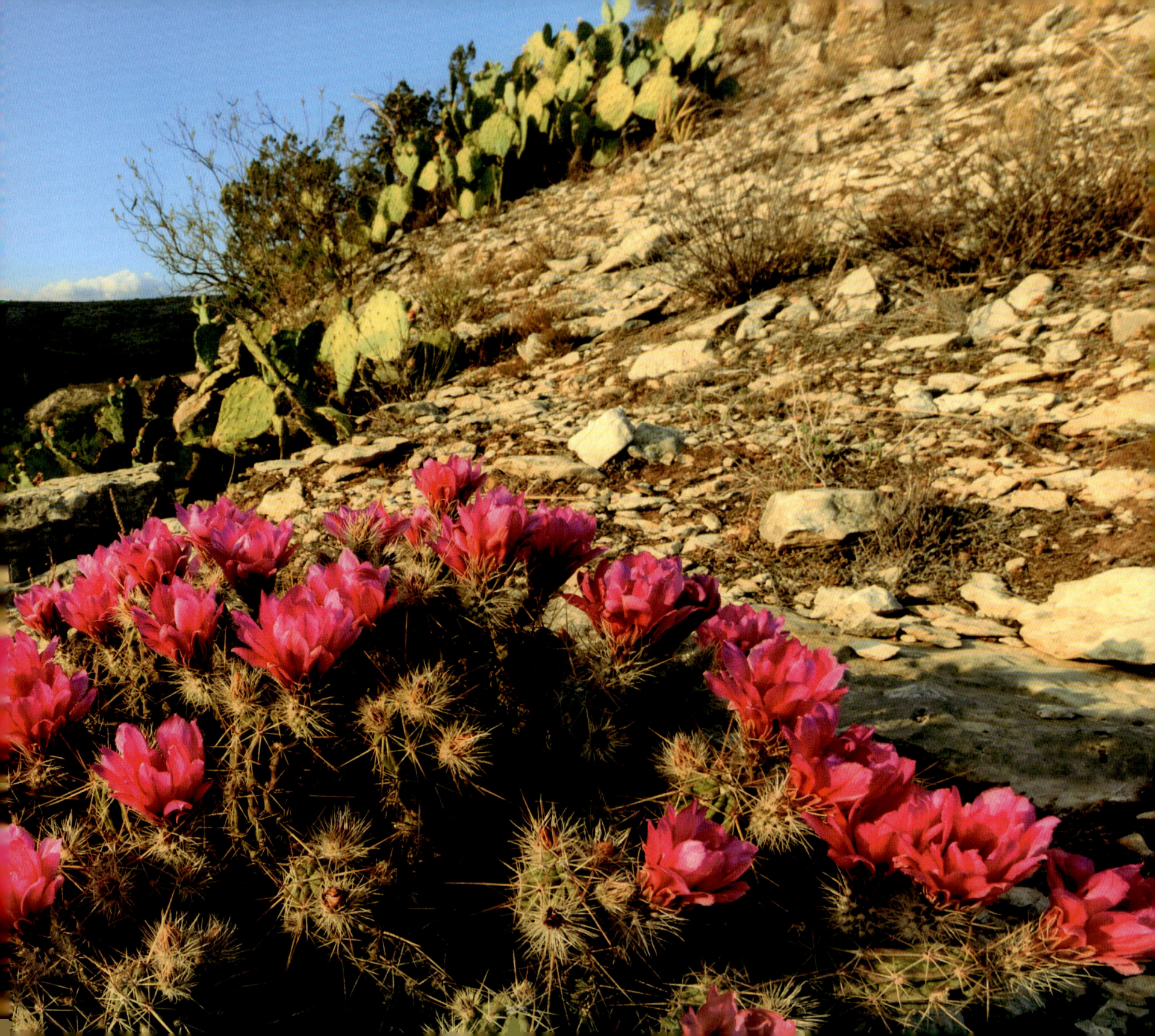

The Rio Grande (Taos)

At the John Dunn Bridge some locals nearly let
their baby drown. He drifted off, face-down,
diaper-up, ten yards, before we cried

our incoherent warning to upset
their lunch. Mid-summer's river's a sluggish brown.
The waters start to clear and rapids subside.

Balloonists dip below the basalt ridge
at dawn to touch the water then rise to crown
the mesa. Just a mile from here, beside
himself, last week, another Gorge Bridge

suicide.

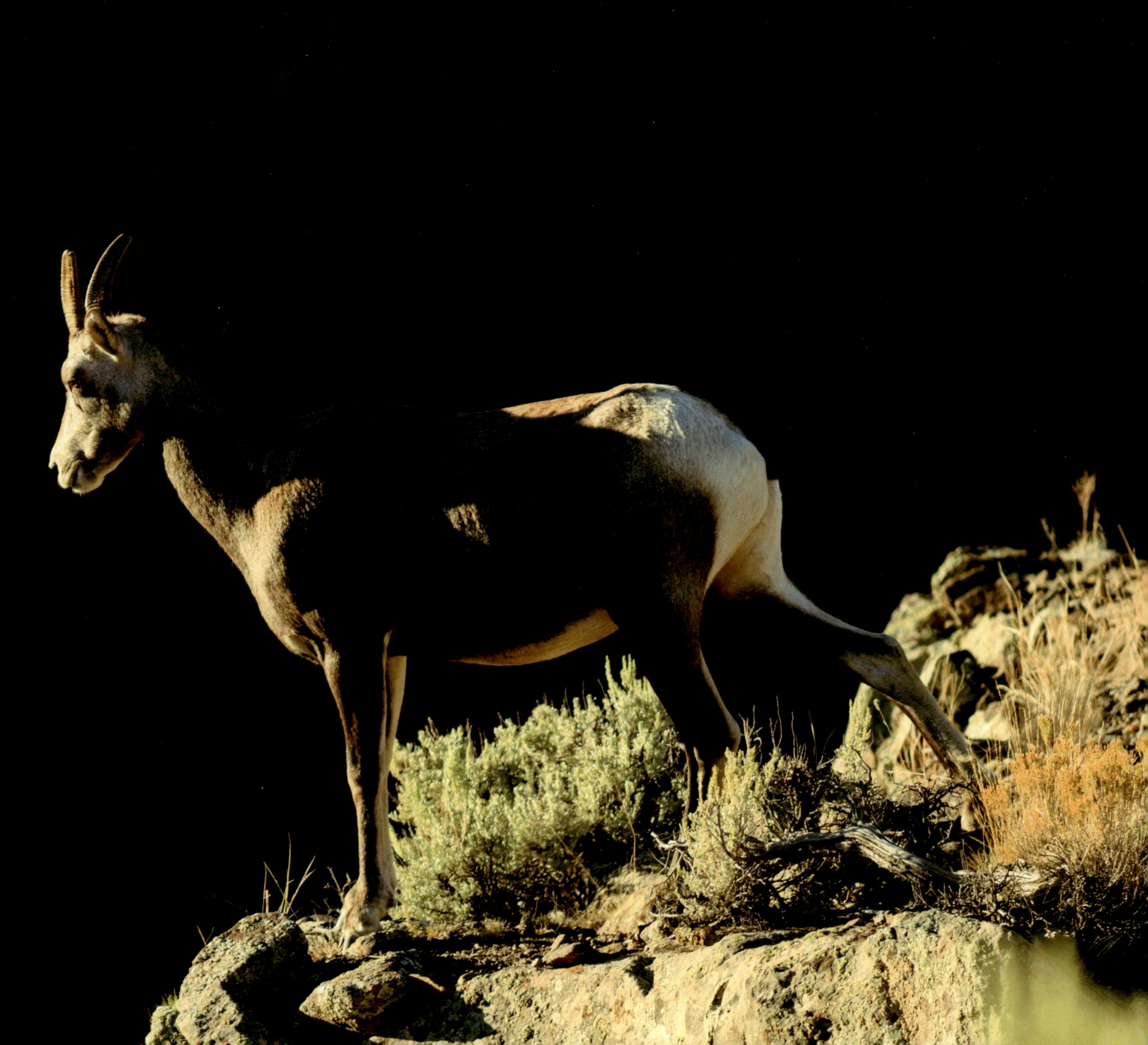

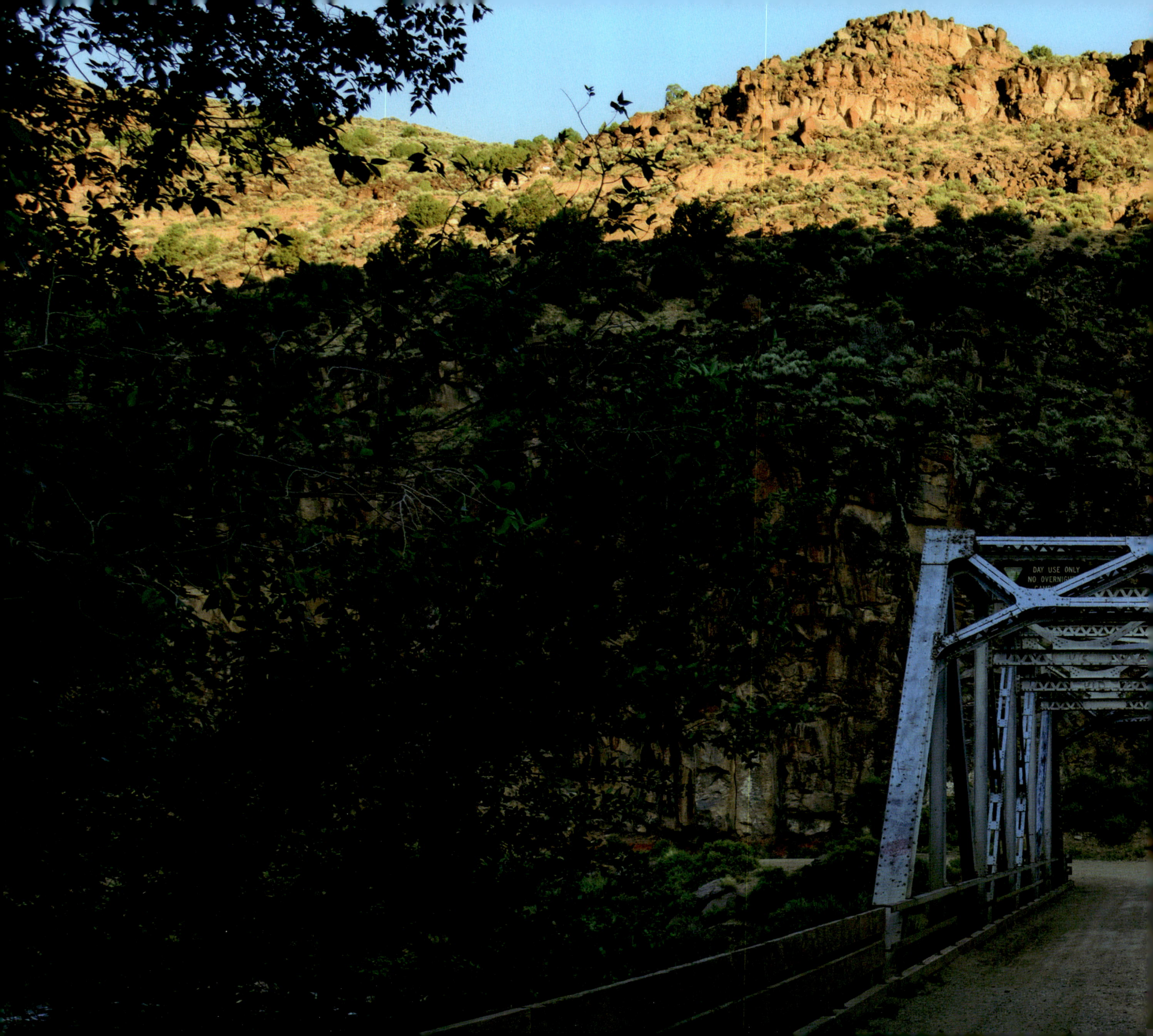

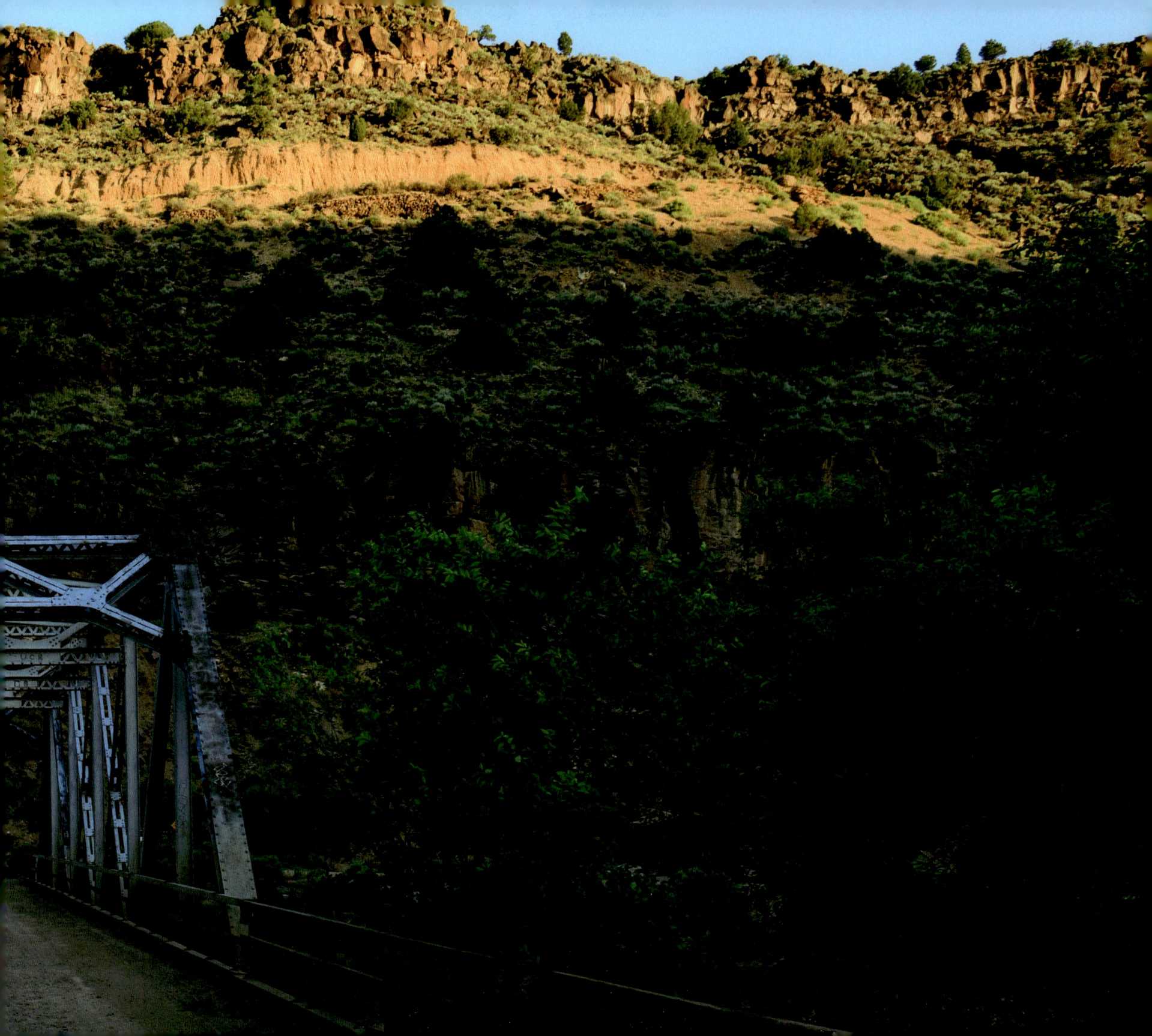

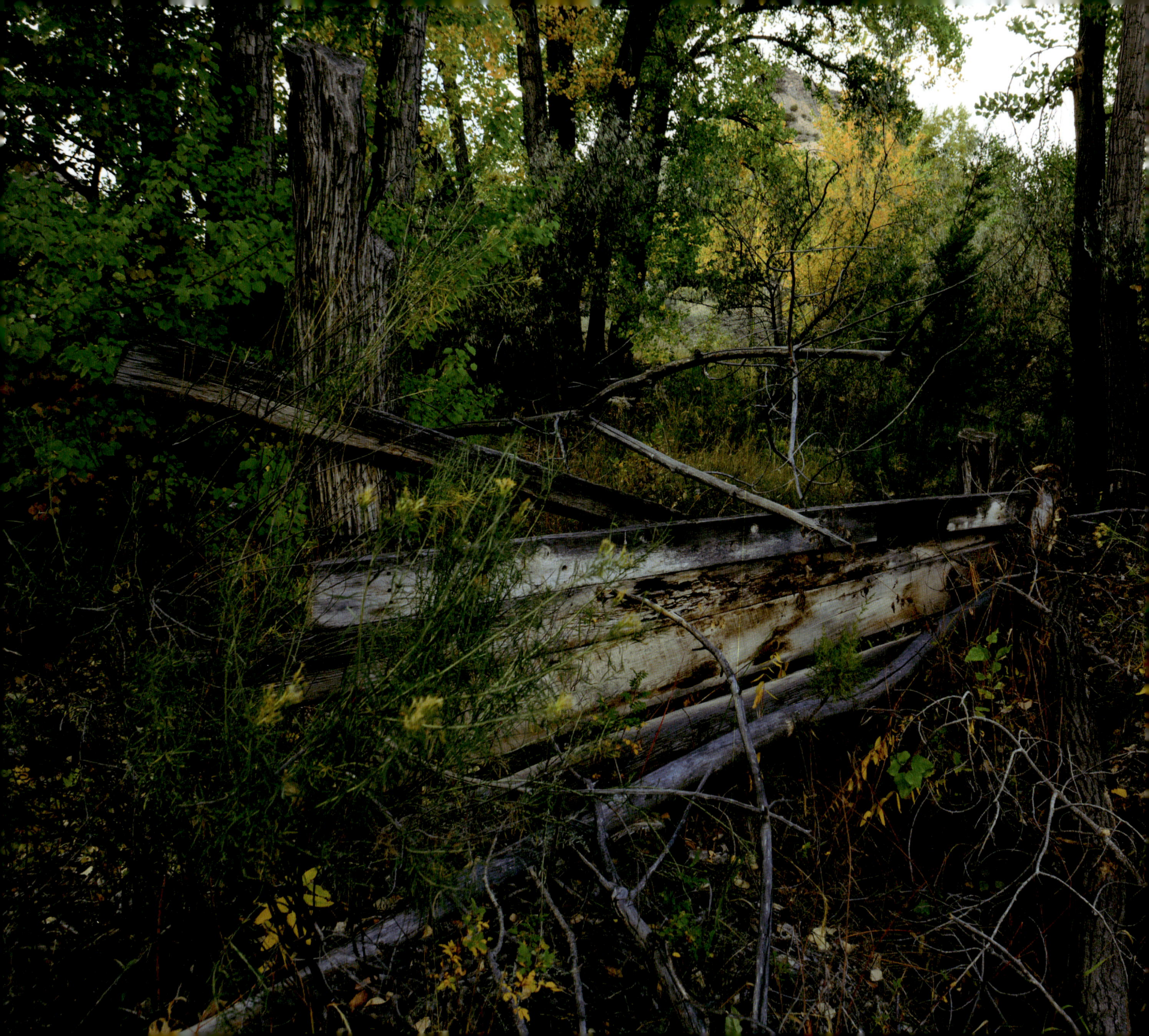

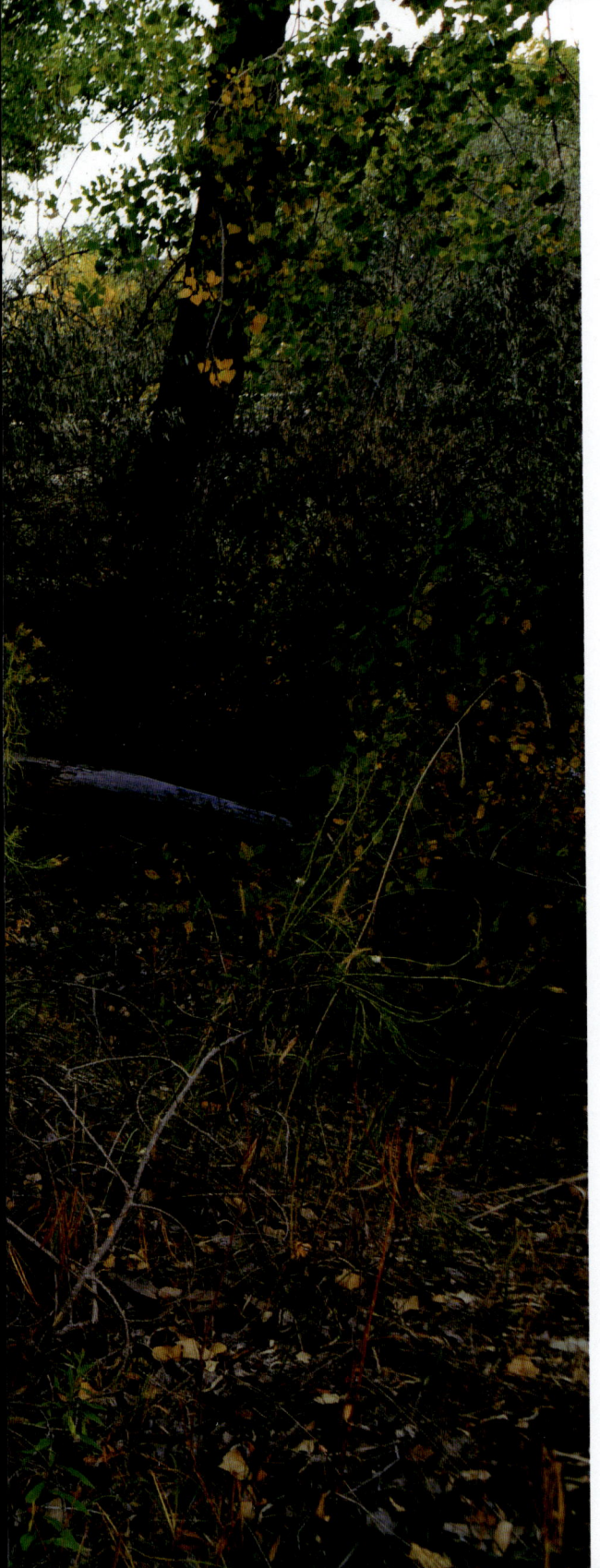

Acequia

He bleeds the running ditch to soak the pasture.
The farmer, shovel-armed, digs trenches where
the water doesn't want to cover and masters
the blue to green his gold high desert square.

Once, Tiwa hunted hares on this sagebrush mesa.
Now blue fingers crawl through dust, and might
is mud all day. The summer sun's eraser
would scribble ought on his land and water right.

A cloud on one ridge ten miles out, a bush
of smoke, of burning forest from a lightning strike
last night, speaks up high noon with a sudden rush
of wind. Where there's fire there's smoke—ghostlike.

White, throbbing fists of storm clouds threaten rain.
His dark indignant muscles flex like Cain.

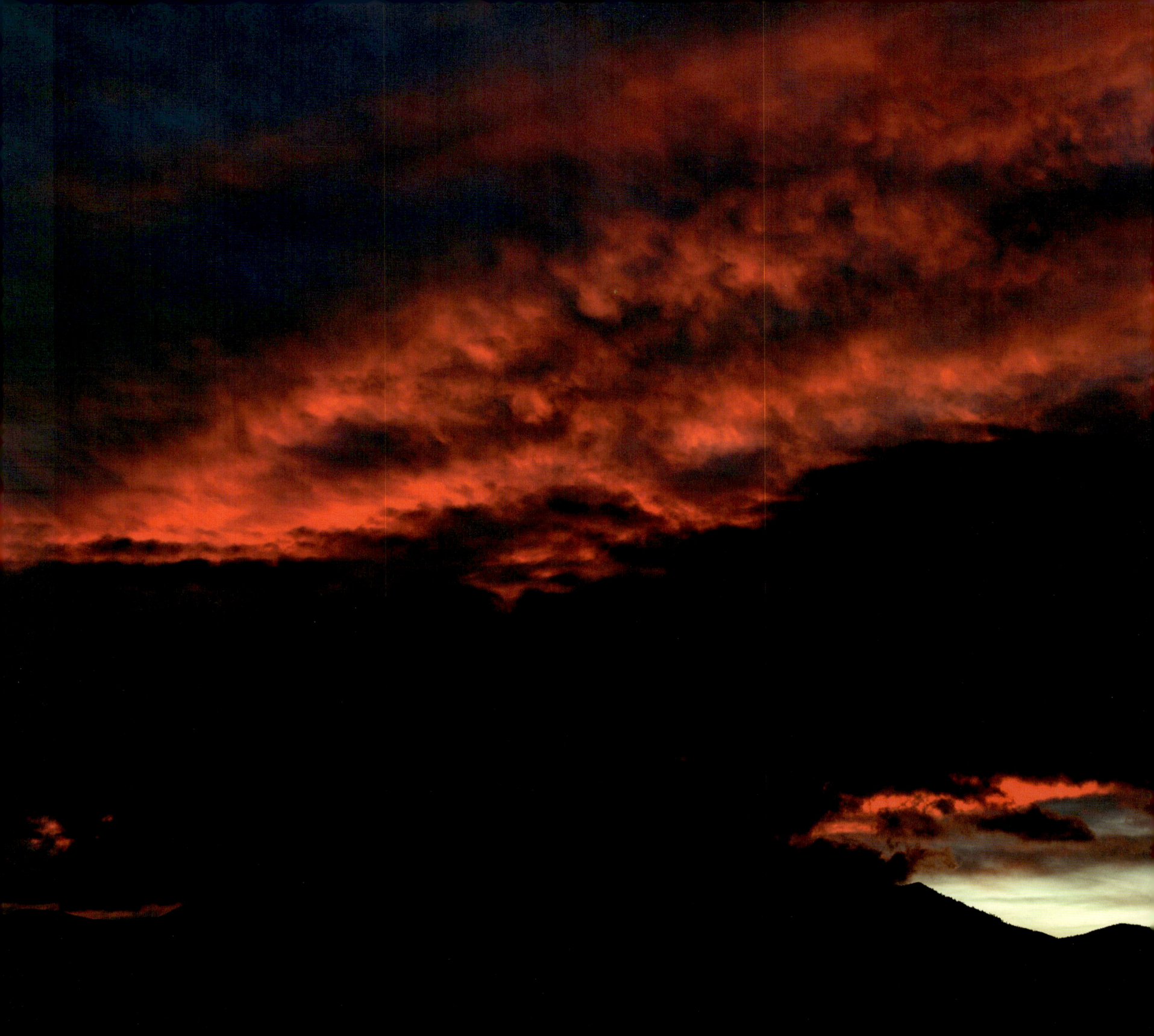

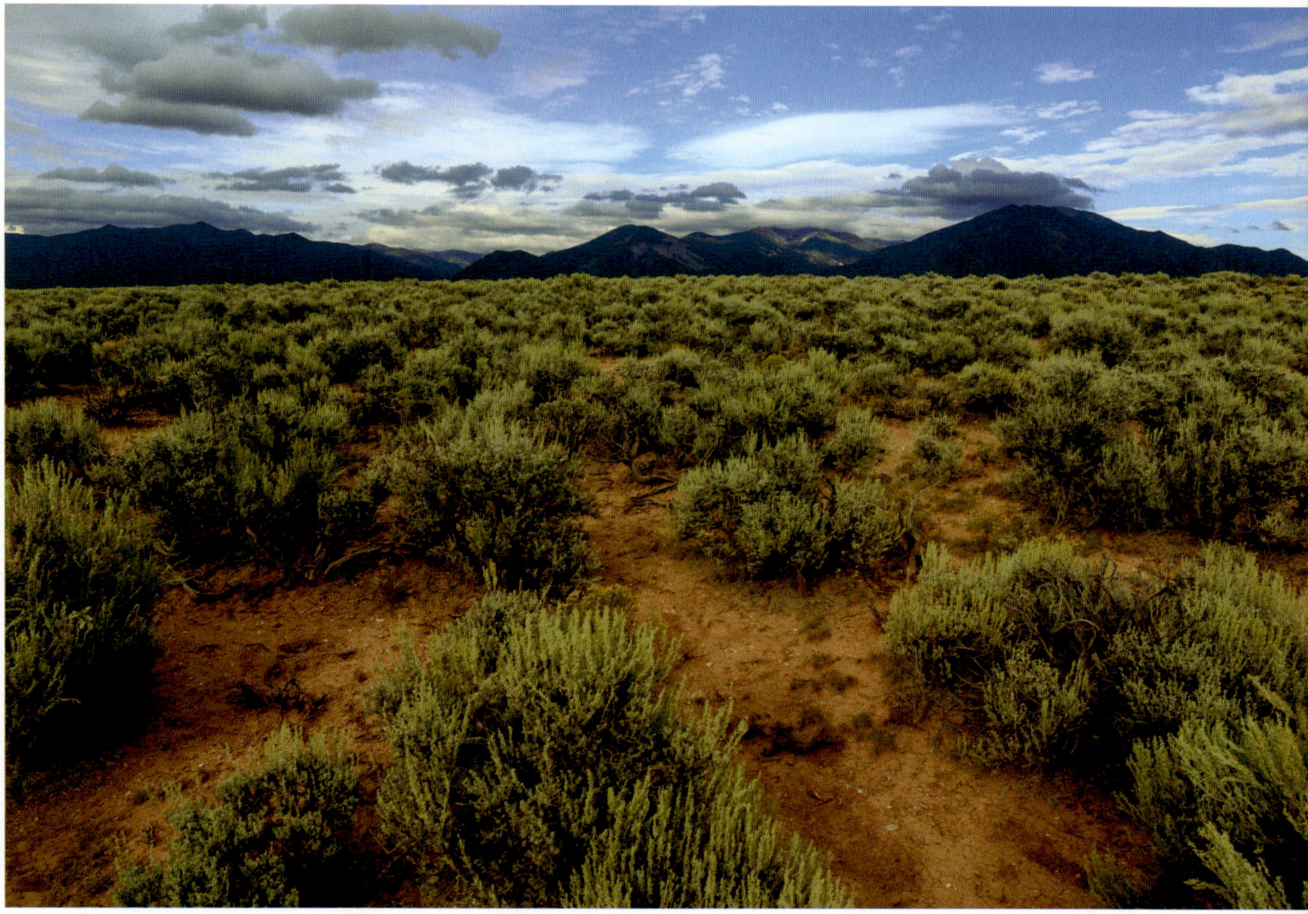

The Secret of Rivers

Standing in this current, trying
to thread a 4X tippet through the eye
of this Woven Stone I've chosen over
a Princess, missing and missing
the eye, sweating, finally through,
and you, tonight,
the secret of rivers,
that long neck of yours panting
in the lamplight coming at that high,
long angle from the hallway to the dark
where I cast a shadow on you
and you don't know it.

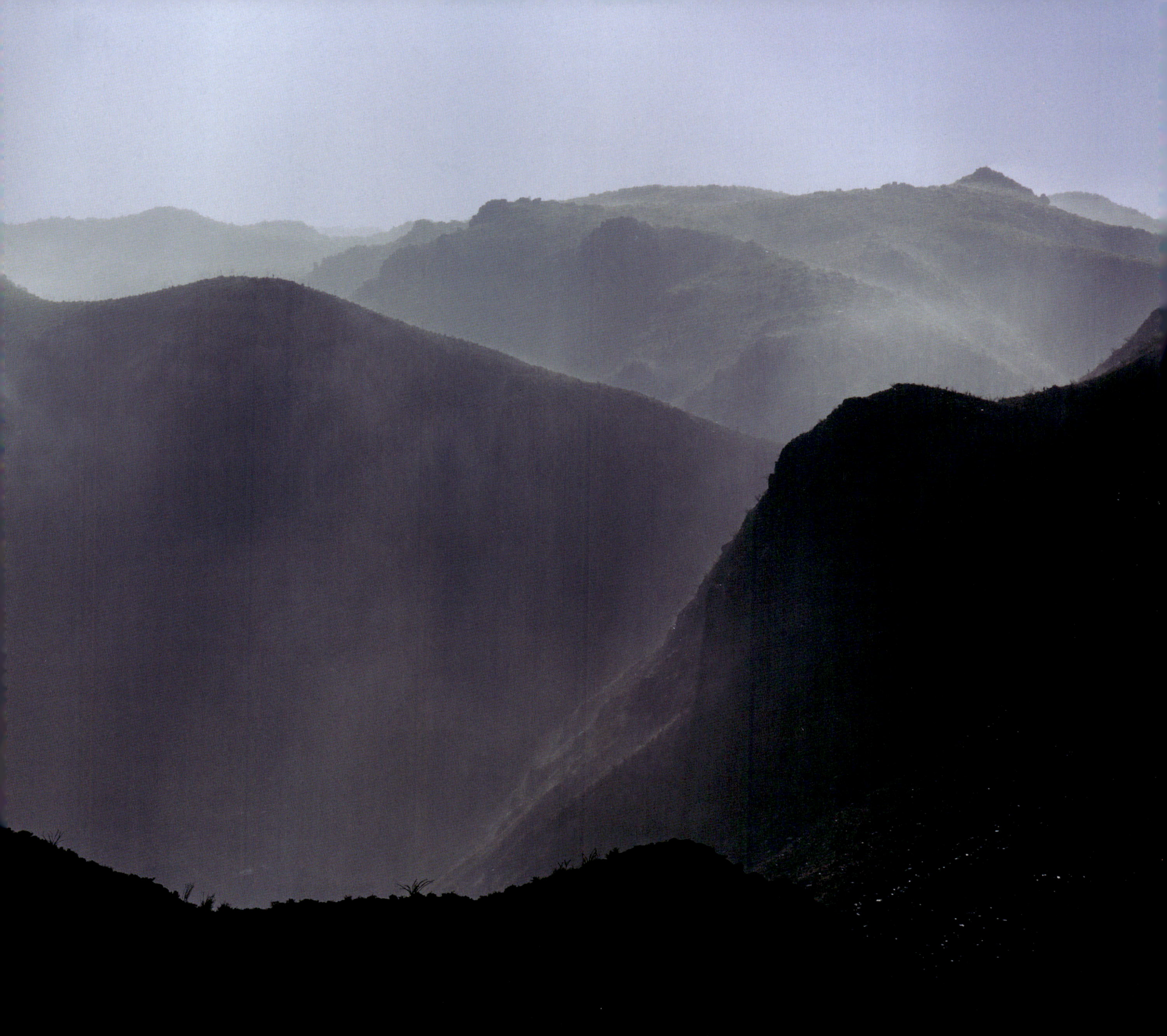

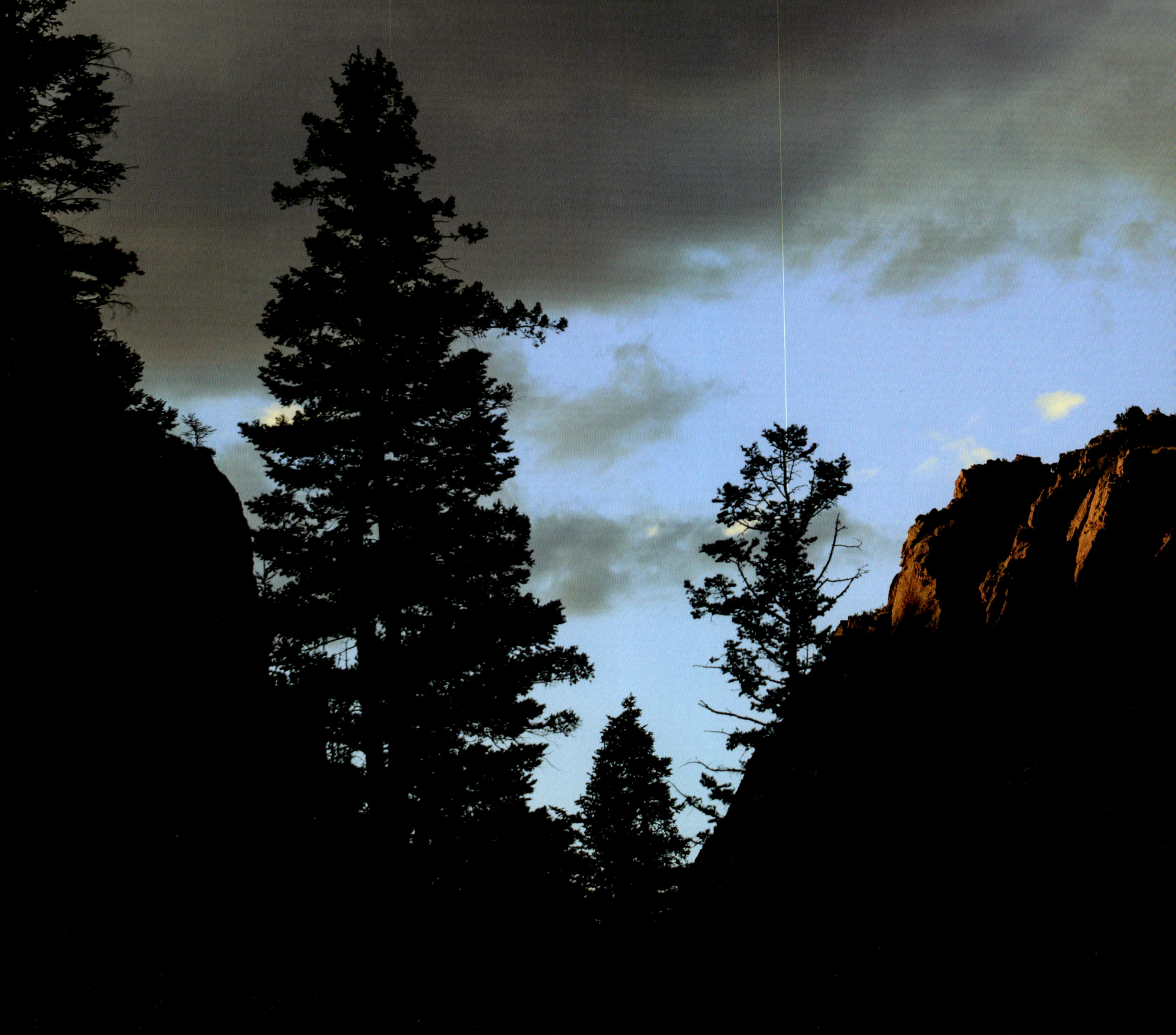

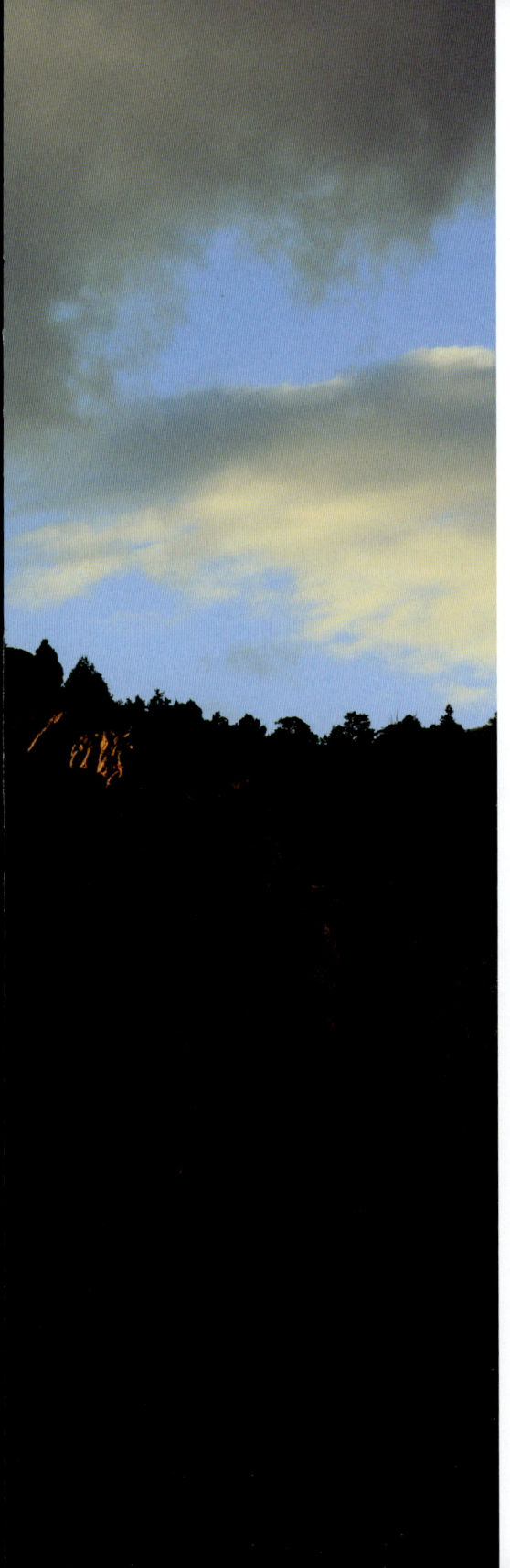

Red River (Hatchery)

I always think they'll stock the river with
a few of the million trout they raise right here.
But mostly, nothing doing. I'd rank it fifth
among my favorite streams in Taos this year.

They've torn away the antiquated dam.
The trout can roam upstream without a flood.
We'll watch for years to come the traffic jam
of rocks and blasted concrete, sand and mud

thin, clarify, the river run its course
within this valley made of vast, stained shoulders
where a Golden eagle big as a little horse
makes refuge high in the crumbling basalt boulders.

A half mile upstream, tangles of wild rose
cut me. This is where almost no one goes.

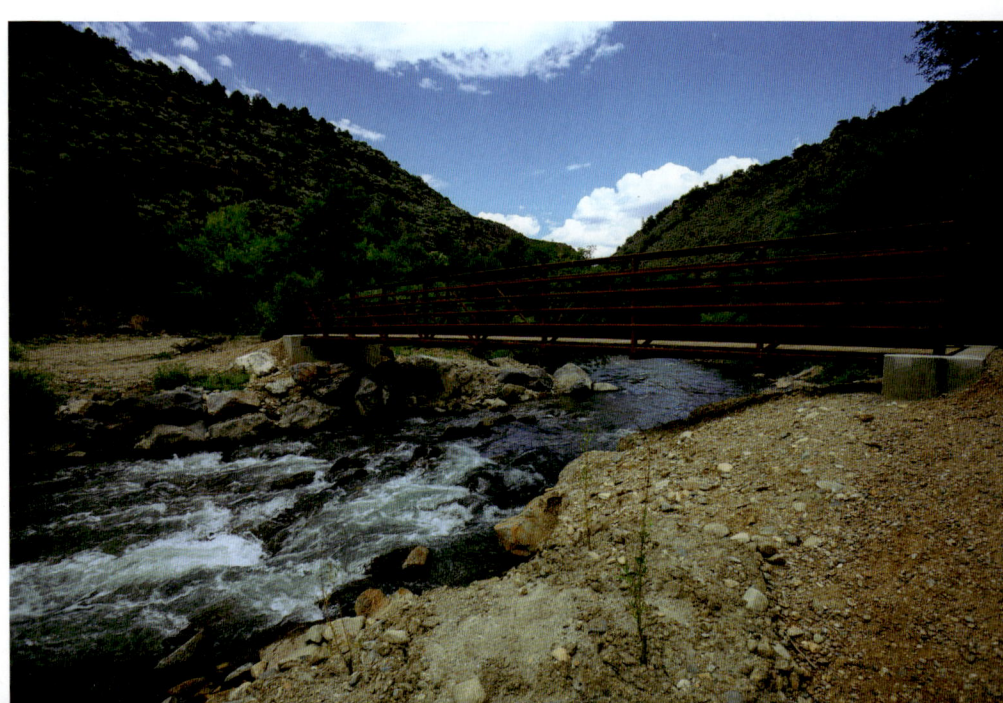

Invasive Species

Some days are better than others.
Yesterday, from a helicopter, I slaughtered
with an AR-15 a couple dozen wild pigs
for miles along a desiccated river.
Nowhere to hide, they fell like dull dominoes
on the limestone bed and dust, with little puffs
of lead exhaust. The biggest boar, tired
of the metal god of constant thunder above,
tired of his own old fat and heaving tusks
that he would have loved to have sharpened
on my thigh bones, he tried to hide below
a thin mesquite he considered a tree of life.
We chuckled as righteous God must have
at modest Adam in his sin. *Where are you?*

We lit up his little Eden with the angel of death.
I wouldn't know, but they say the flesh
of any wild pig over a year old
tastes rancid no matter how you cook it,
ham or loin or meaty shoulder. Some say
it tastes like human flesh, but who would know?
You couldn't hear the laughter over the roars
of all our hovering power poured out.
I admit we paid a lot to get those kicks
and free beer at the cabin after, watching
the sun set. Later, someone by the fire asked
a question: *What is the glory of God?*

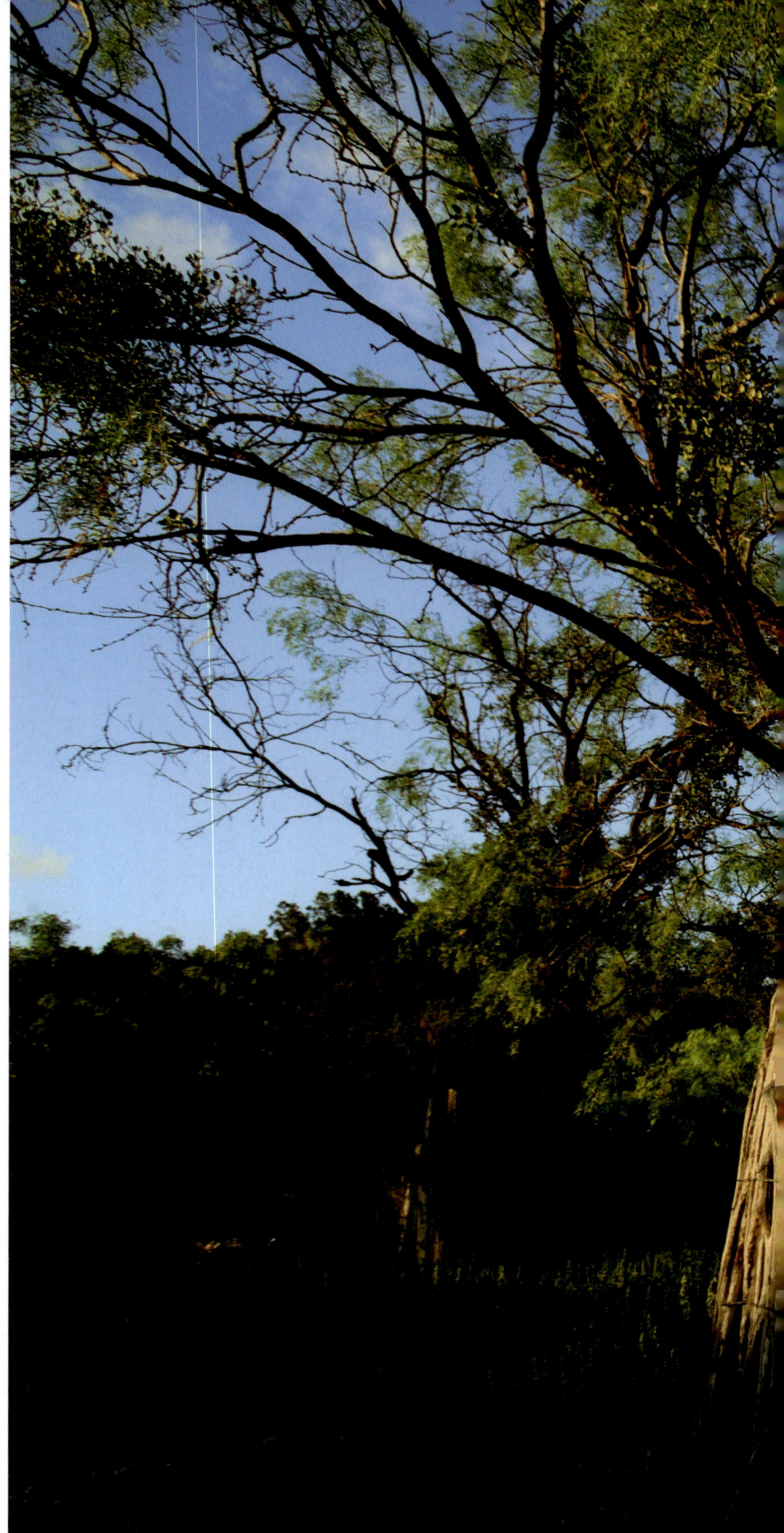

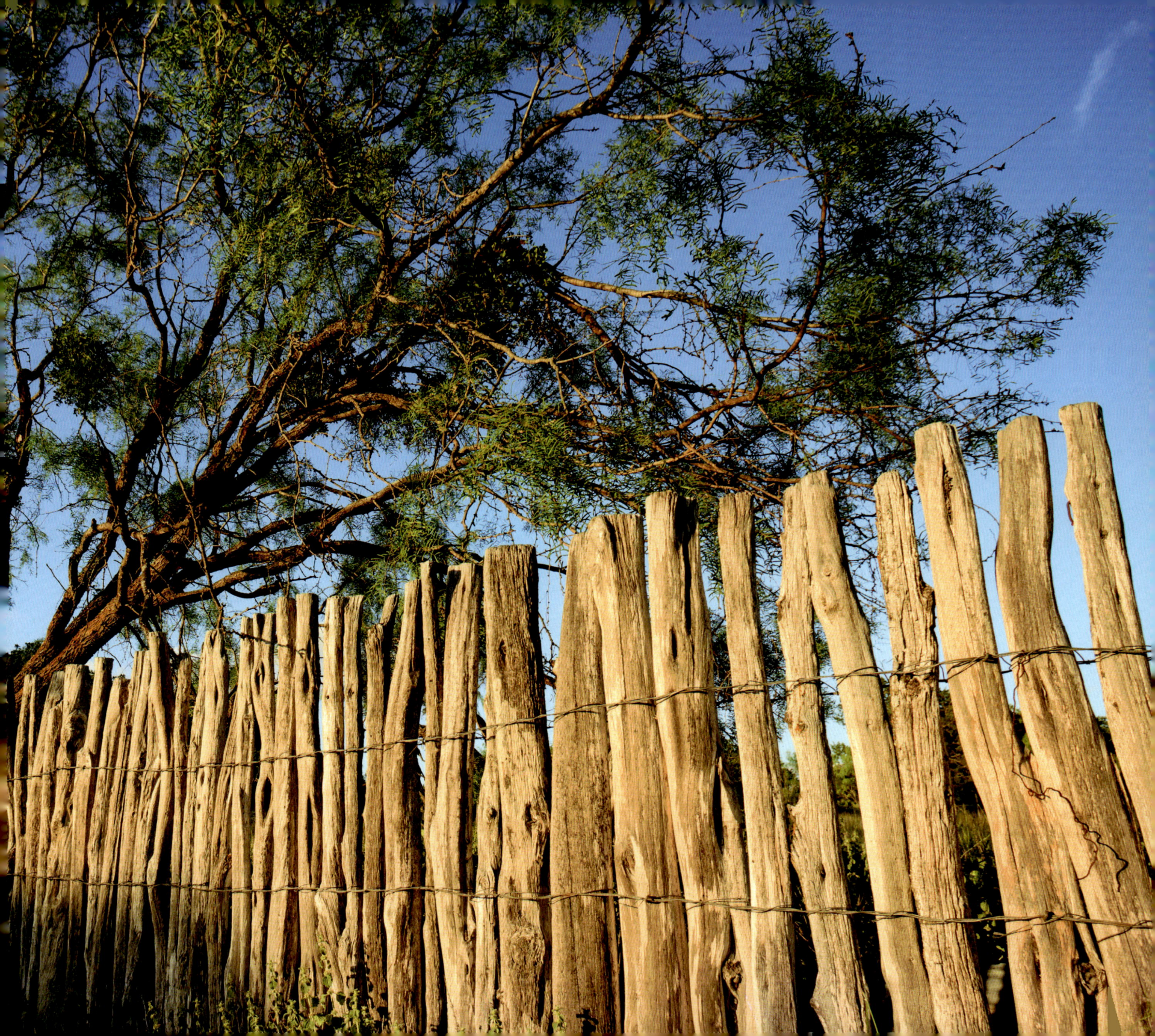

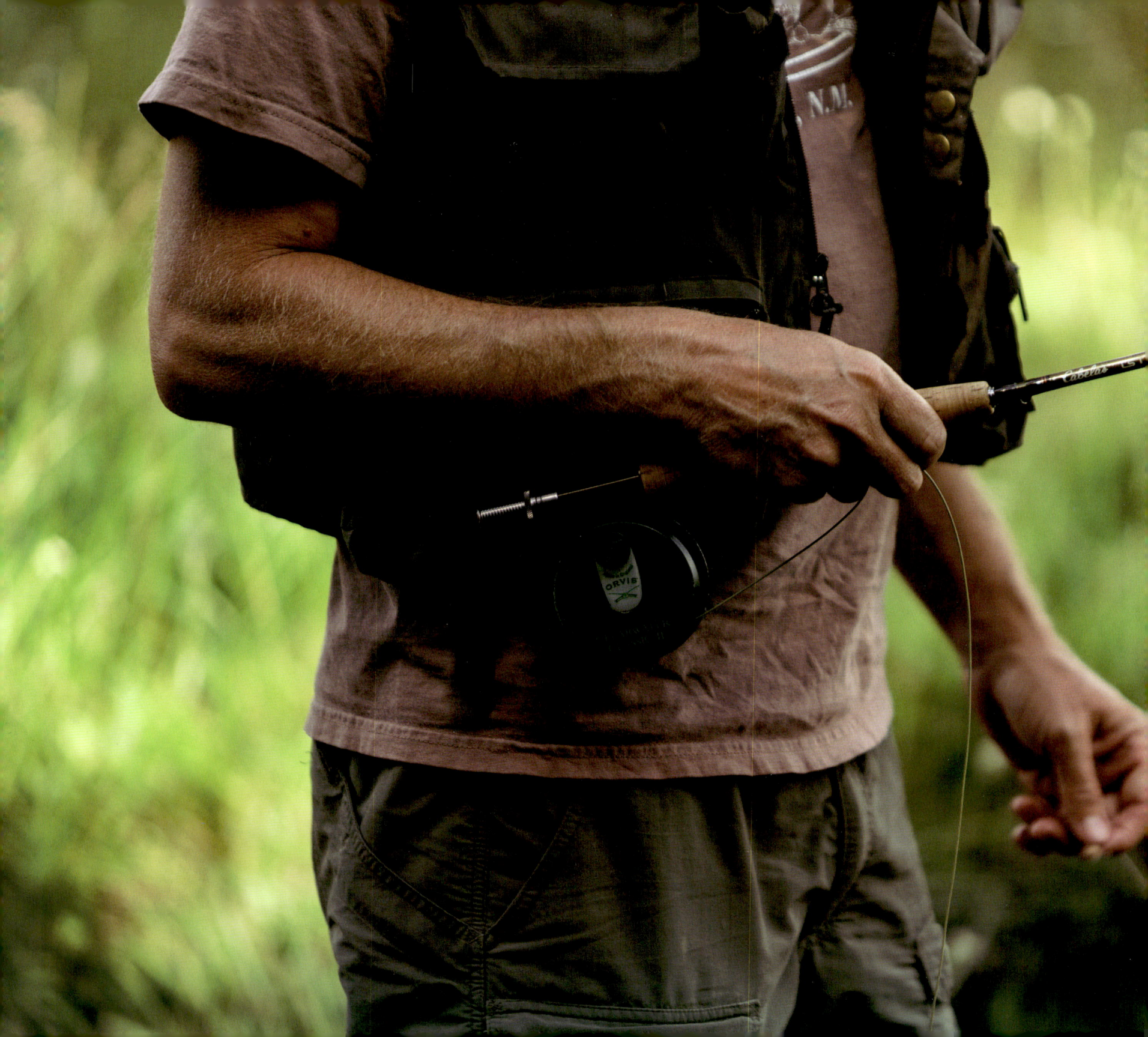

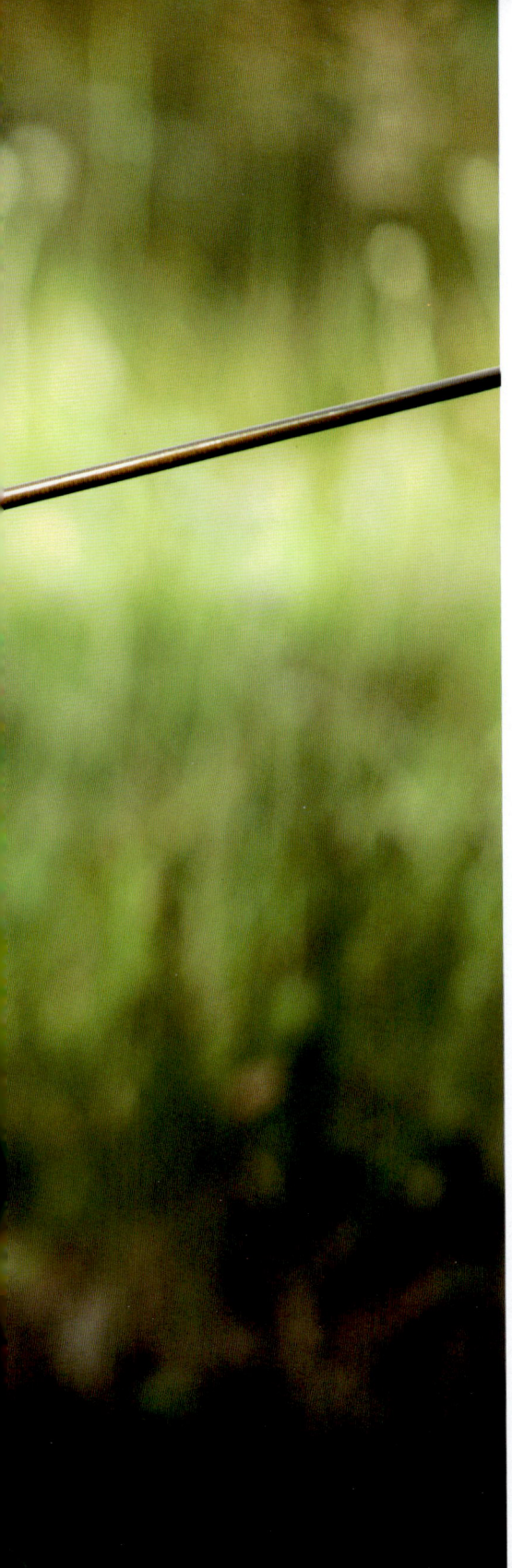

The Colorado River (Texas)

Close to Lampasas on one half-mile stretch
in early March, the water clarifies
almost. The purple mountain laurels sass

the rotting browns of winter. You think you'll catch
not fish so much as a God who loves disguise
and a great spill of tea with milk—and pass

the boredom, please—with gray skies dropping mist
then spitting rain. Cold, you realize
you forgot your waders. You wade and ache. You cast,

surprised by the strike, the electricity-kissed
white bass.

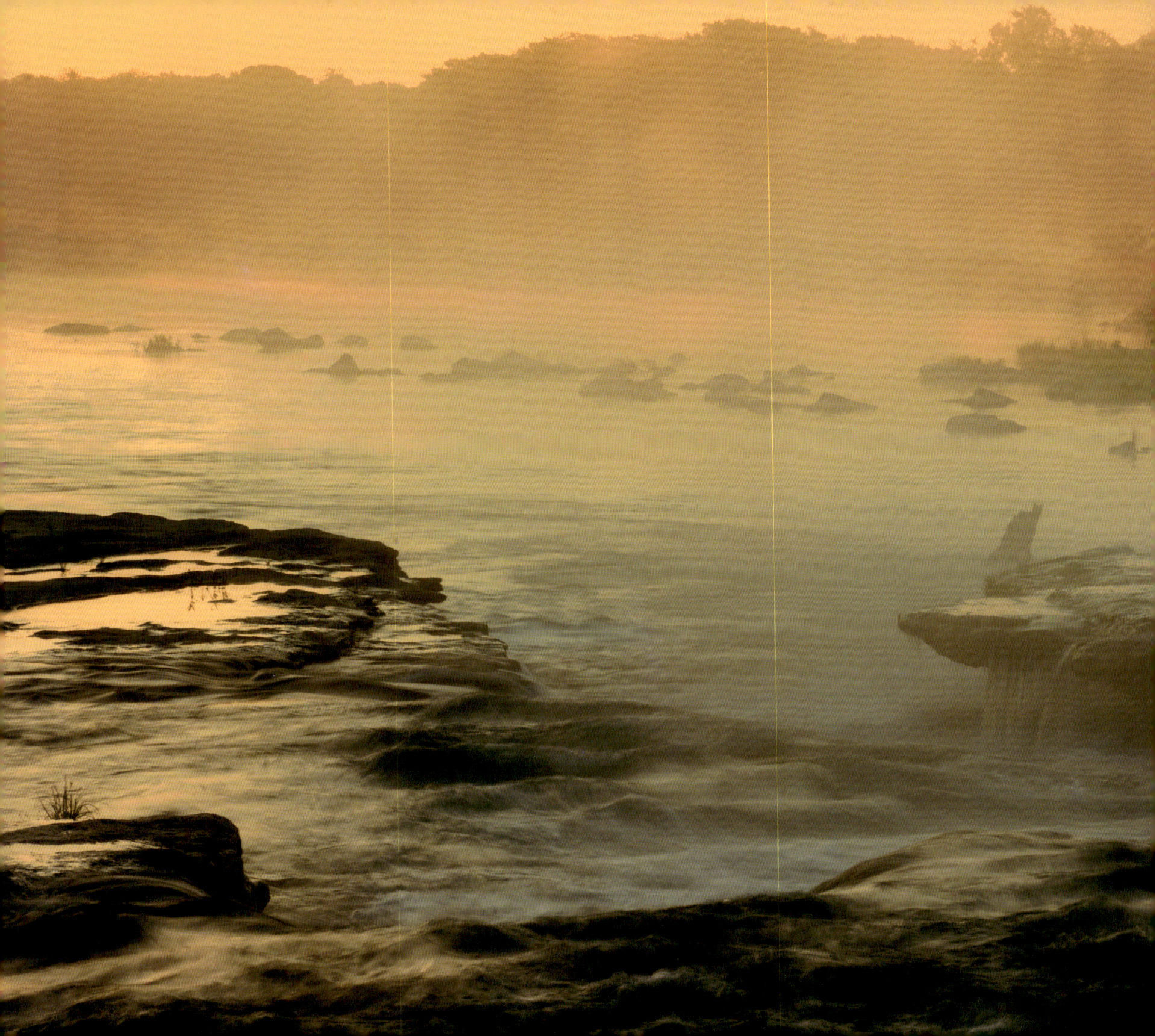

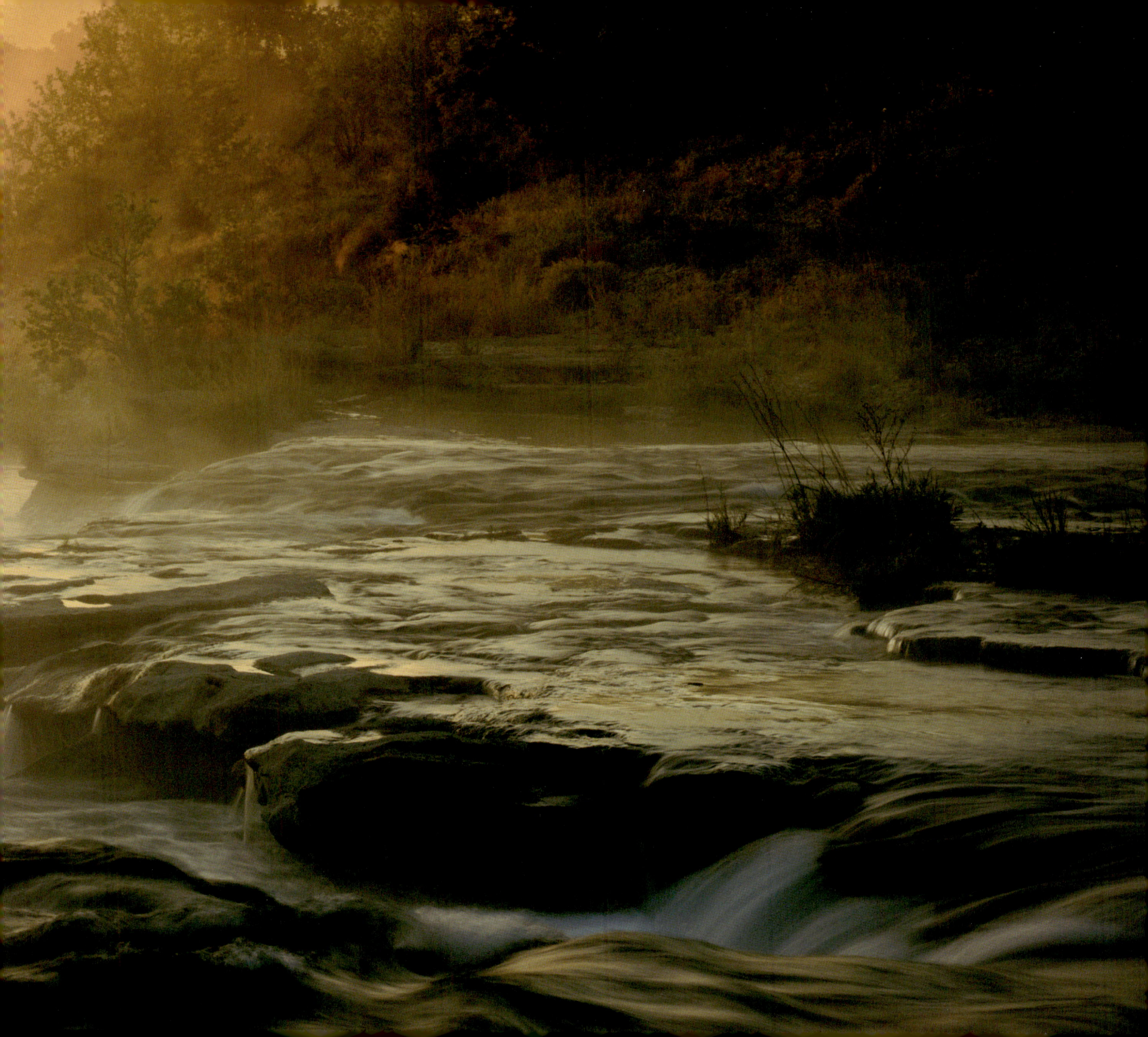

The Llano River

In a pile of mesquite debris in the field
not far above the river, the cotton rat twitches
in its sleep, dreaming of a Sharp-shinned hawk.
At the river bottom, the giant stands
of pecan trees canopy a trampled deer path
which is its own small stream carried away
with her footsteps. The wind moves through
the grass at the bank like three deer, and then
three deer move through the grass like light wind.
They are three does the color of rotten twine,
and they lift their heads when a single mesquite leaf
shakes loose from its tree fluttering as if
it had wanted this long spiraling downward.
Her path leads from the field to the river,
and I have followed with my book in which
none of this appears, not one wooden giant
or a path or a woman I must follow with my book.

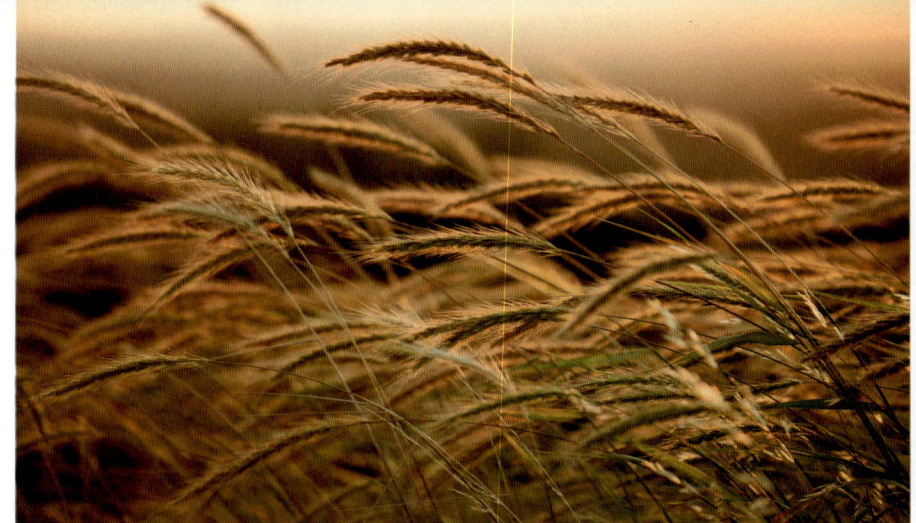

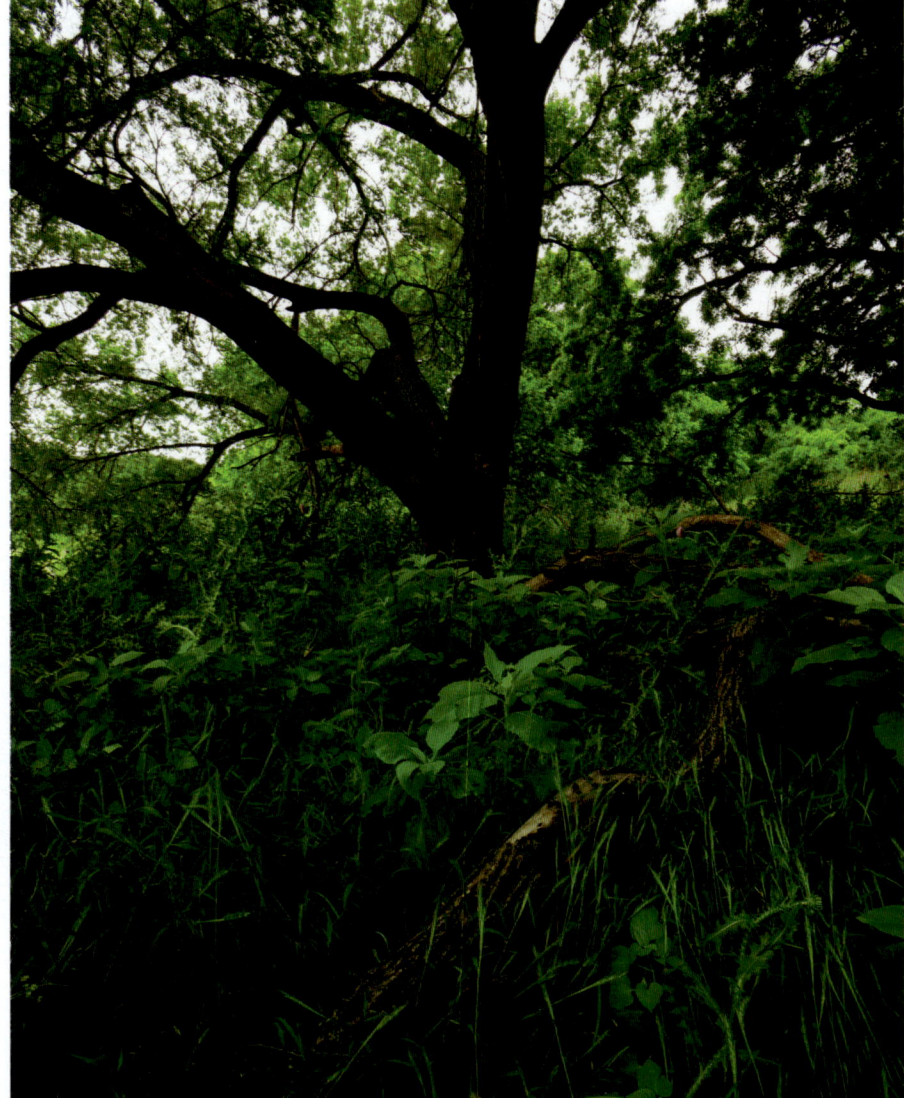

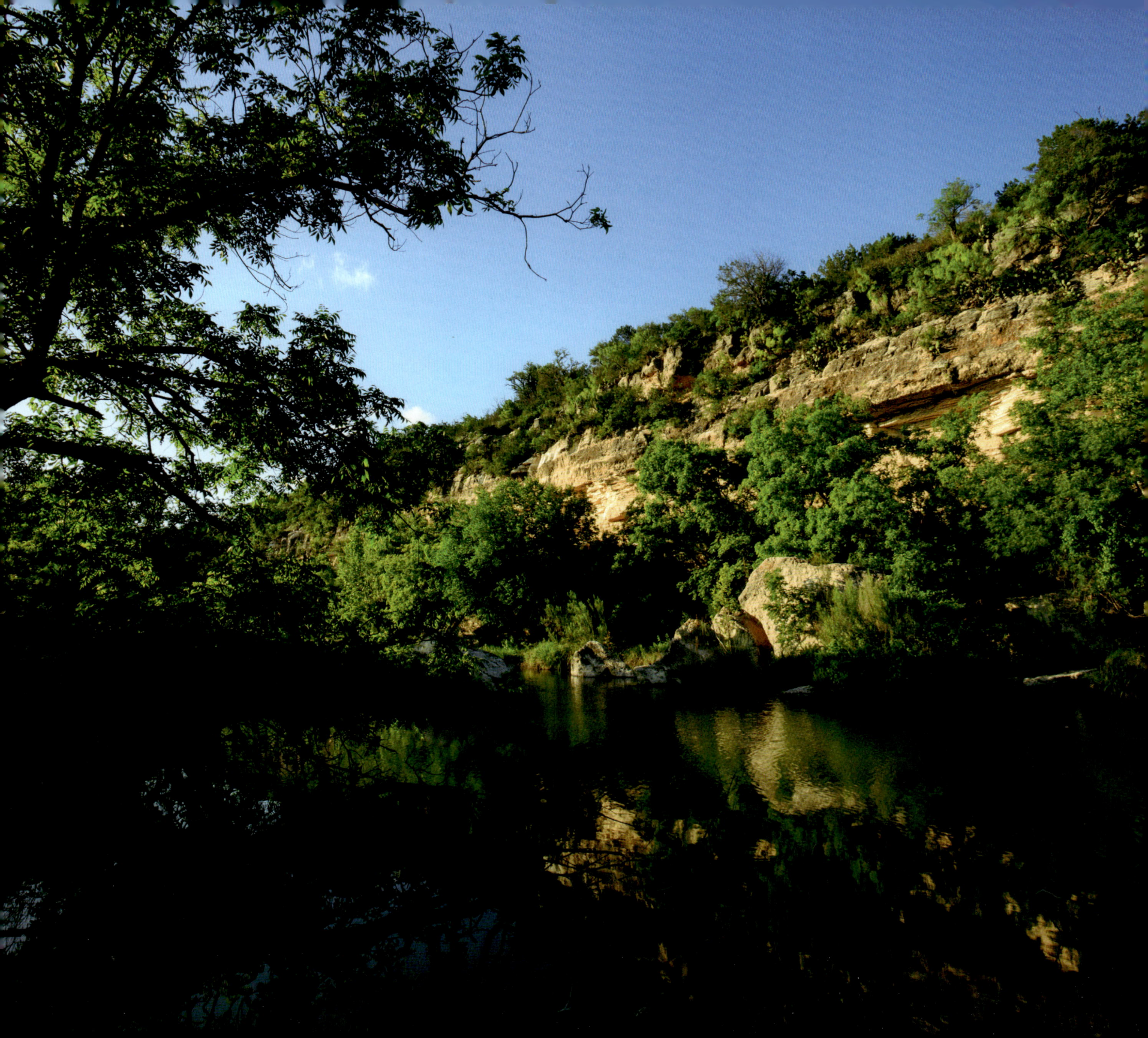

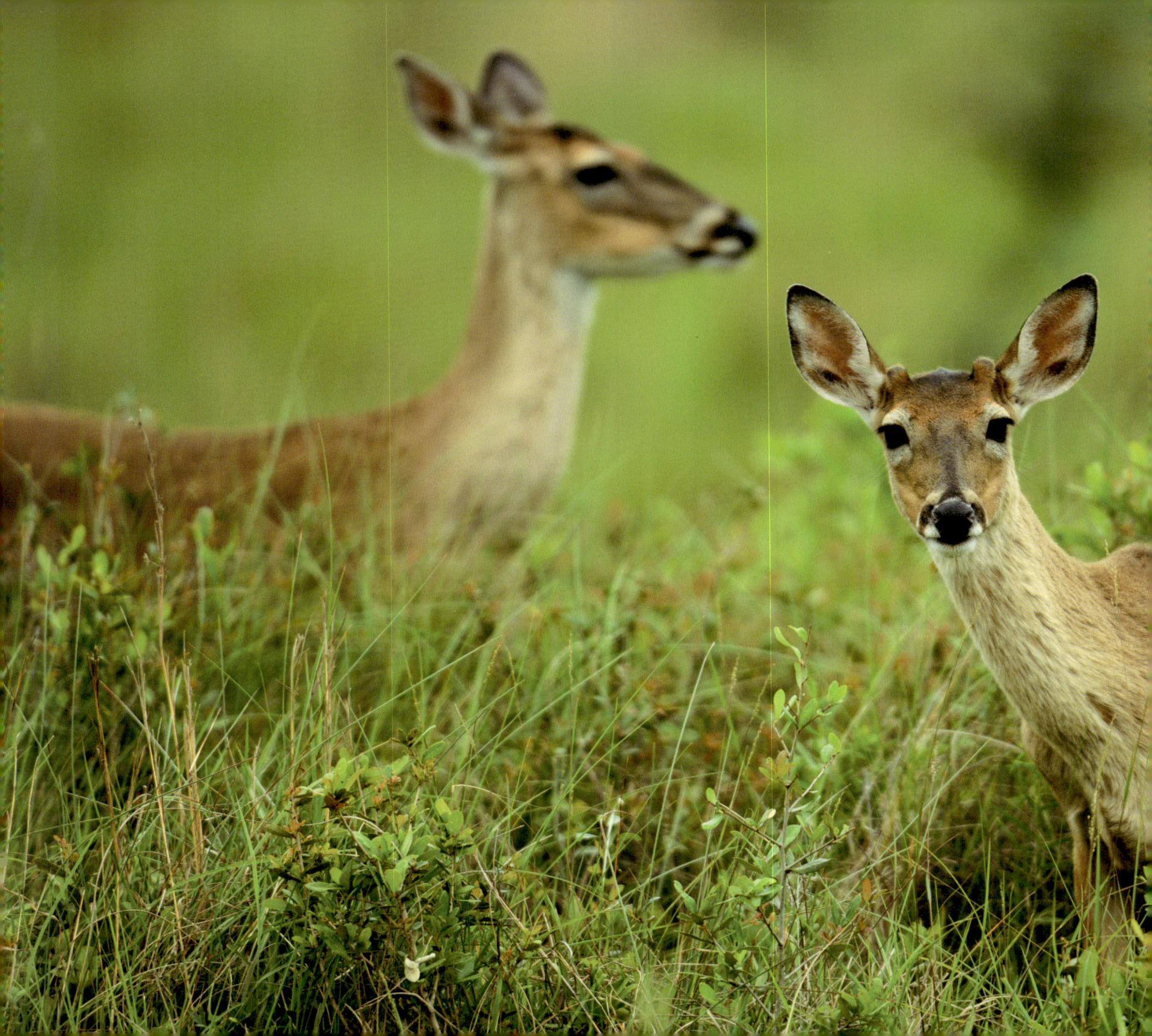

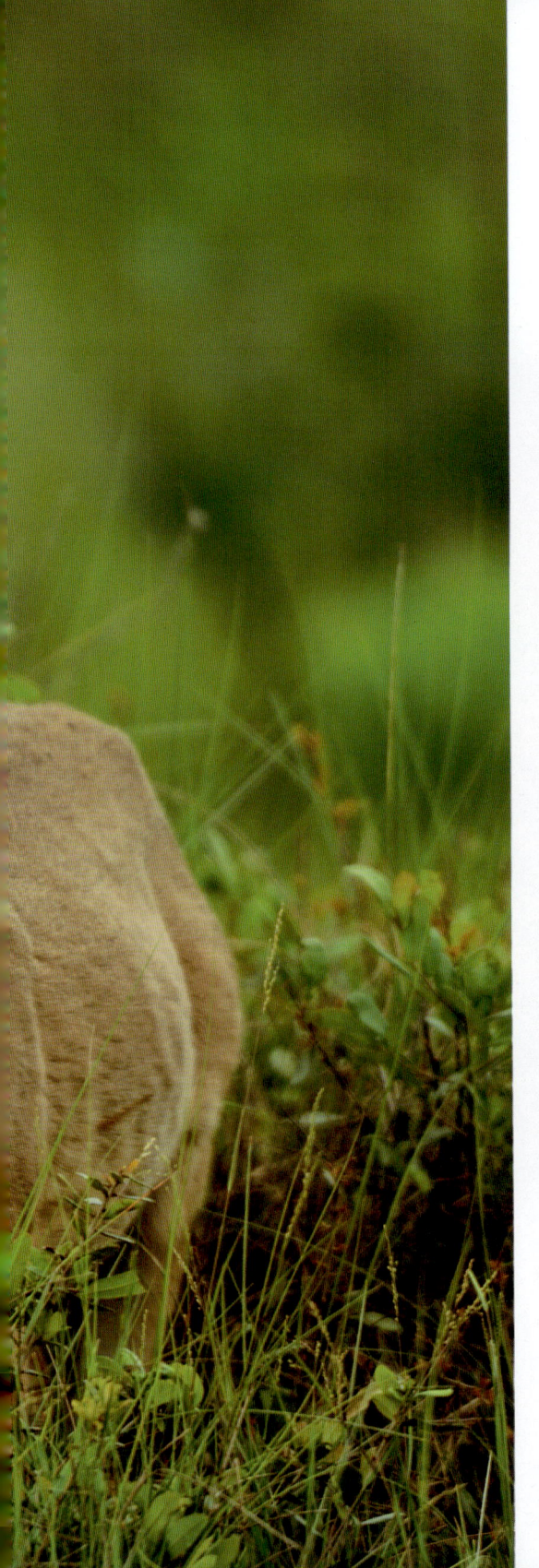

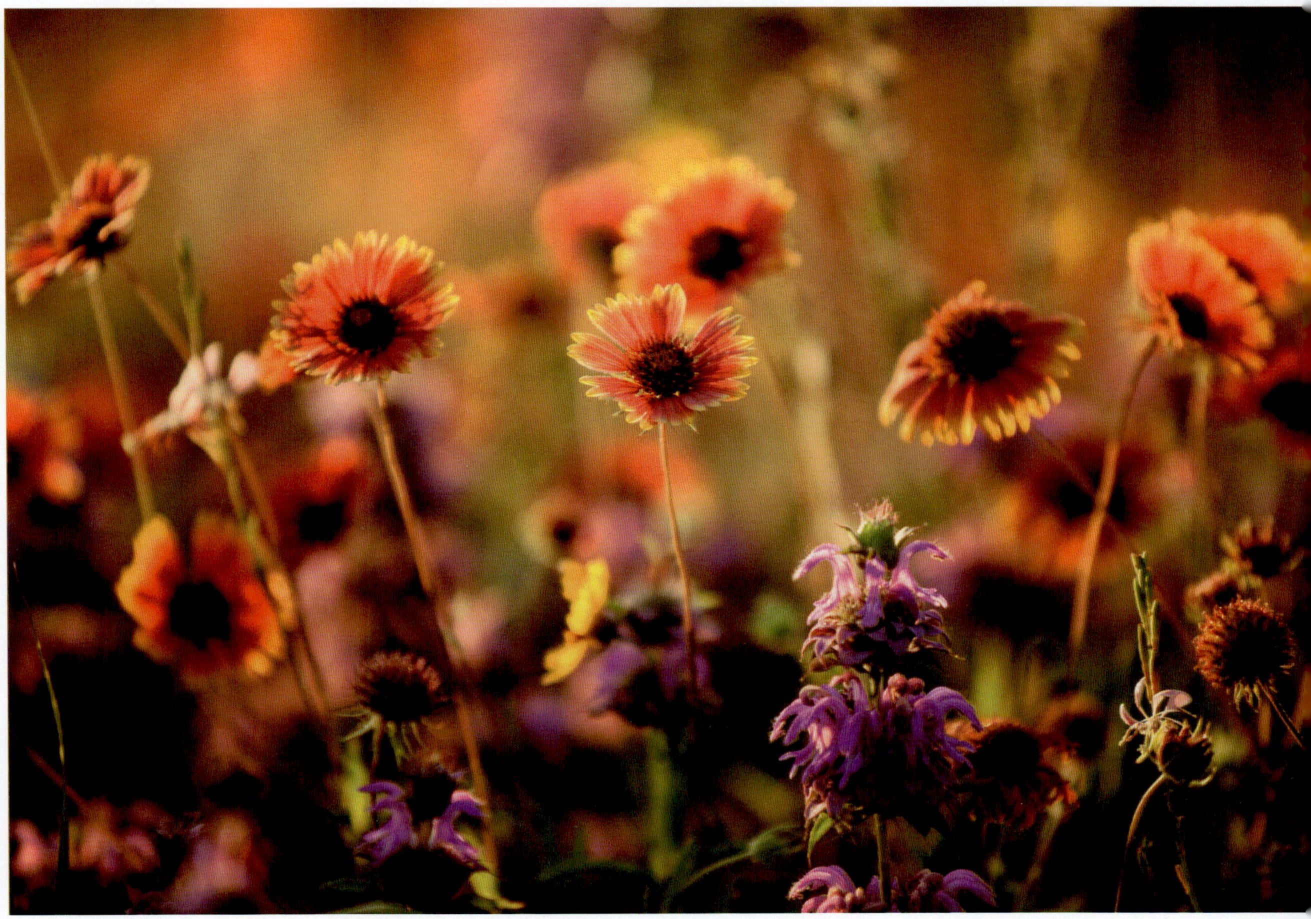

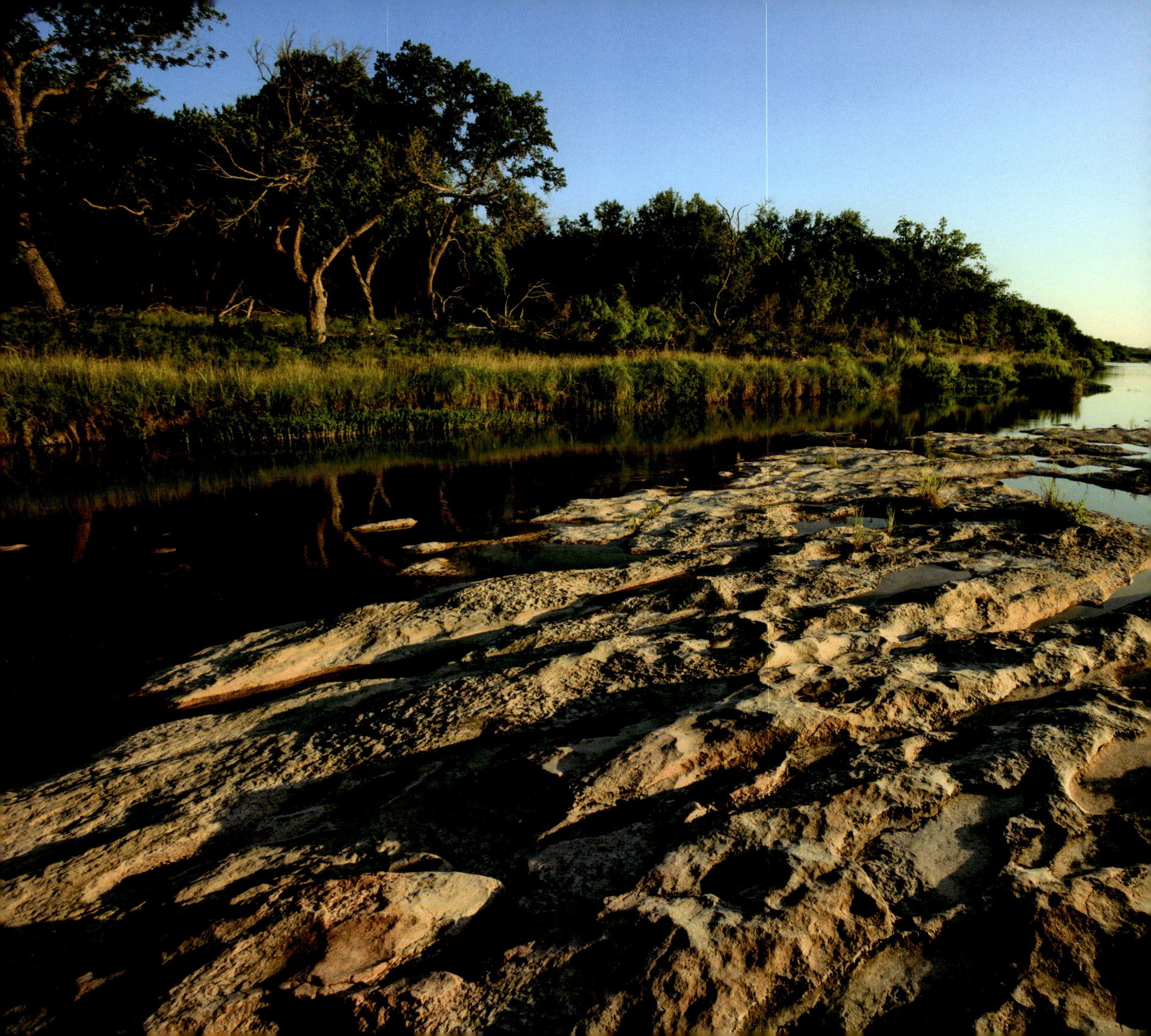

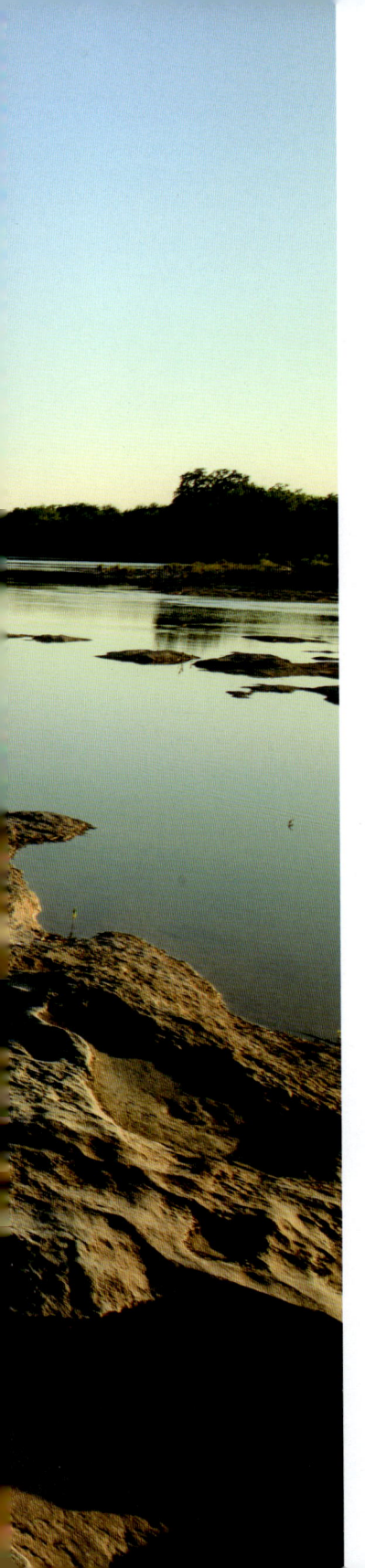
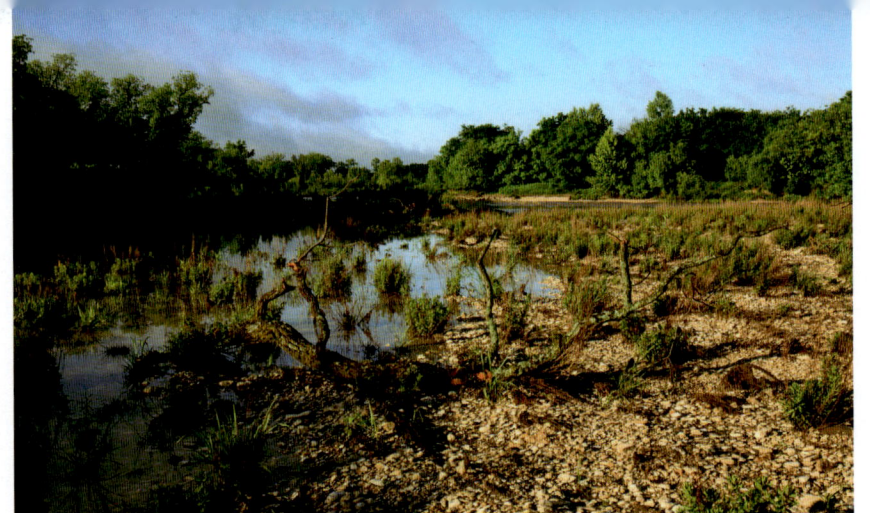
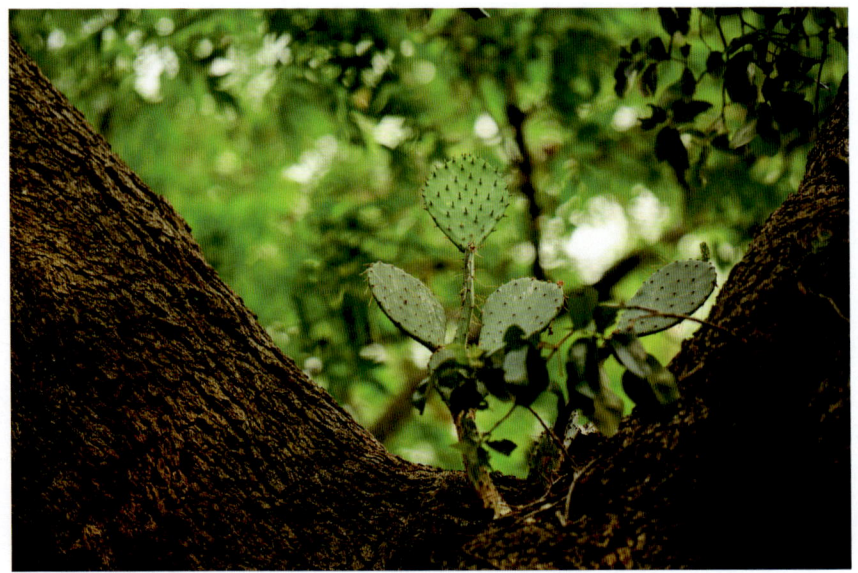
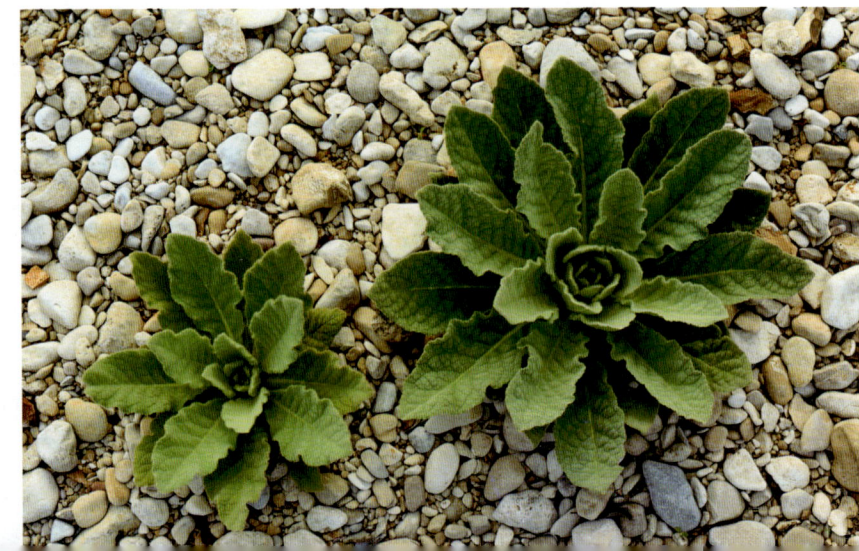

Hill Country Drought Along the South Llano

Despite the prickly pear anchored
in the crook of the old pecan
parched and sprawling in the high branches
like nature's monster ears hanging
on any word of man's frail failure,

and despite ten thousand catkins curled
and desiccated in the half-
hearted shade of the noon pasture
grasping at the absence of grass,

in this stricken field
two invisible angels have concocted
a game with painted buntings.

They toss them from a crippled mesquite
to an old mullein flower stalk and back,
and those neon bouquets even sing.
And sing to the new mullein leaves
soft as the ears of sleeping deer.
And sing Happy Birthday to the dust.
And sing *fire fire where where here here*
to the reluctant cuckoo who brings
his three big gulps of water.
Please pour them in my ear.

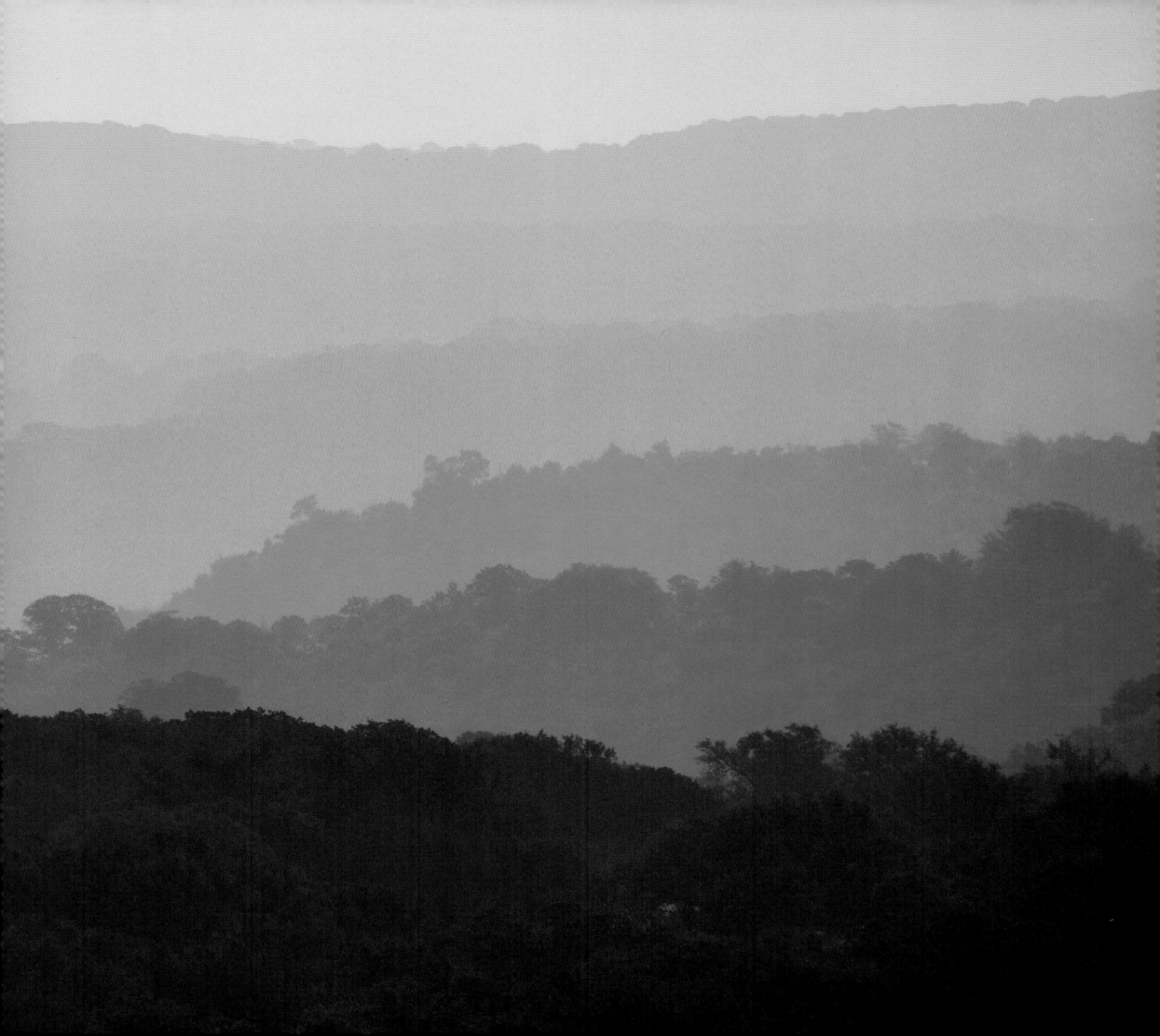

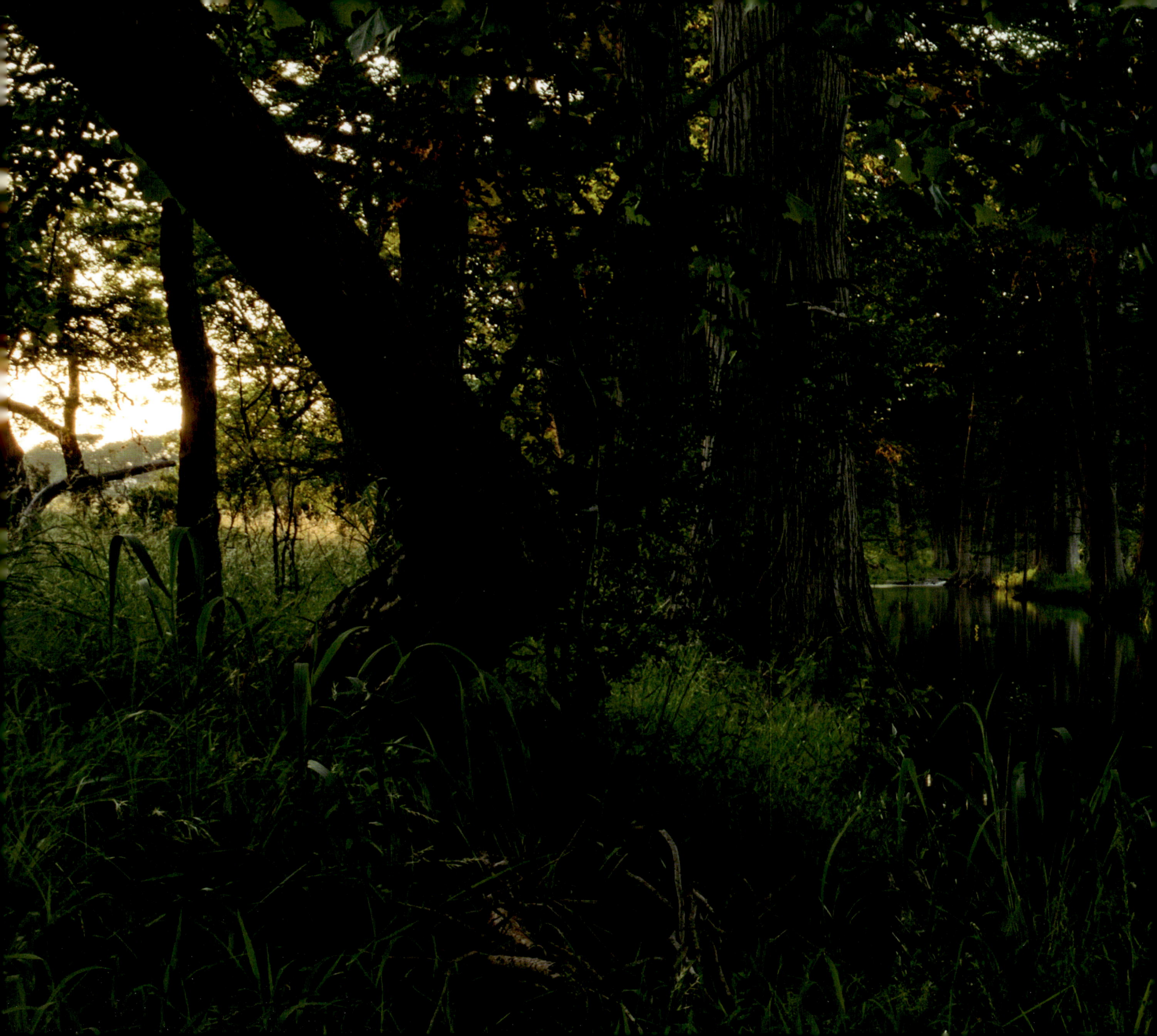

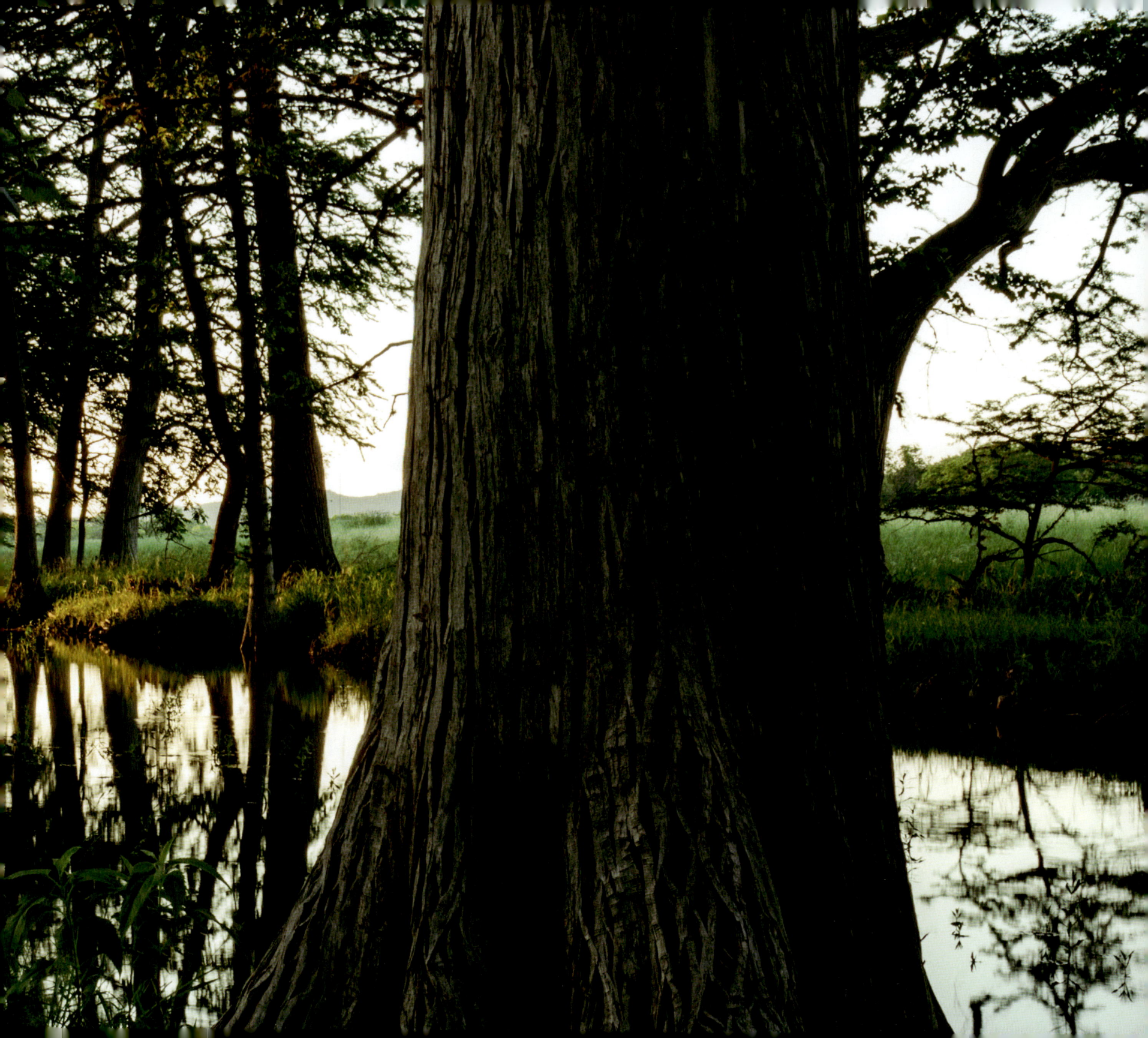

Escape on the Sabinal

Like a river, we flashed and flooded to schools
toward some imagined paradise, as yearned
our own kinfolk who fled their parents' rules.
We were exactly right to go! Those fools
can't see—for us, back home is where the heartburn
is, was, where romance is a butter churn.
Humidity of the Texas Hill Country cruels
the summer days with sweat while winters earn
their solitude. Cold almost freezes, cools.

So girls became our toys and books our tools
at college. We learned to judge the jewel
God is, saw Earth's insides like Jules Verne
and Eden lost was not so bad. Adjourned,
we had traveled East!—But snow helped us discern

we missed the constant sun, the heat, affirmed
the good of cypress shade to rest our souls.
Too hot? Stay still until the evening fuels
a breeze. We know now we didn't know, confirm
this thread might lead us to original pools
where we might lie among the spring-fed ferns
and watch for the orangest orchard orioles.
Our canyon loves; the city ridicules.

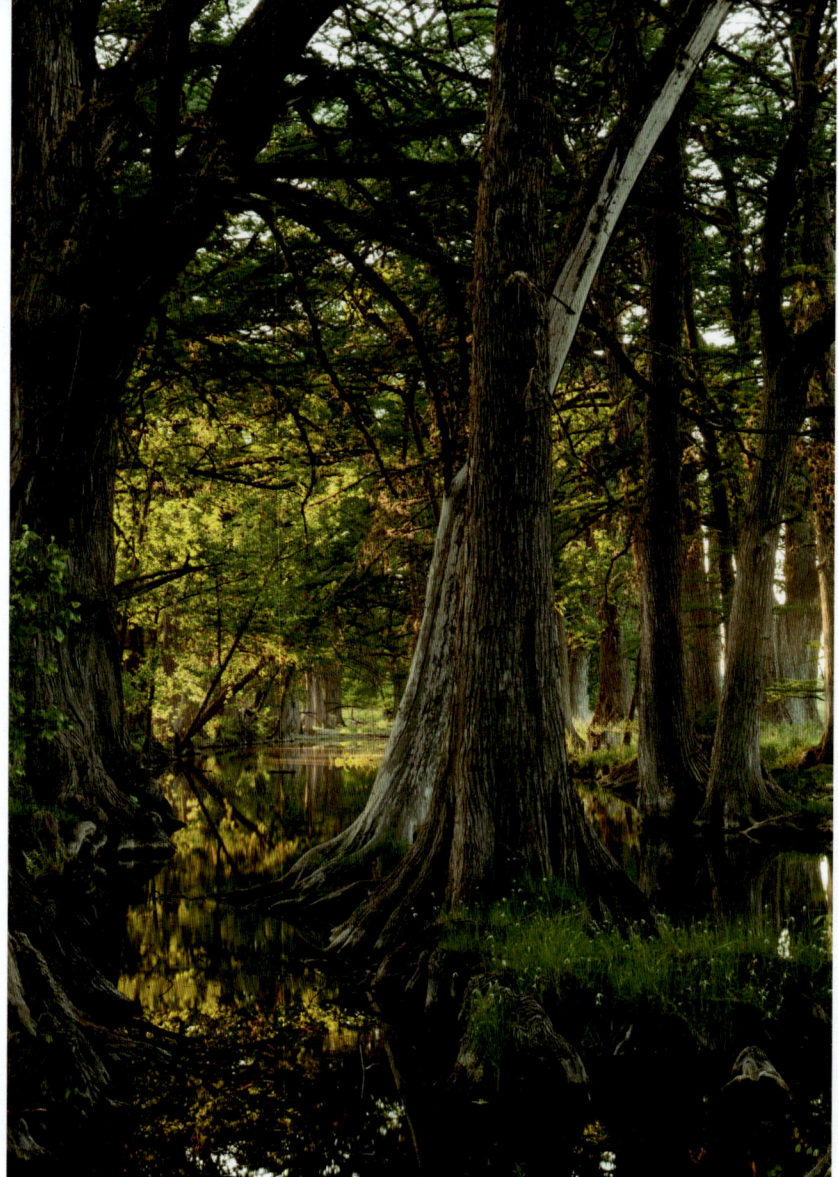

To fish, as well as fathom we're food for a worm,
is to accept a river's unconcern—
how it surrenders water molecules,
and rains, drifts, calms, distills, reflects, unspools.

We leave as soon as we can, only to learn
we spend our whole lives trying to return.

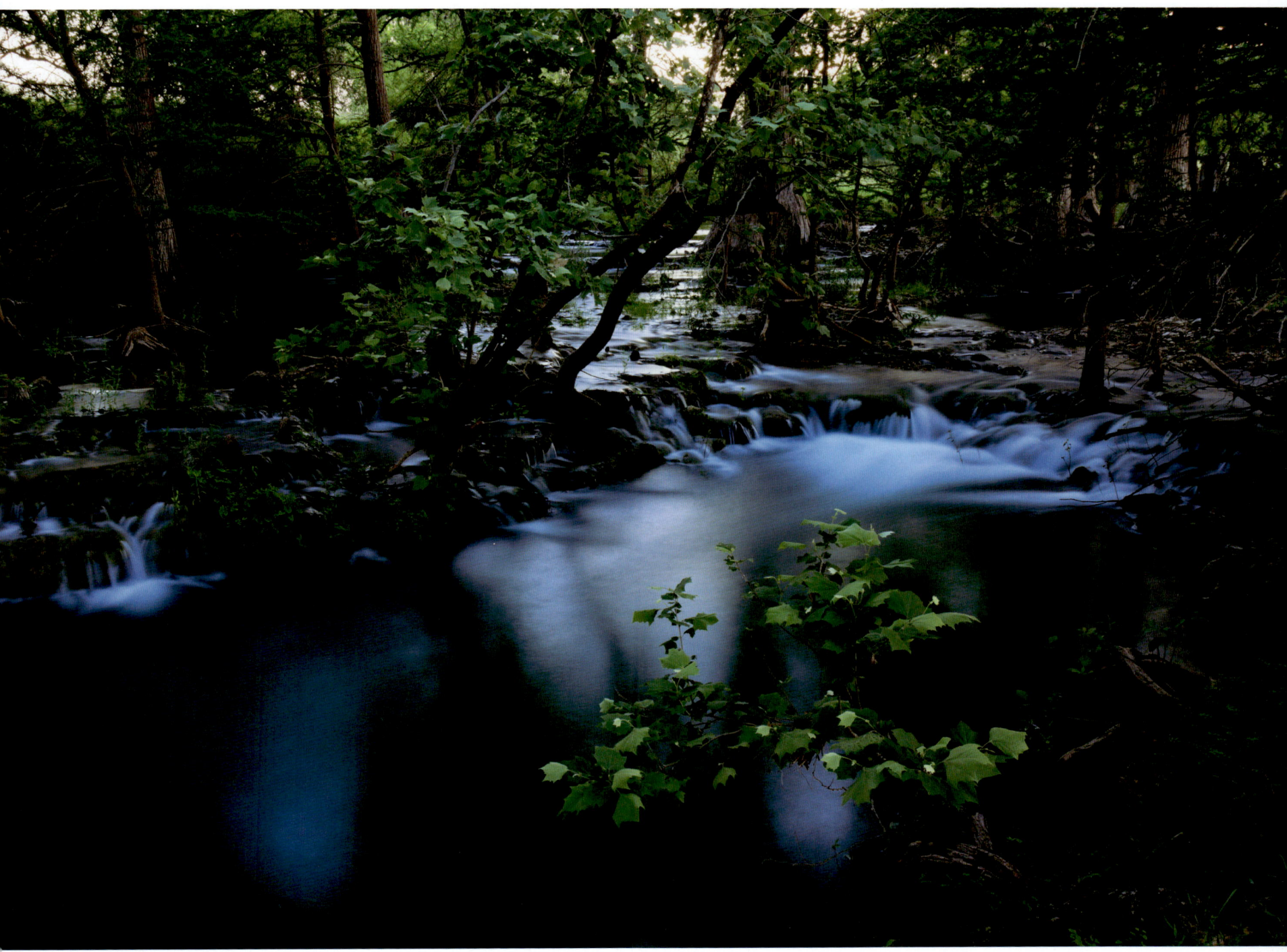

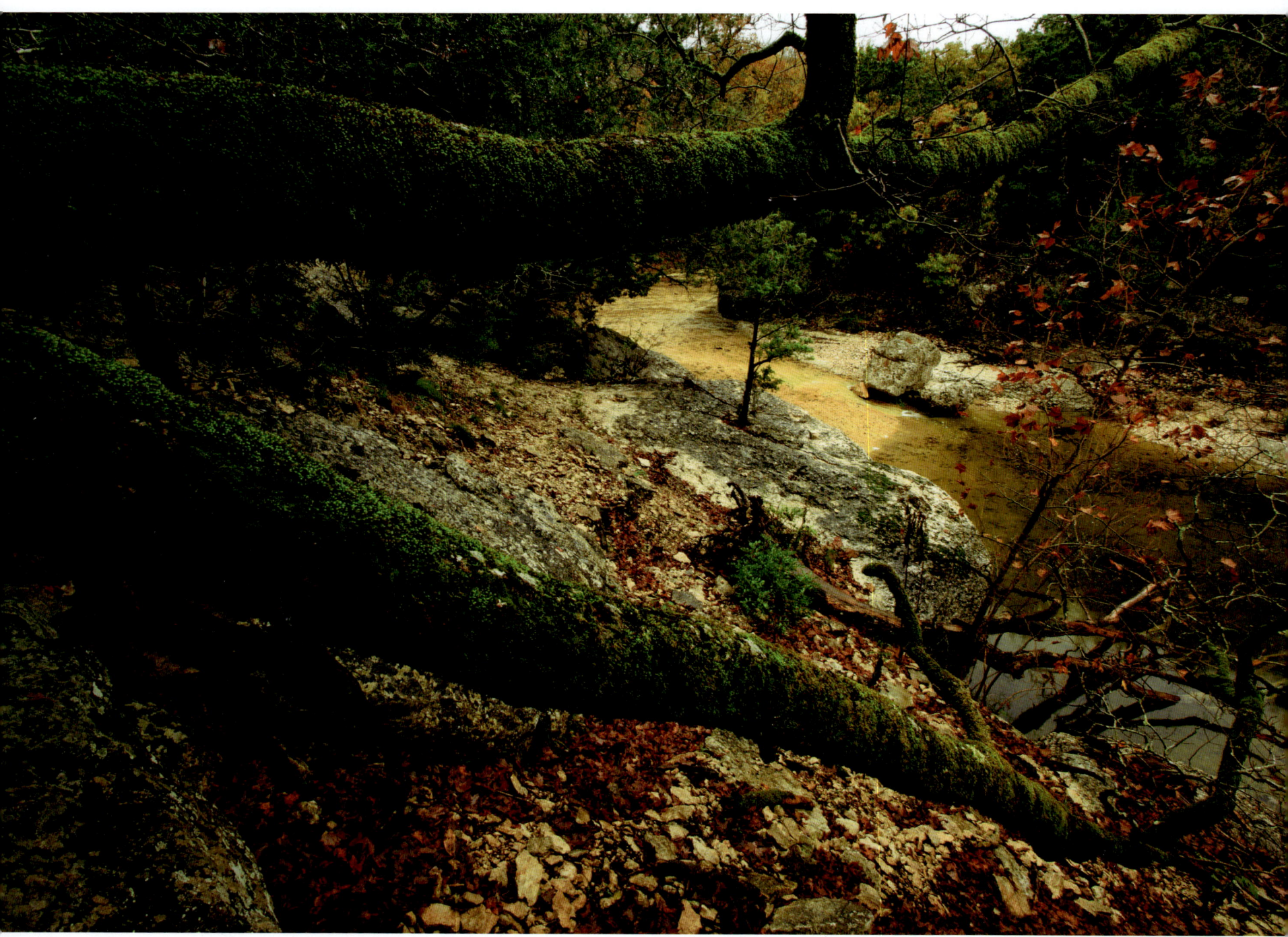

Love Creek

Is there water better than a secluded creek
where cold springs rise in warm late spring through layer
on layer of limestone rock? We hide and seek
the real Hill Country south and find like prayer

the solitude we need. The overflow flattens
wide as a church, a millimeter deep
like a Slip 'N Slide for giants. Nothing happens
for a hundred yards, but then, my love, Love Creek

narrows, tumbles, and drops to a cool pool
where, ahead of you, I place on the darker sand
an invitation, a limestone chunk (I'm a fool
for signs) I found: a heart the size of your hand.

You descend the trail like the song of a canyon wren.
You smile at my offering. We enter in.

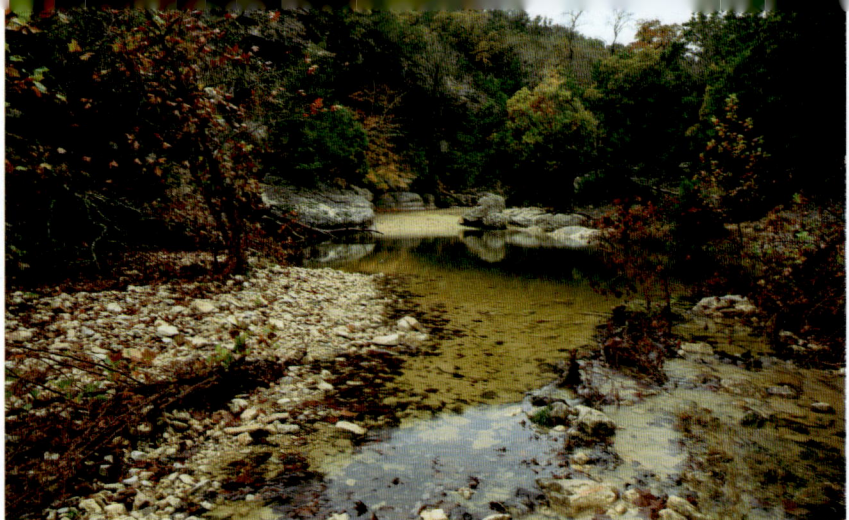

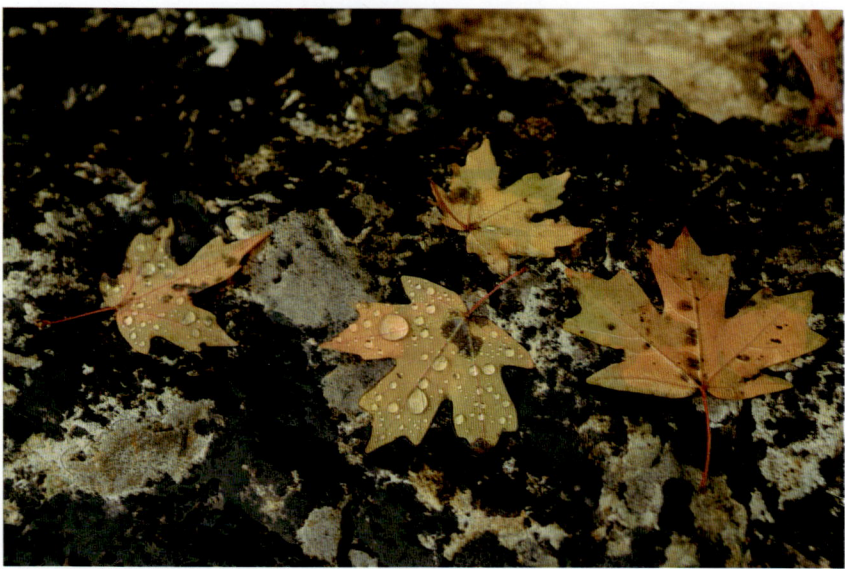

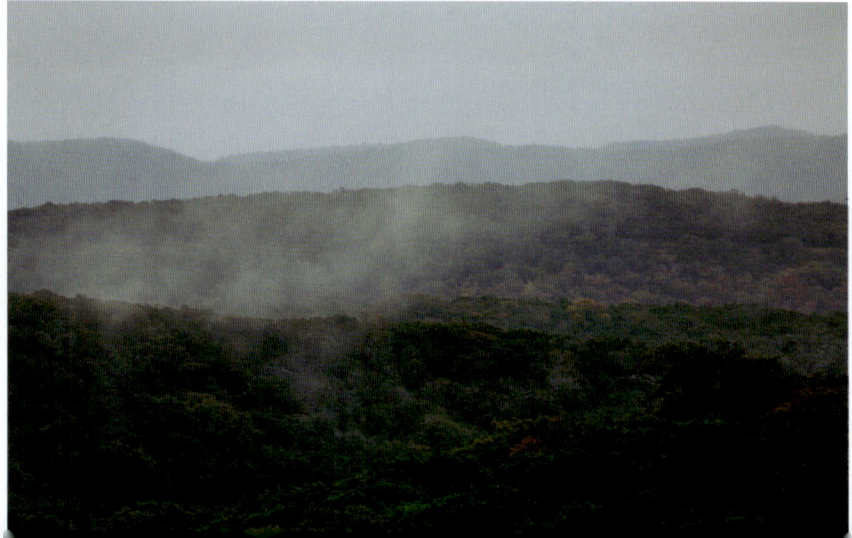

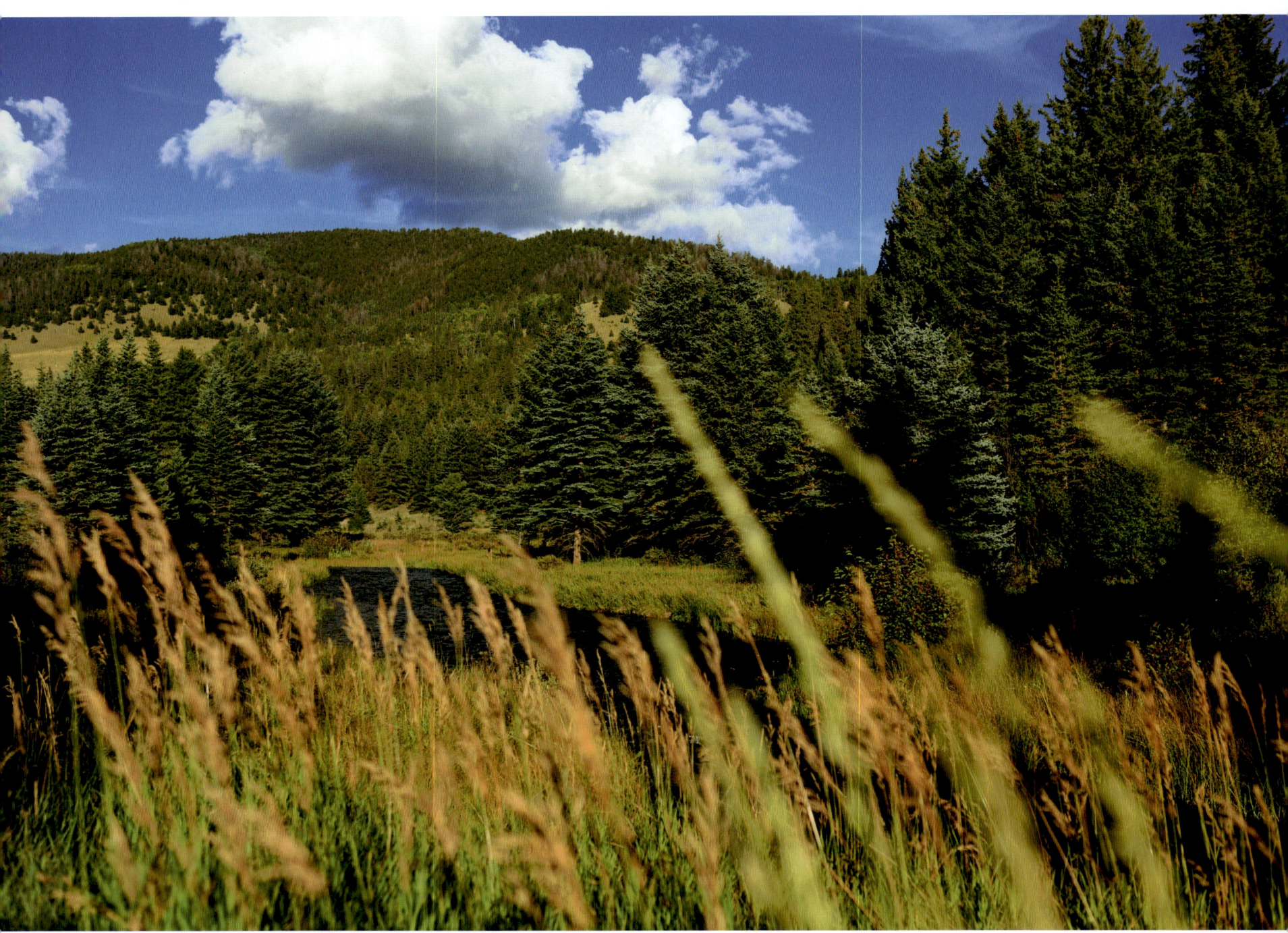

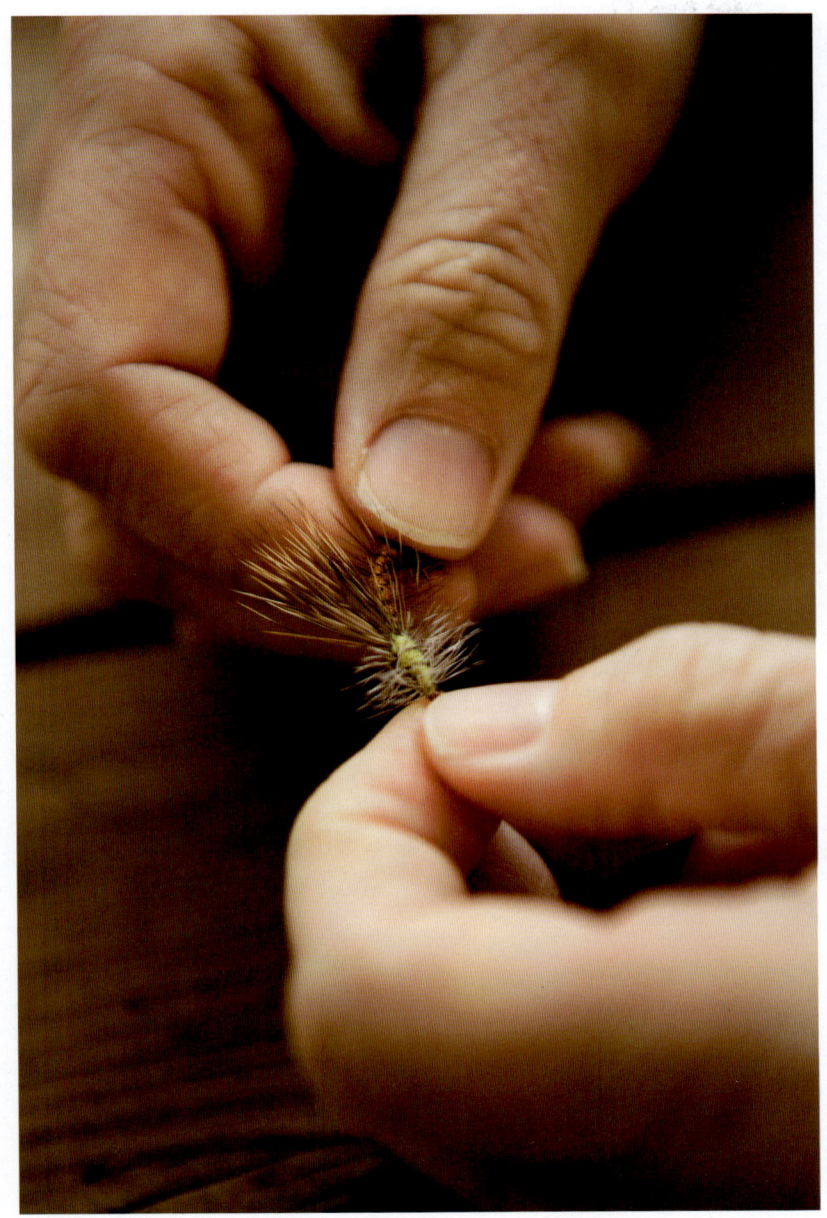

Invisible Fish

The guide at the slideshow asks us
who can see the fish.
Each, in our own Alaska,
could guess, but only a wish

we could be surer rises.
Reluctant to raise a hand,
our total silence comprises
the fear of reprimand:

an ax-headed thought might swim:
a stone mistaken for a trout
below the ruffled scrim
of the run would leave no doubt

how Texan, how far we are
from nature. The hush confirms
our ignorance: we'd mar
the world with hooks and worms.

His silhouette's afloat
behind the projector's boulder,
light swirling hotel motes
before him: silt, lit golden.

If he's the fisherman,
then we're the fish aware
of shadows, movement on
the shore, hunger and fear

—

our needle north from birth
and sex to death. He waits
as patiently the earth
holds steady on its plates

till a laser pointer now
points *fish fish fish*, discloses
just who we are from how
we hid within our guesses.

The last few slides, and on
come the lights. The river
evaporates. We're gone
like fish out of water shiver.

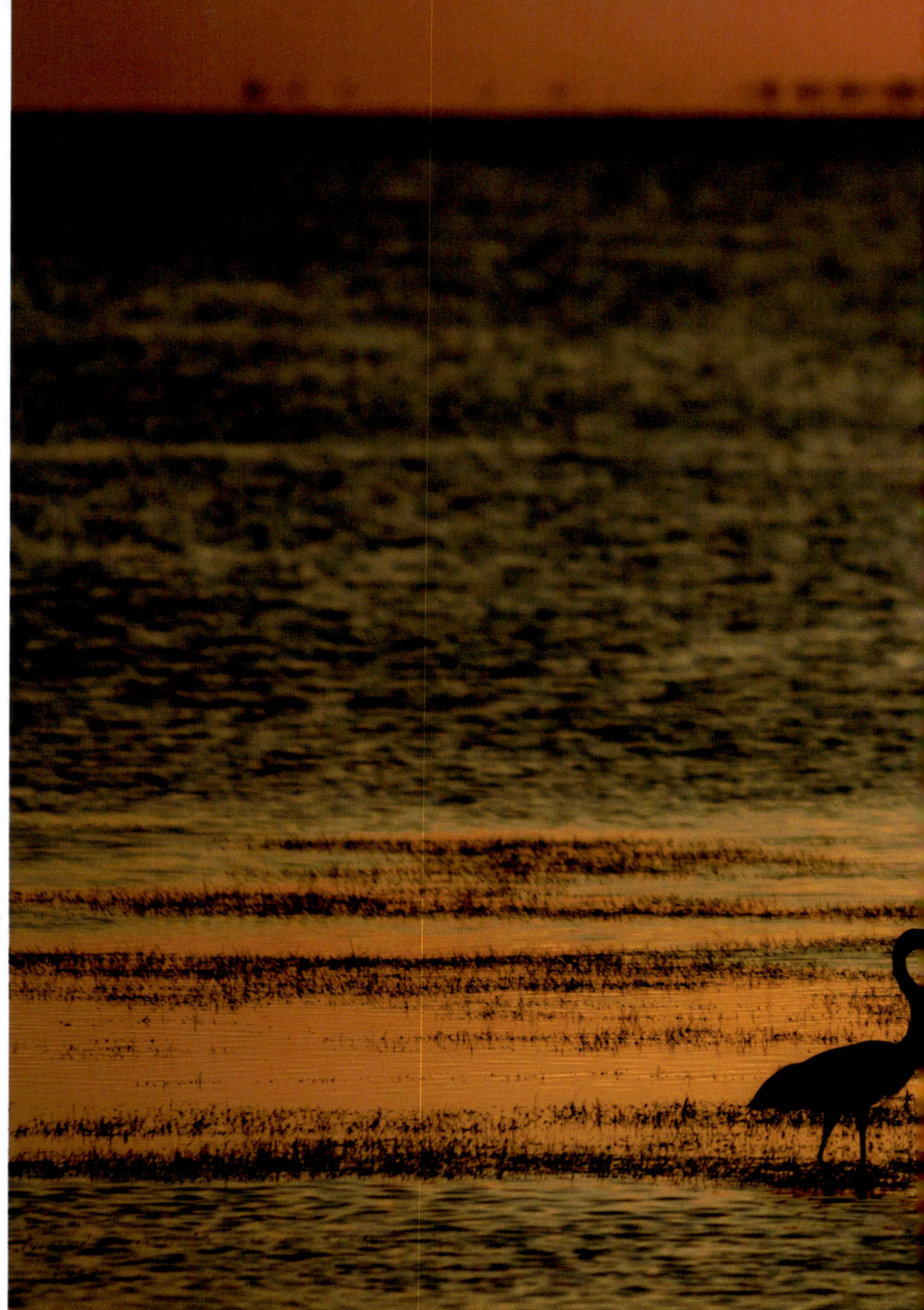

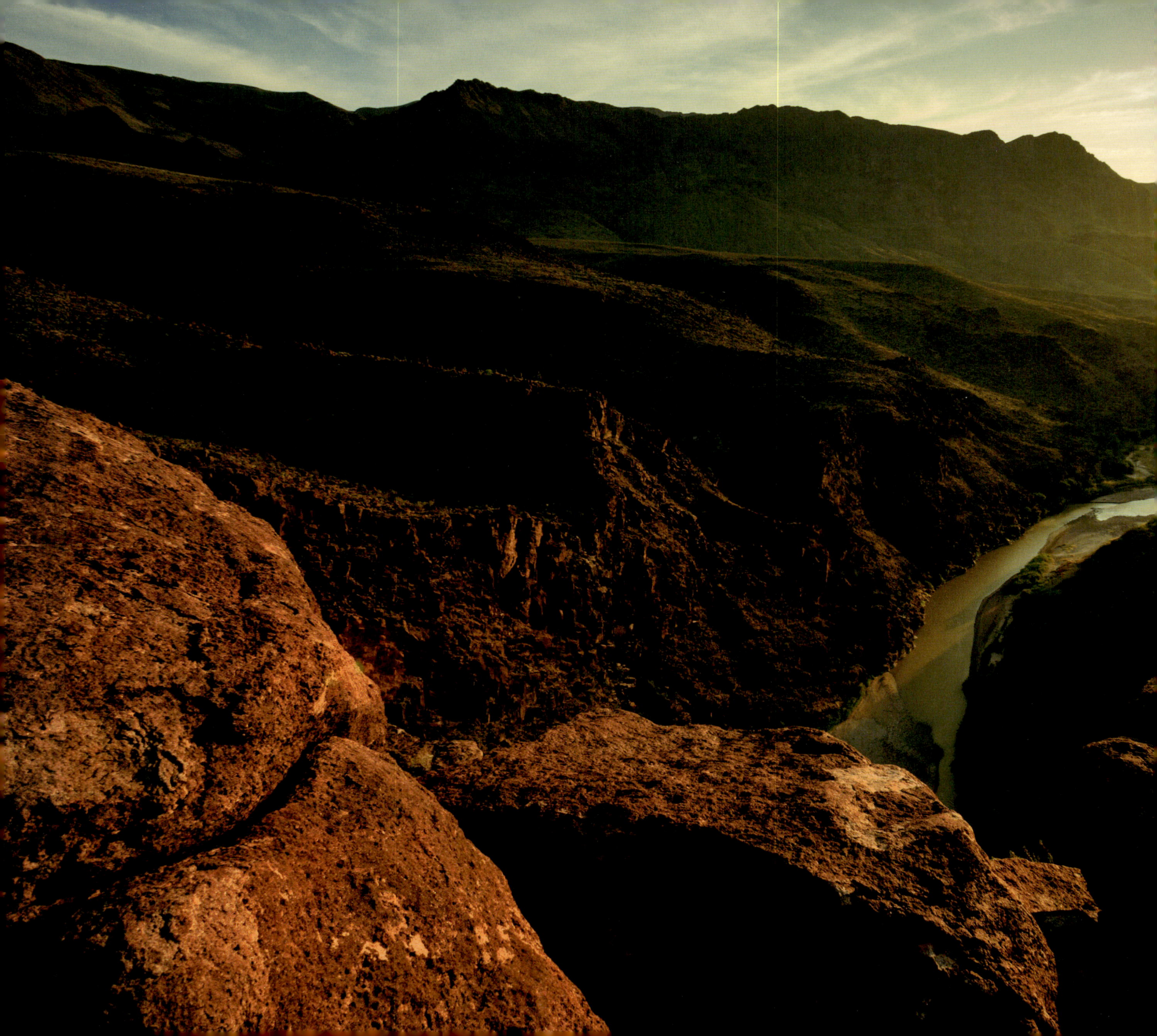

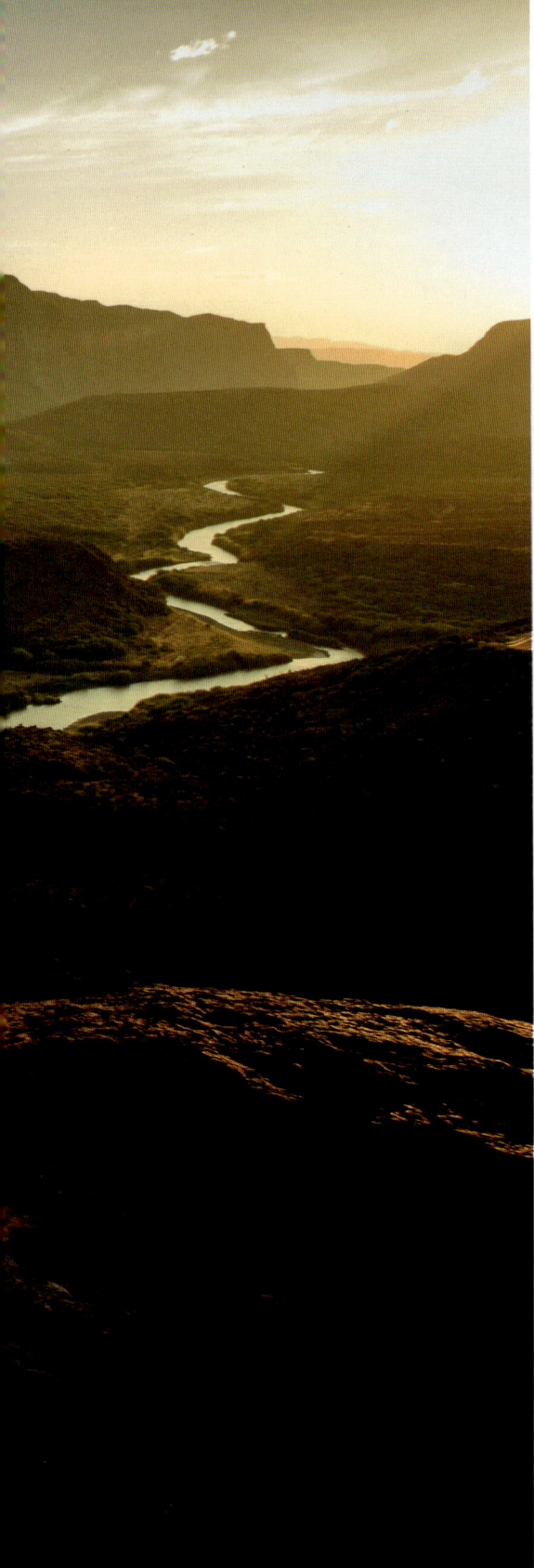

River Prayer

Non è fantin che sì sùbito rua
col volto verso il latte, se si svegli
molto tardato da l'usanza sua
Paradiso XXX 82-84

Our river, which art might make known your powers
other than prayer, the mouth where all the falling
ends in a whisper? The shell of the aural sea

might not at first receive the crafted hours,
the cries that turn back in a tidal crawling
toward a source as the child delivered, free,

rejects his freedom in the world, devours
love and loves. Graceful mother, do not grieve
when your child at last moves toward eternity

from home. He will return in time. Believe
you me.

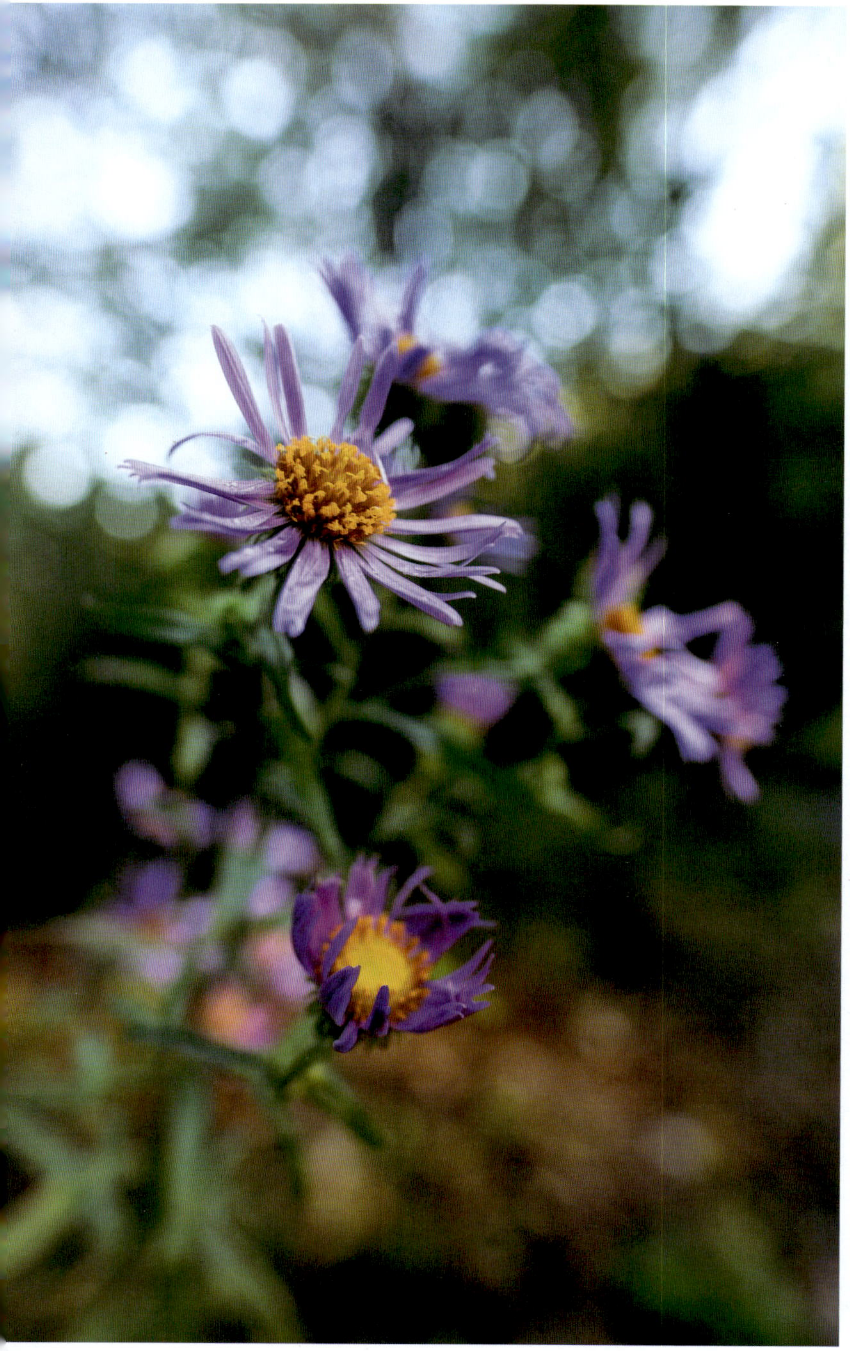

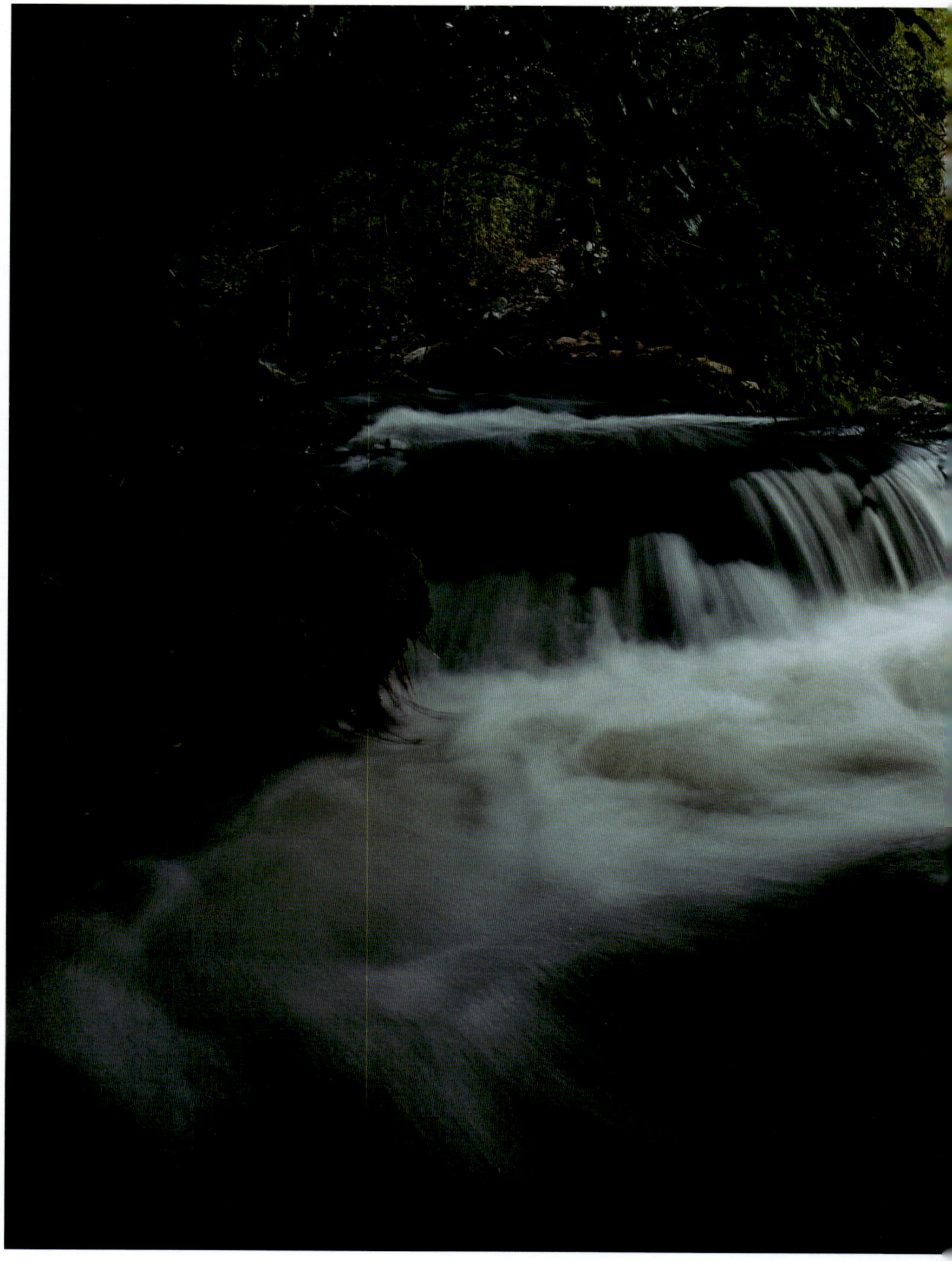

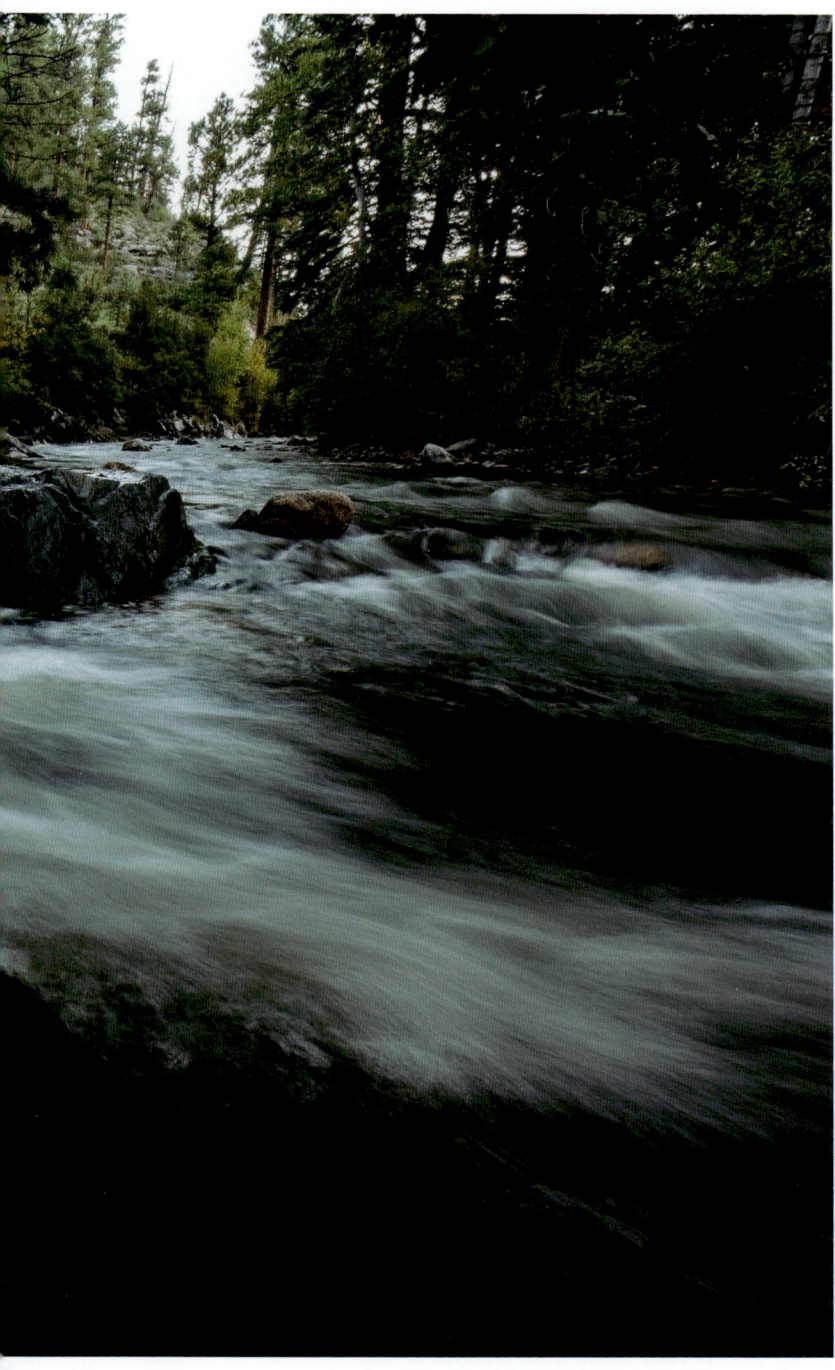

The Pecos (at Holy Ghost Creek)

State road sixty three tends to chase
the river, the way a sinner's turpitude
turns back for his redemption, upstream toward
the mountain source. Where this anointing weighs
into the murky Pecos, brown trout worry
with their sixty spots of fire in the stillnesses
beside the currents. We crave the wilderness
beneath each flat black beside the hurry.

Below my line, trout long in the sunshine
of dreams. The Spirit makes these flames almost
real when this vision wakes within my wrist.
In the white way falling through a blue place the sign
points travelers to Cowels or Holy Ghost.
Which direction do you think I fished?

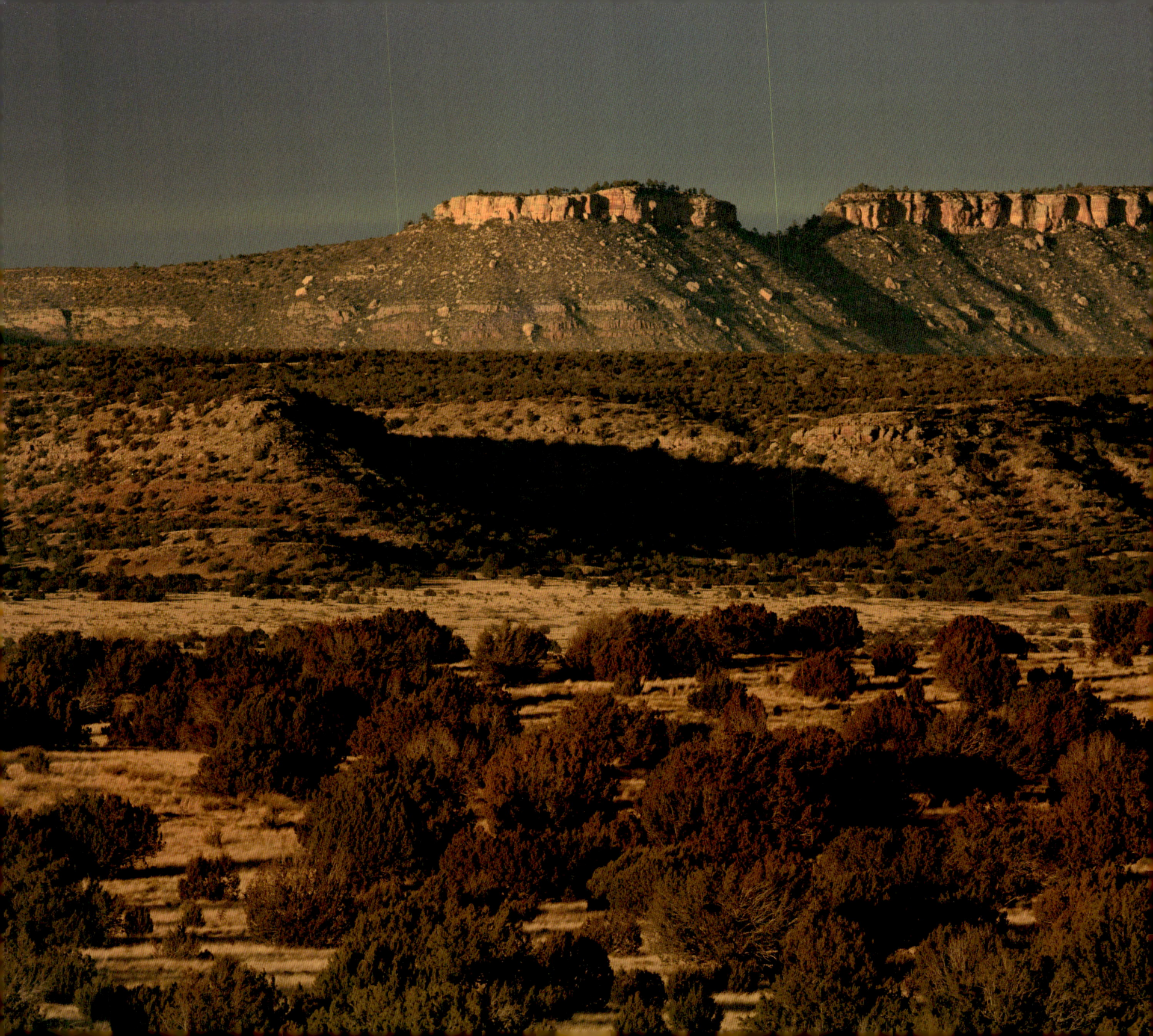

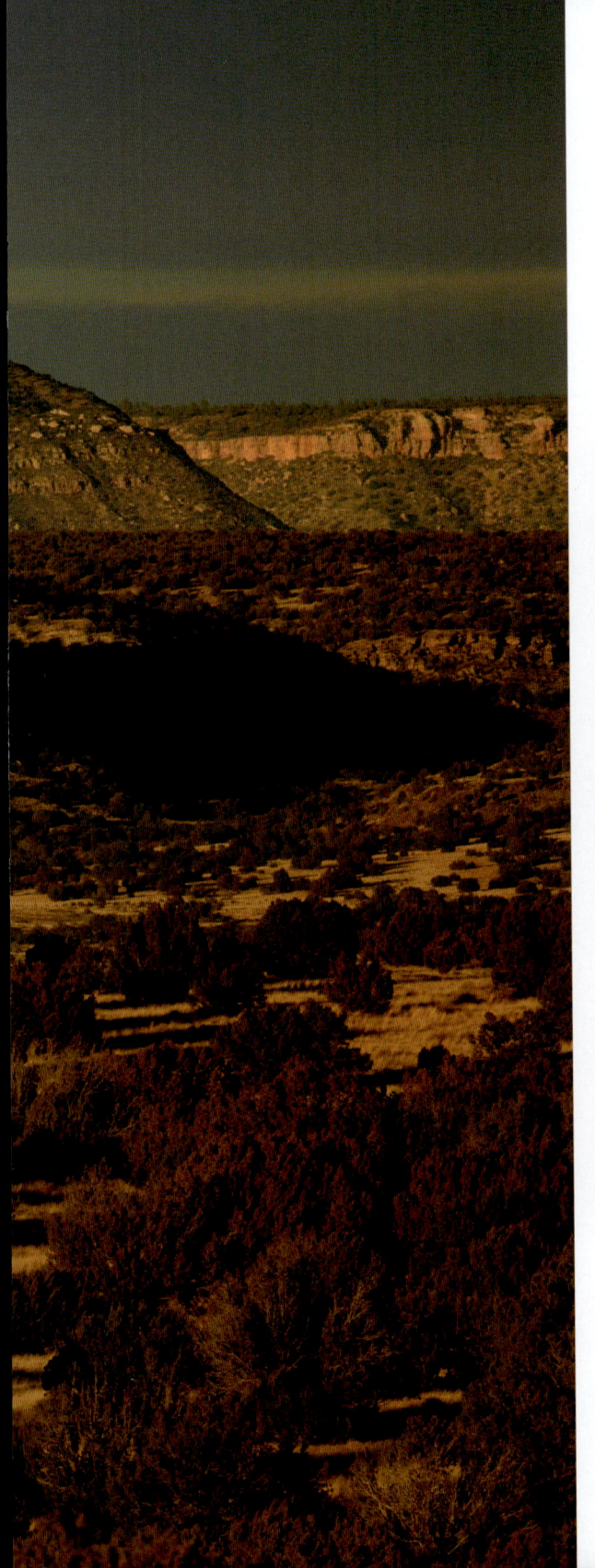

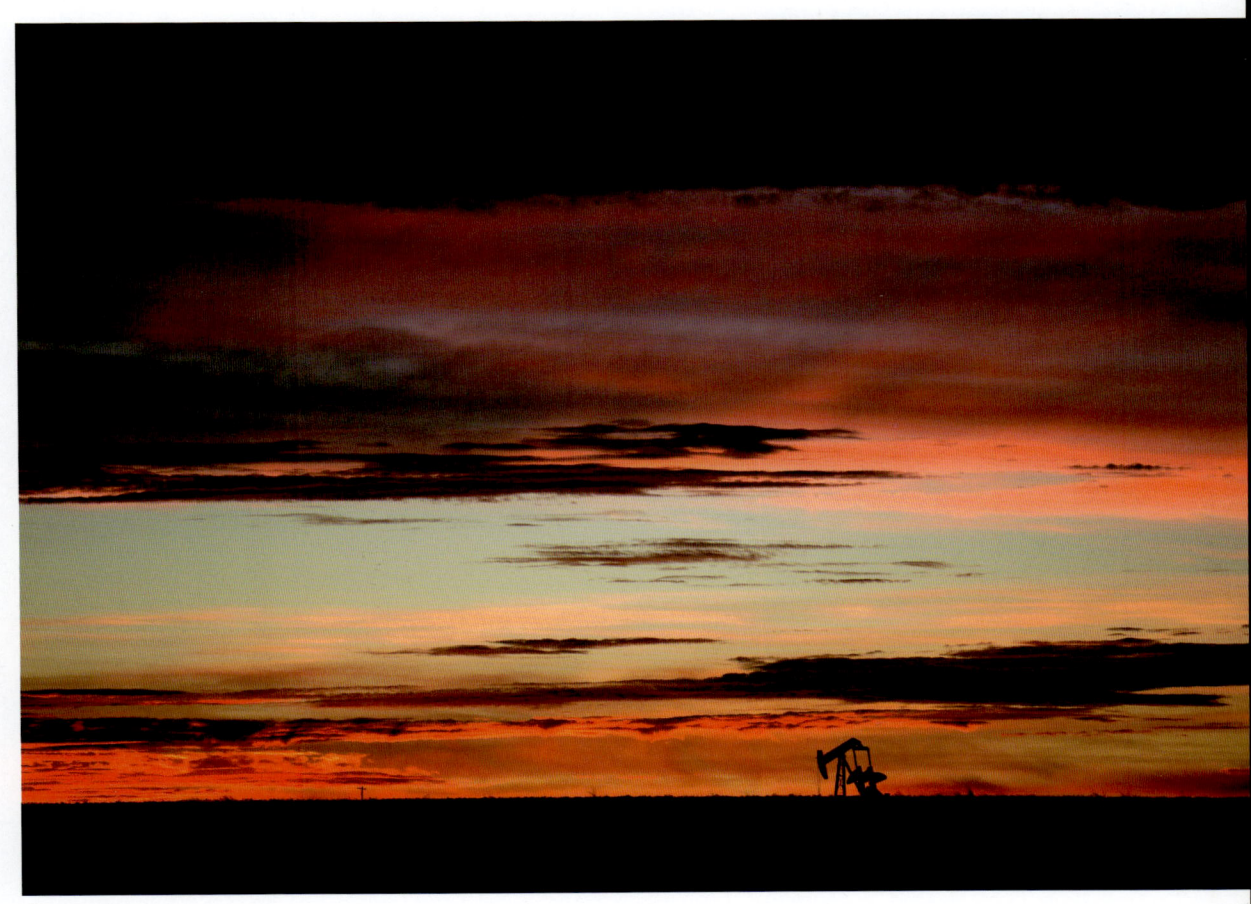

Loving and Goodnight, Goodnight and Loving

This roadside Western placard marks the blind,
bleached turf that claims a history. Some keys
might rust out there, lost, prairie-buried, find
no purchase, no hand turning by degrees
a mechanism toward a hinge, no lock
at all. You must outlast the grief, laugh, station
yourself like some poor town's long depot, chock-
full of childhood's golden dust motes. Prize privation

at the Ranching Heritage Museum: Less
is. Thirst would always map the trail. To win
was to, despite the sun, refuse undress-
ing till night, good night, keeping the moisture in
and loving the distance like nothing's pleas.
The trickling Pecos brings us to our knees.

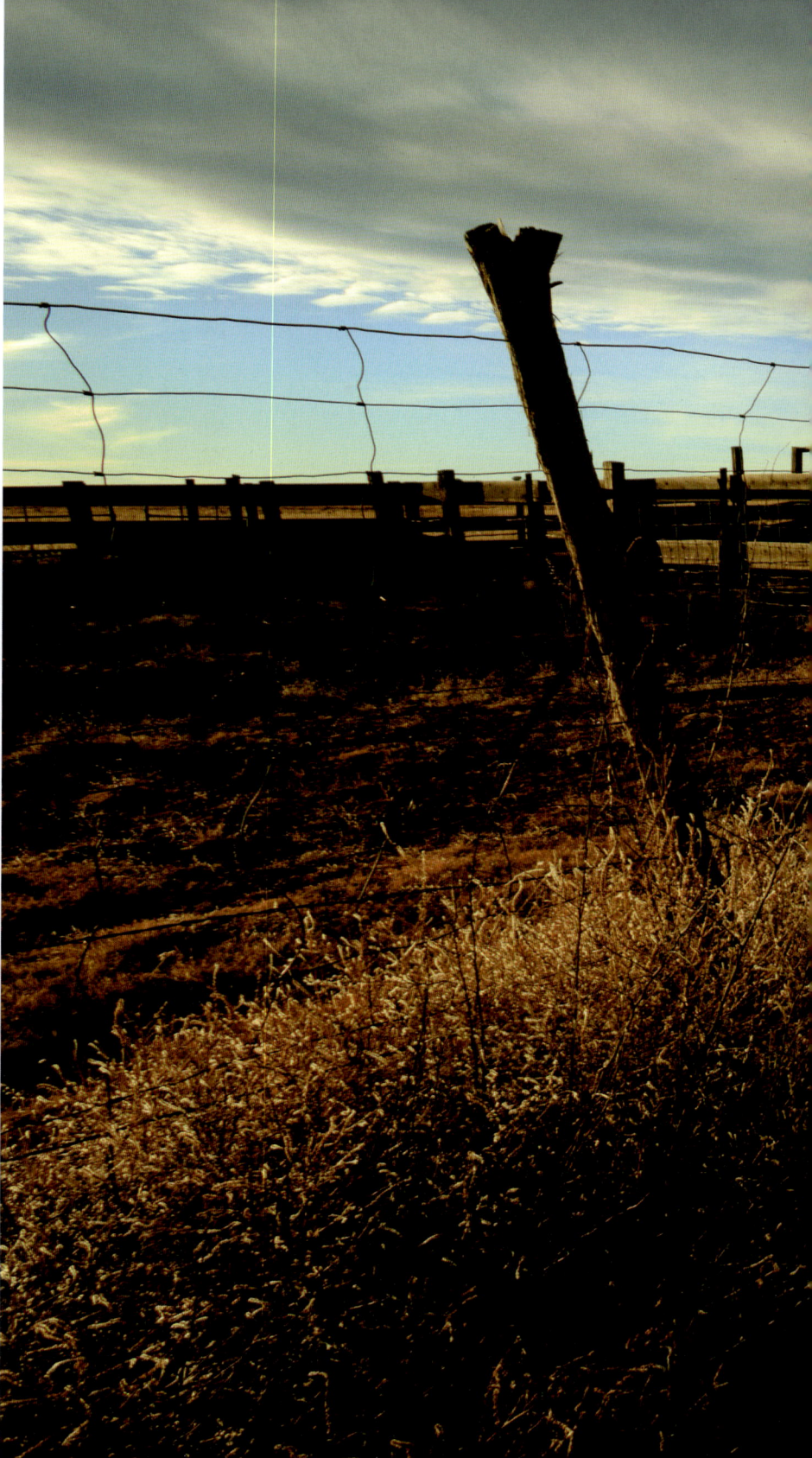

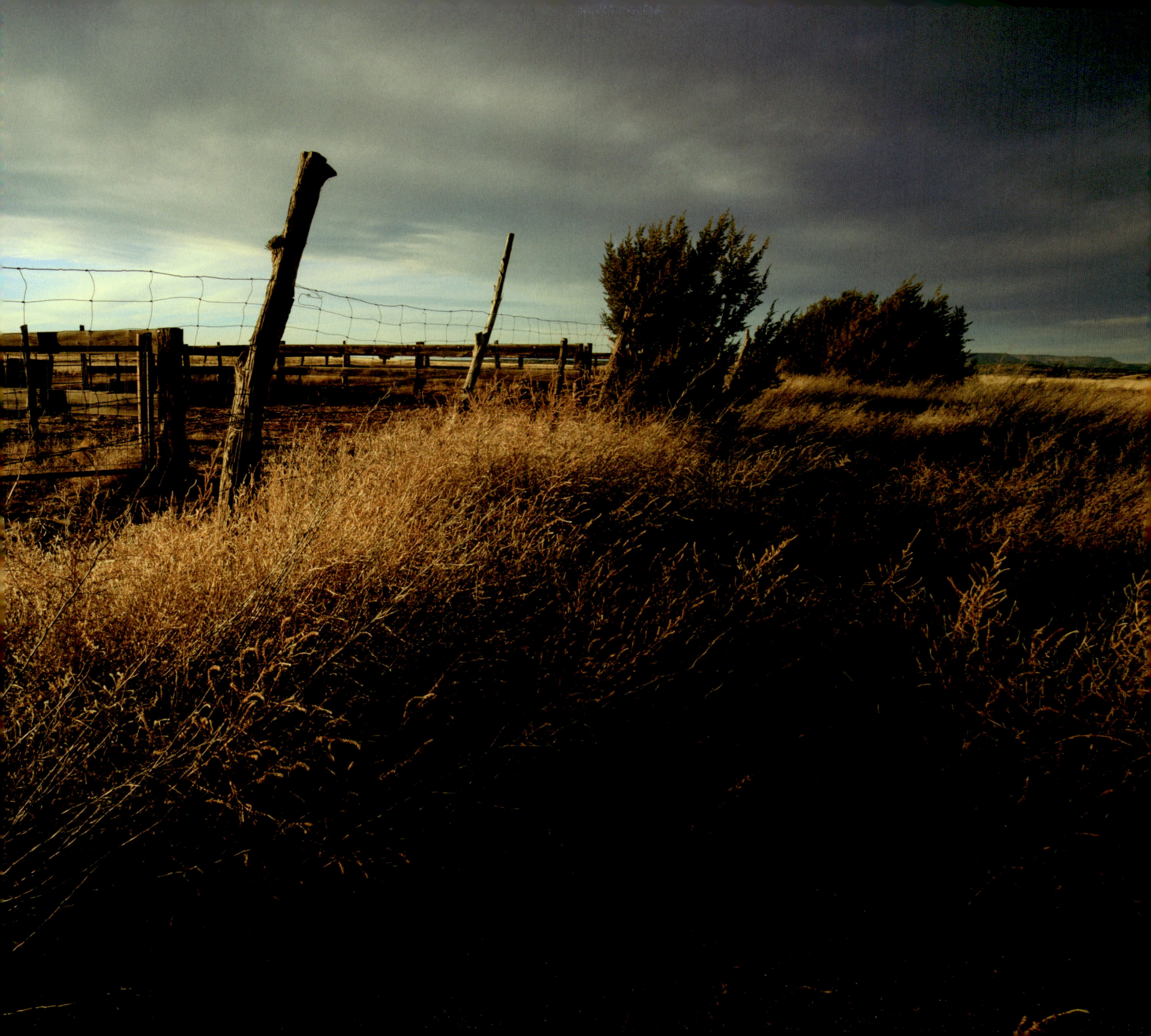

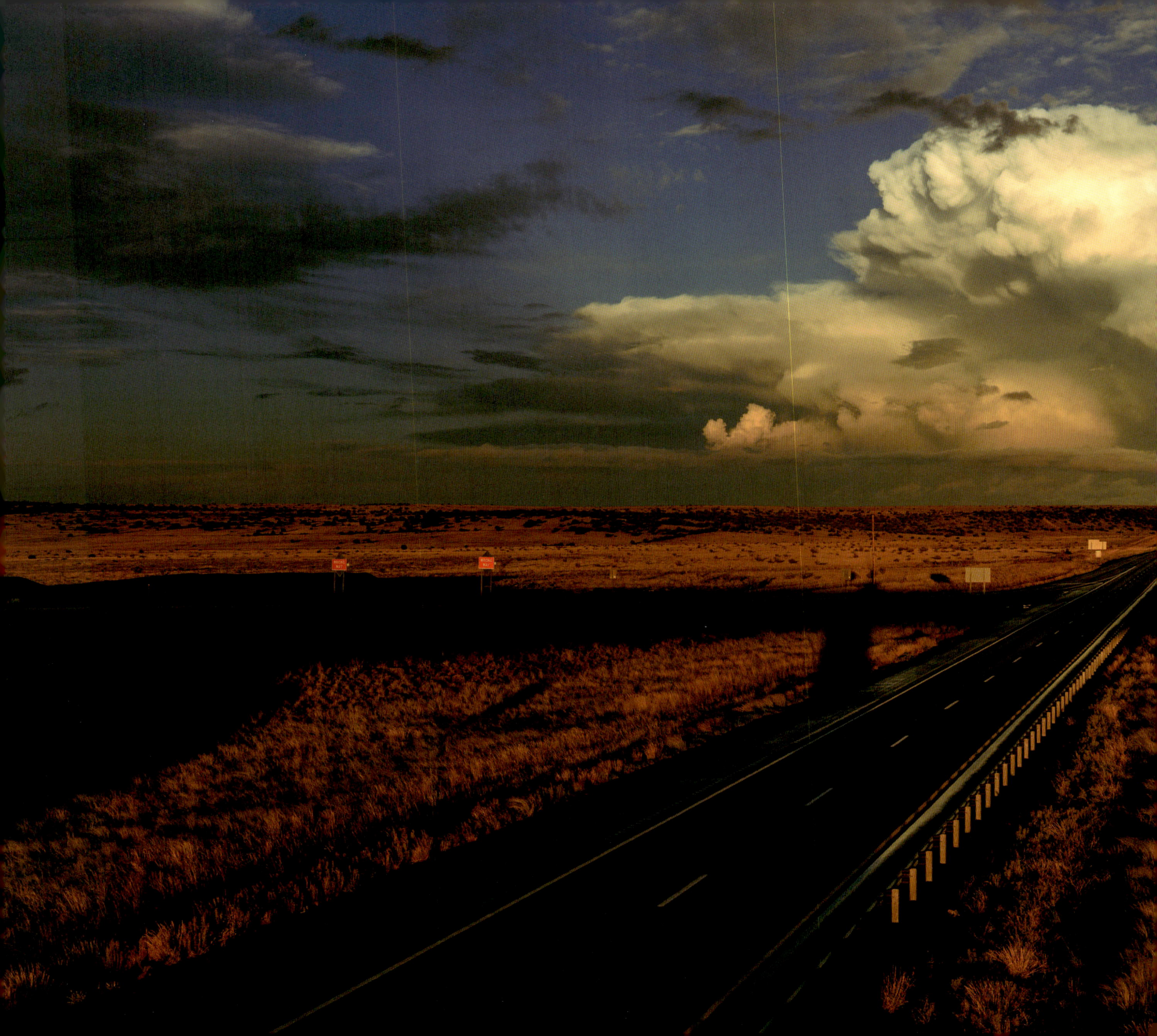

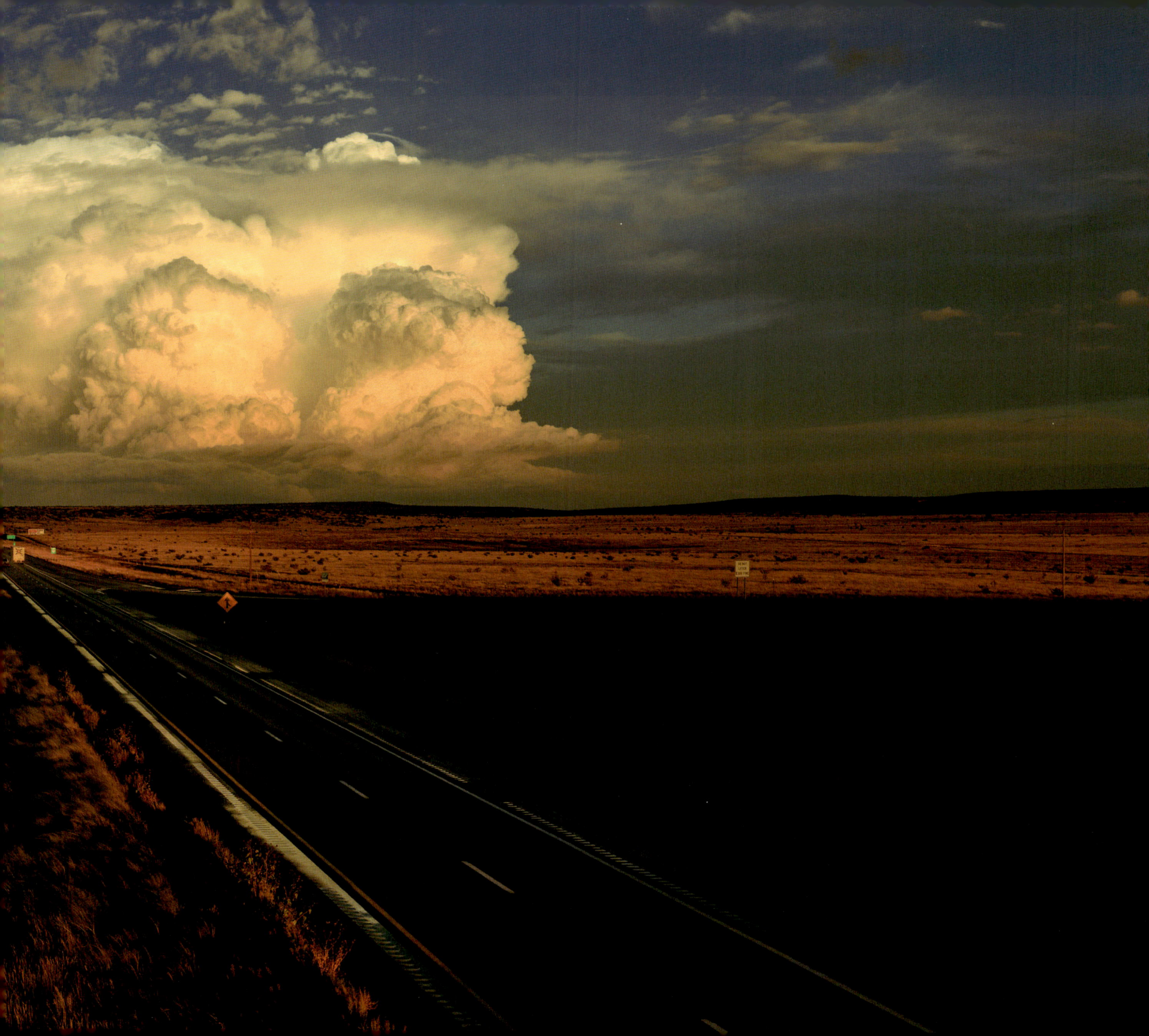

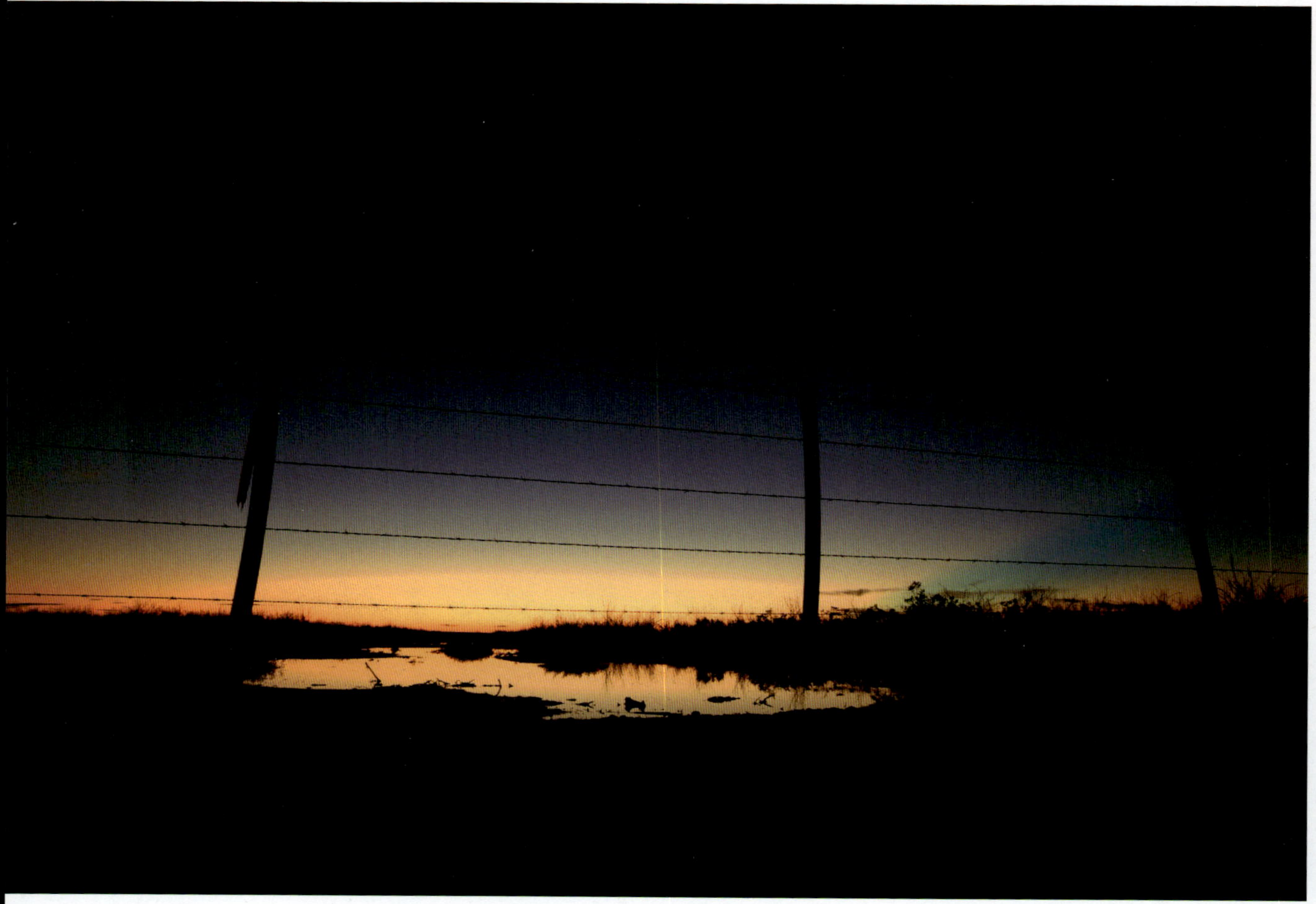

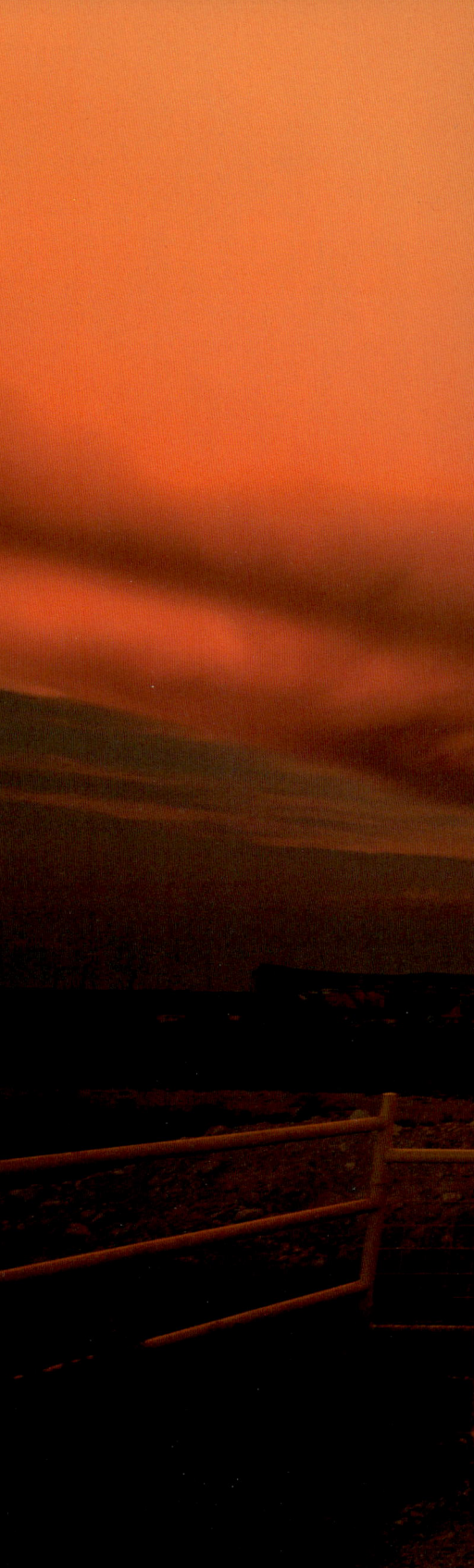

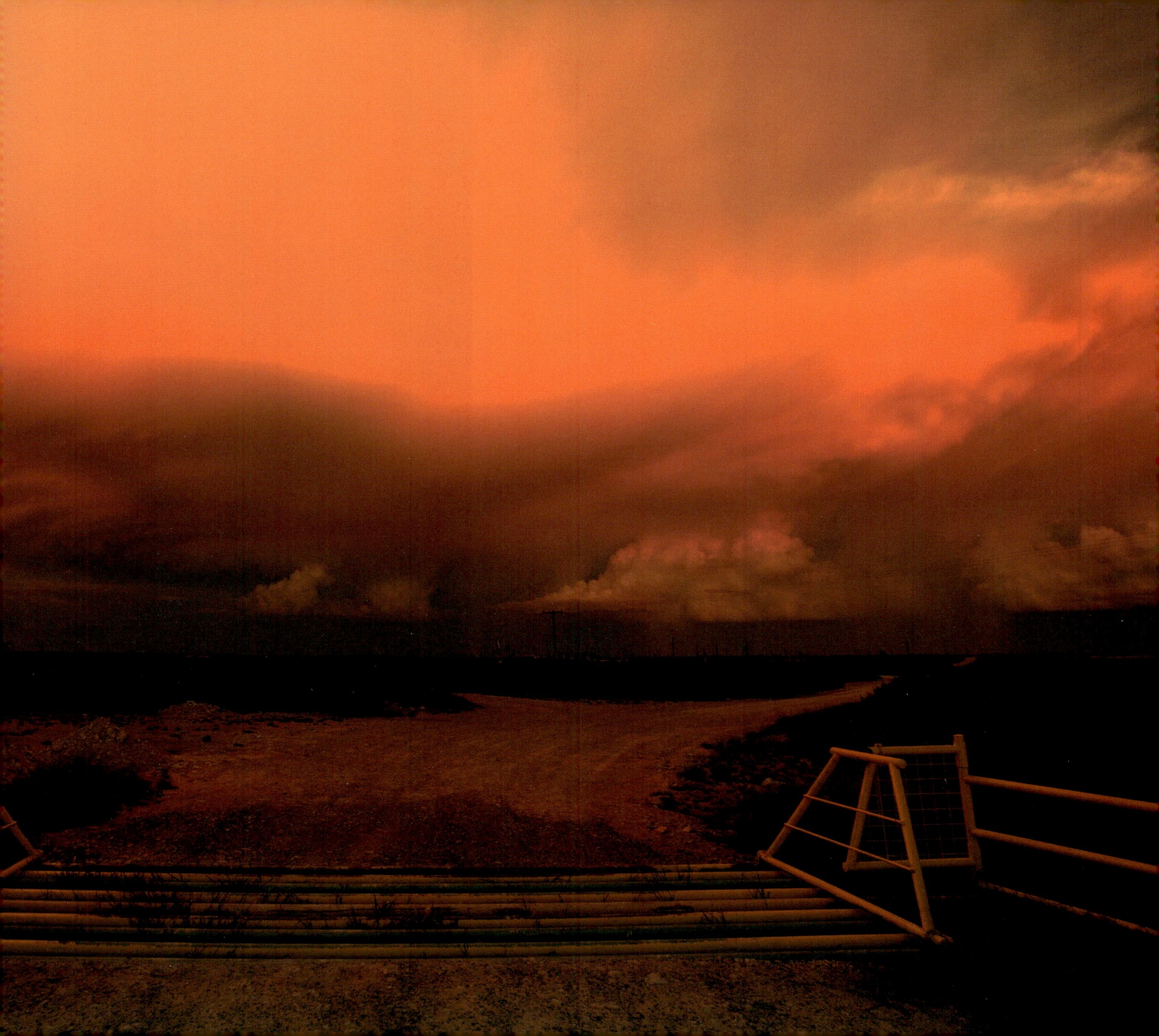

Lullaby

We are our own the way a river swallows
itself. The need that need follows follows.

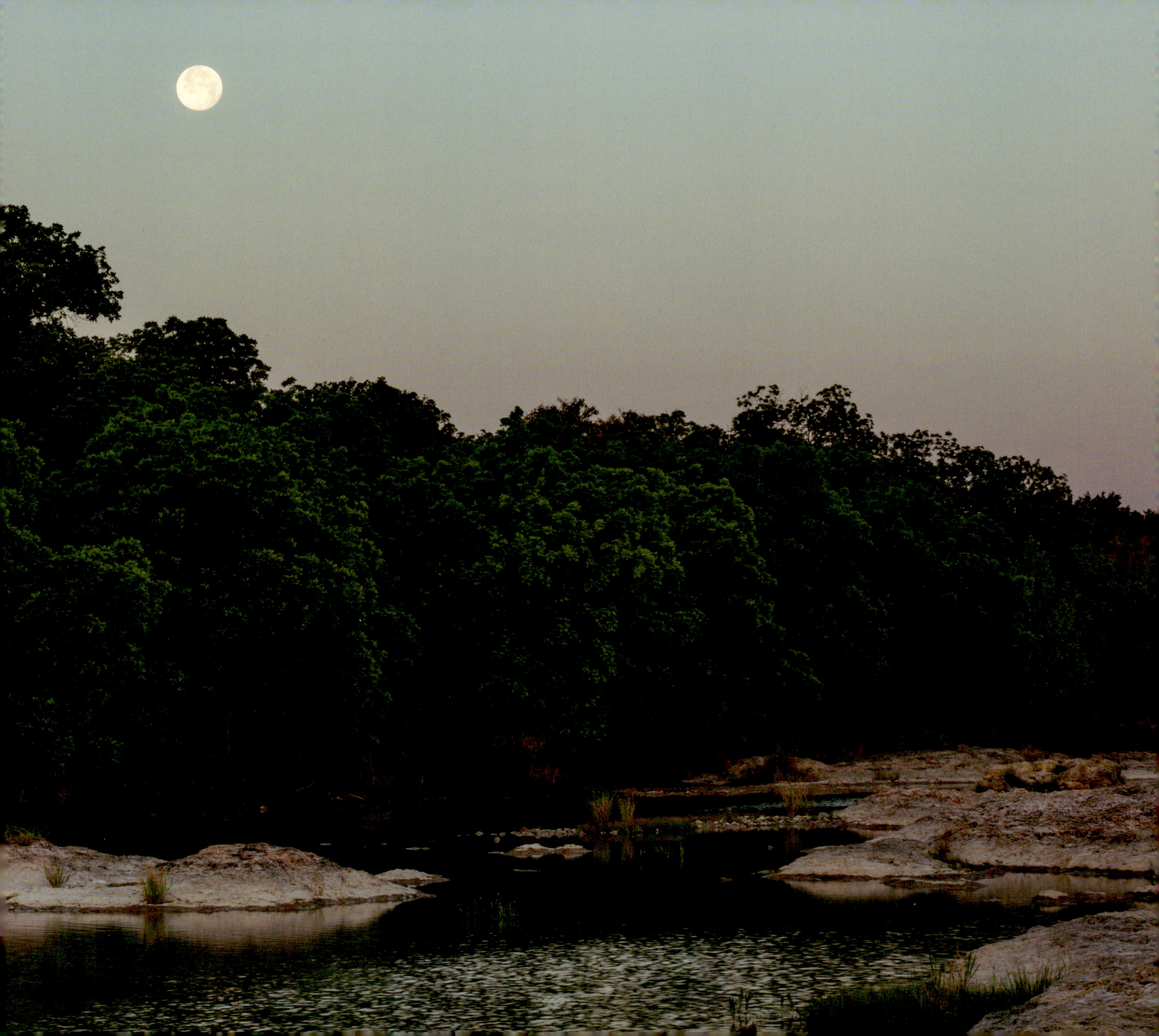

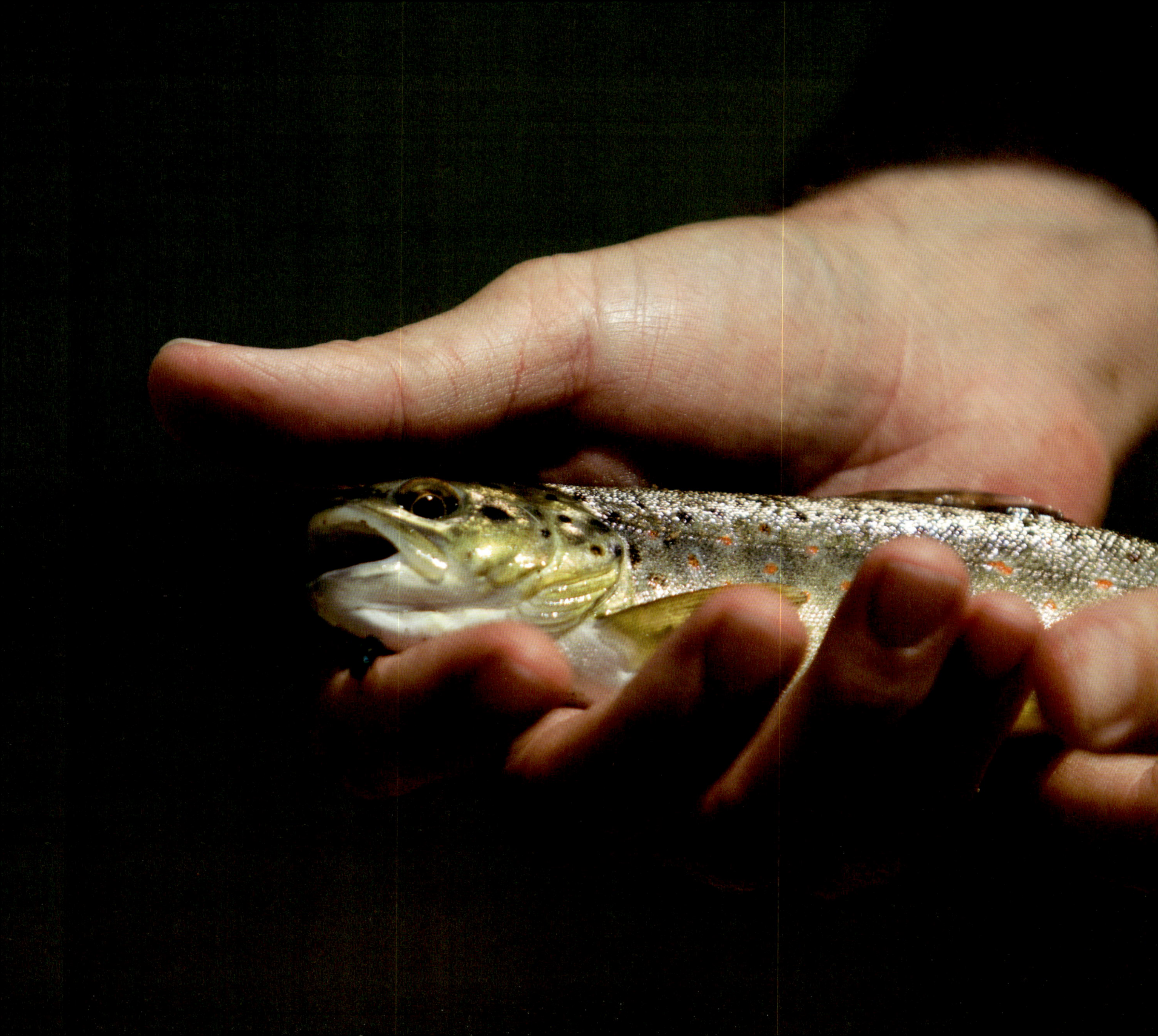

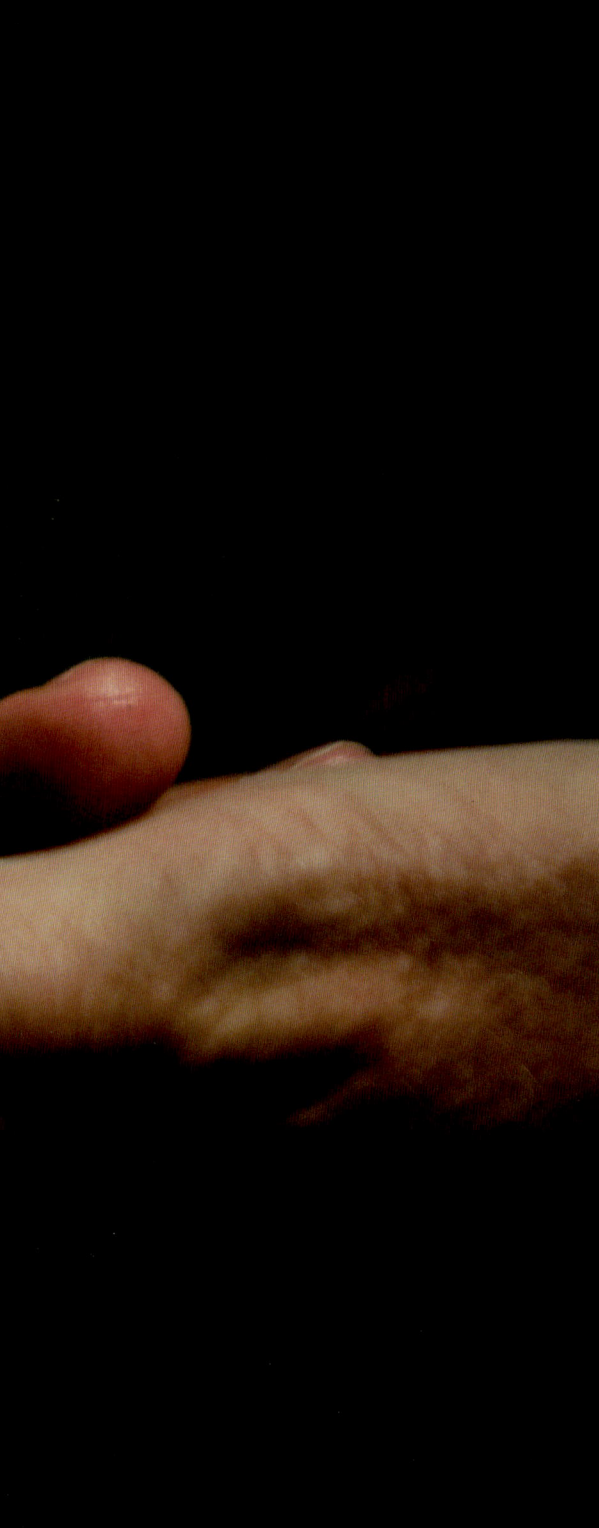

"Trout that swim"

Wait to wade. Streamside, kneel, retrieve a stone
from the wet edge. Beneath slither the nymphs
of flies, a moving prehistoric sketch.

They scuttle their inept attempts at bone
to undermine the light, your sight, and hints
of what will cast successfully. Yet you catch

that shine, that peacock herl. A small refusal
whets wish, is charming as a timid prin-
cess. Understand a rock if you would match

(undistracted by the bobbing ousel)
this hatch.

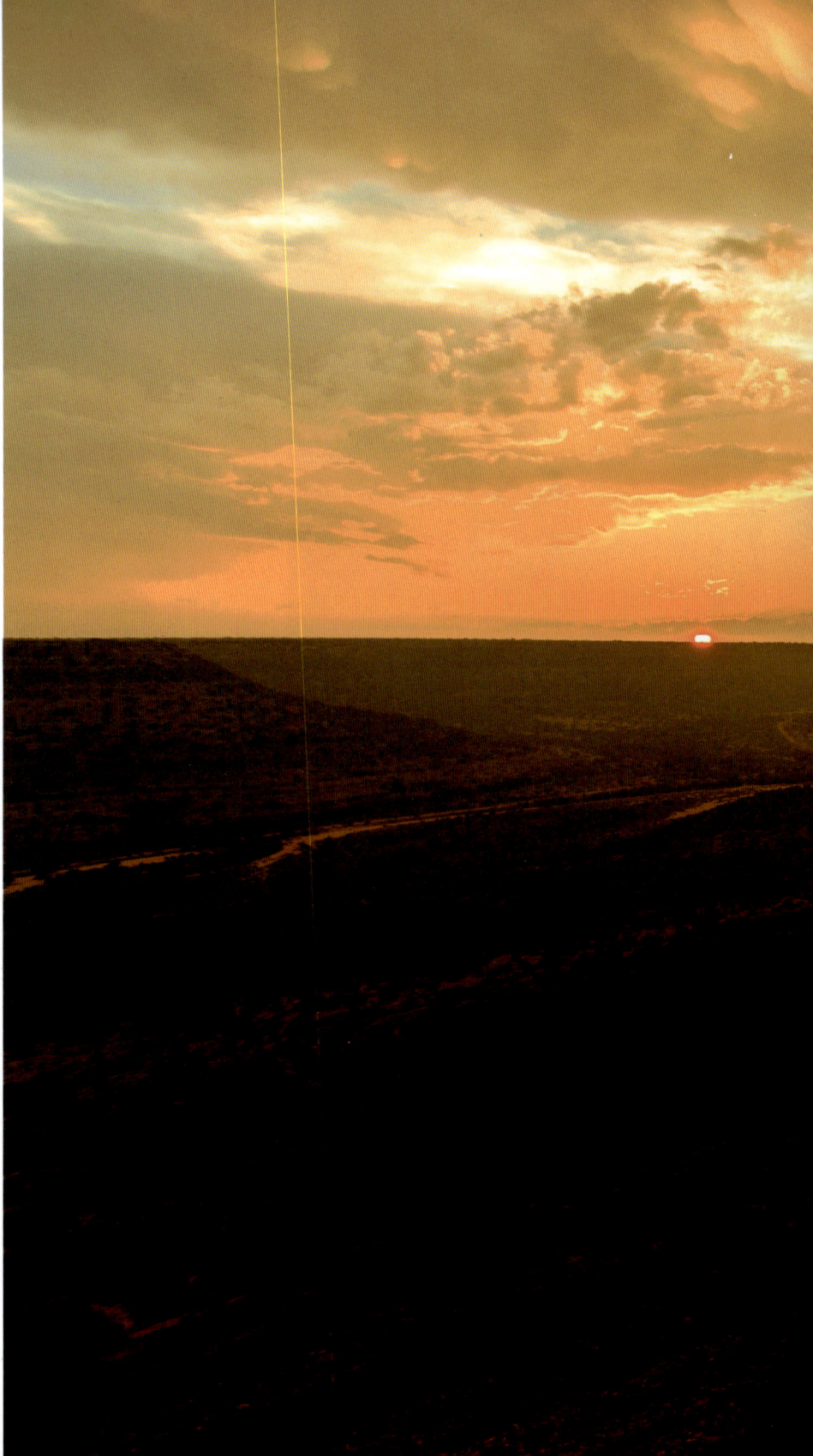

Independence Creek

Down around Independence Creek, the plateaus below I-10
are all the same height. If you take a photograph from the crown
of one on a humid day, the air is so white, my friend,
it may seem someone has cropped the entire top of the terrain,
and that right there is Texas sky so clean and long you disdain
the ceilings of your house and any tree that might hinder heaven.
Between the plateaus of crumbling rock grow mostly mesquite
and prickly pear and a billion centipedes in a rarely wet May
crawling among limestone rubble and jackrabbit-fur coyote scat.
Drop down to the valley floor, and up from Caroline Spring
comes the clear hovering of a smallmouth bass and his tail waving
a black flag like a lazy dog waiting for small trespass to raise his ire.
The Canyon live oaks are few and far between except where
the springs and creek can keep alive the struggle and grip.
The low clouds of morning scud along like driven ghost steers
drifting in search of grass until, at its height, the sun is a whip
and makes of the wind a long fire to purify the idea of distance.
You can't measure the gratitude of the Proserpine Shiner
in the shallows of the impossible water praising the Refiner
in the Chihuahuan Desert limestone stretches and big vistas.

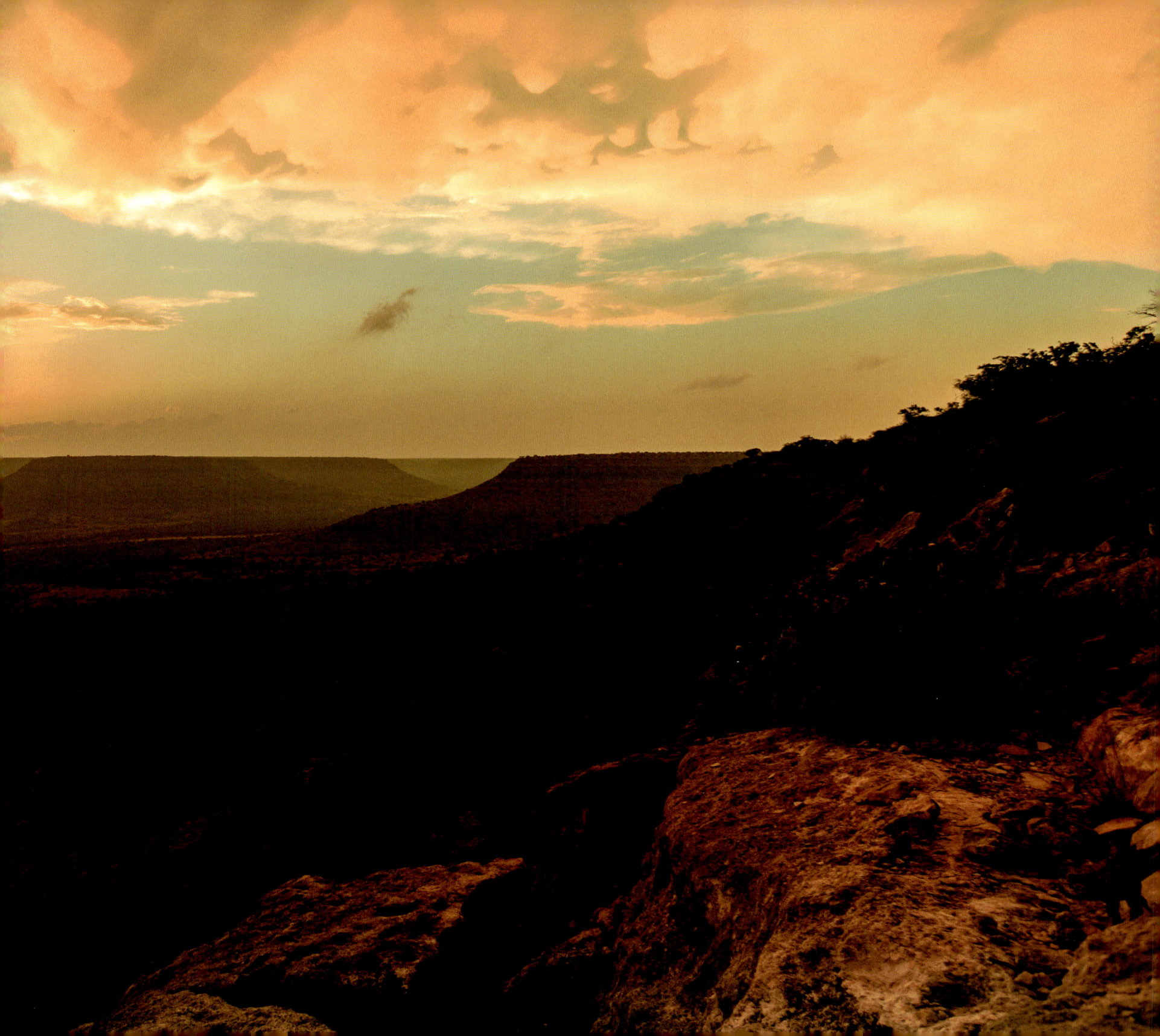

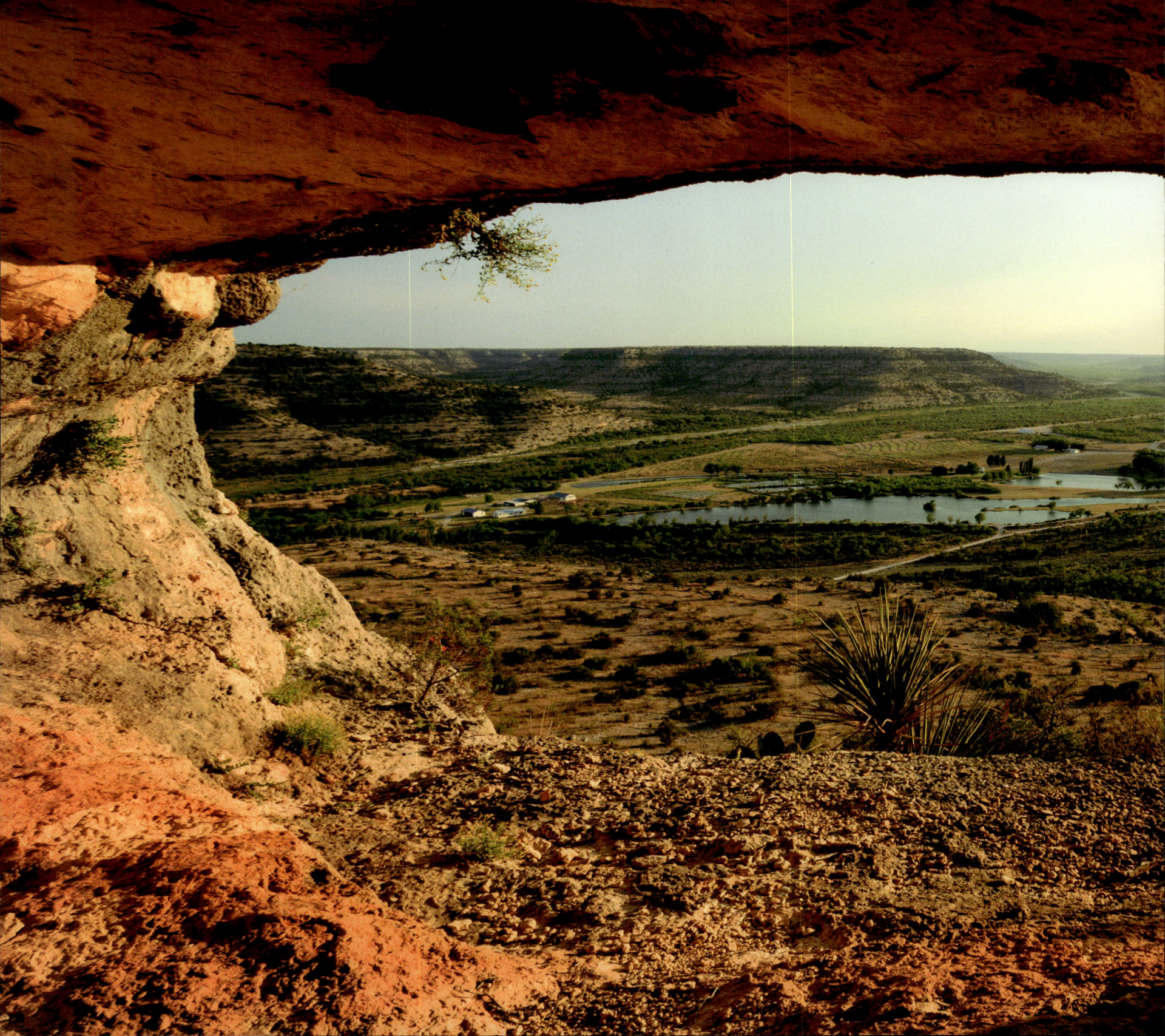

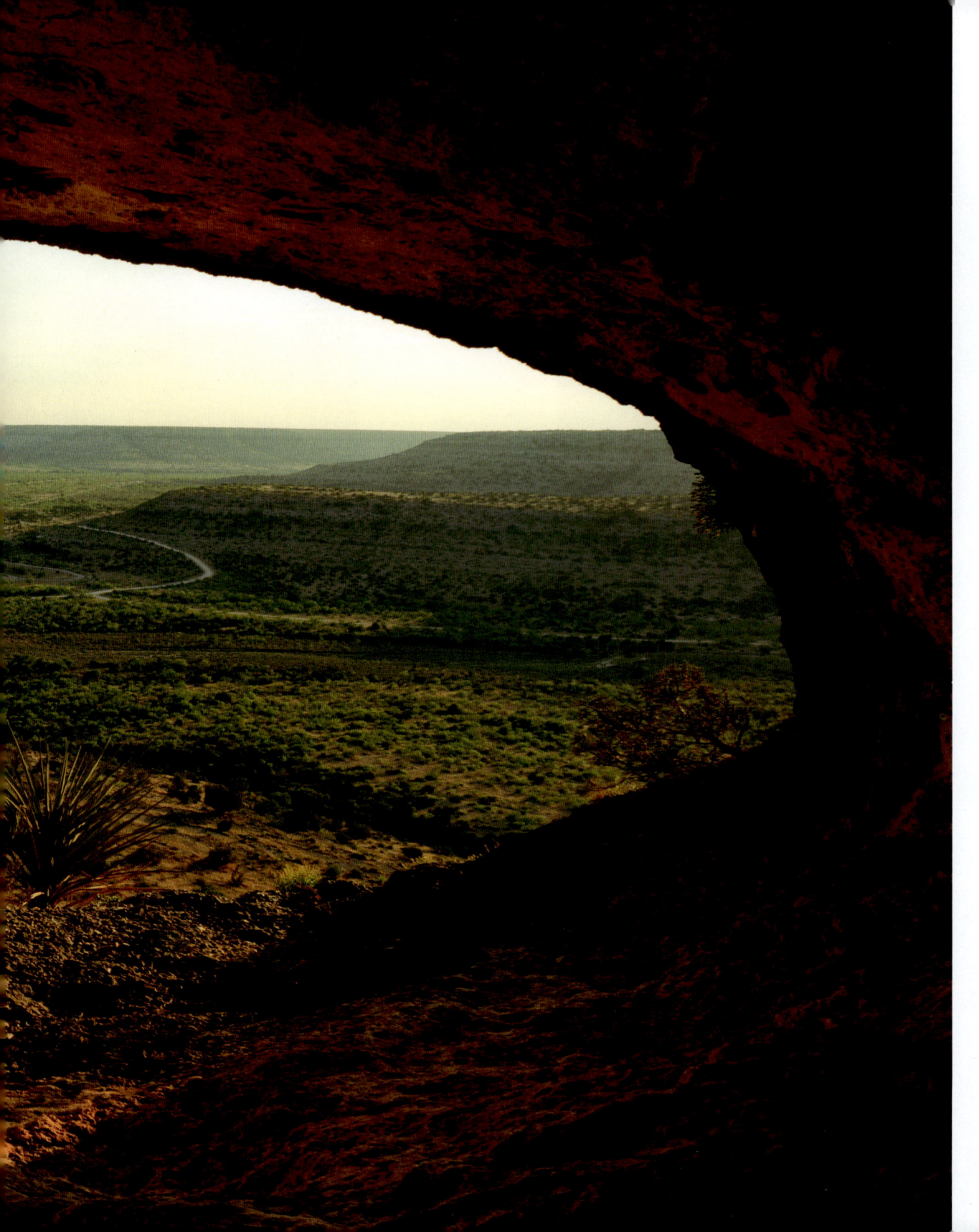

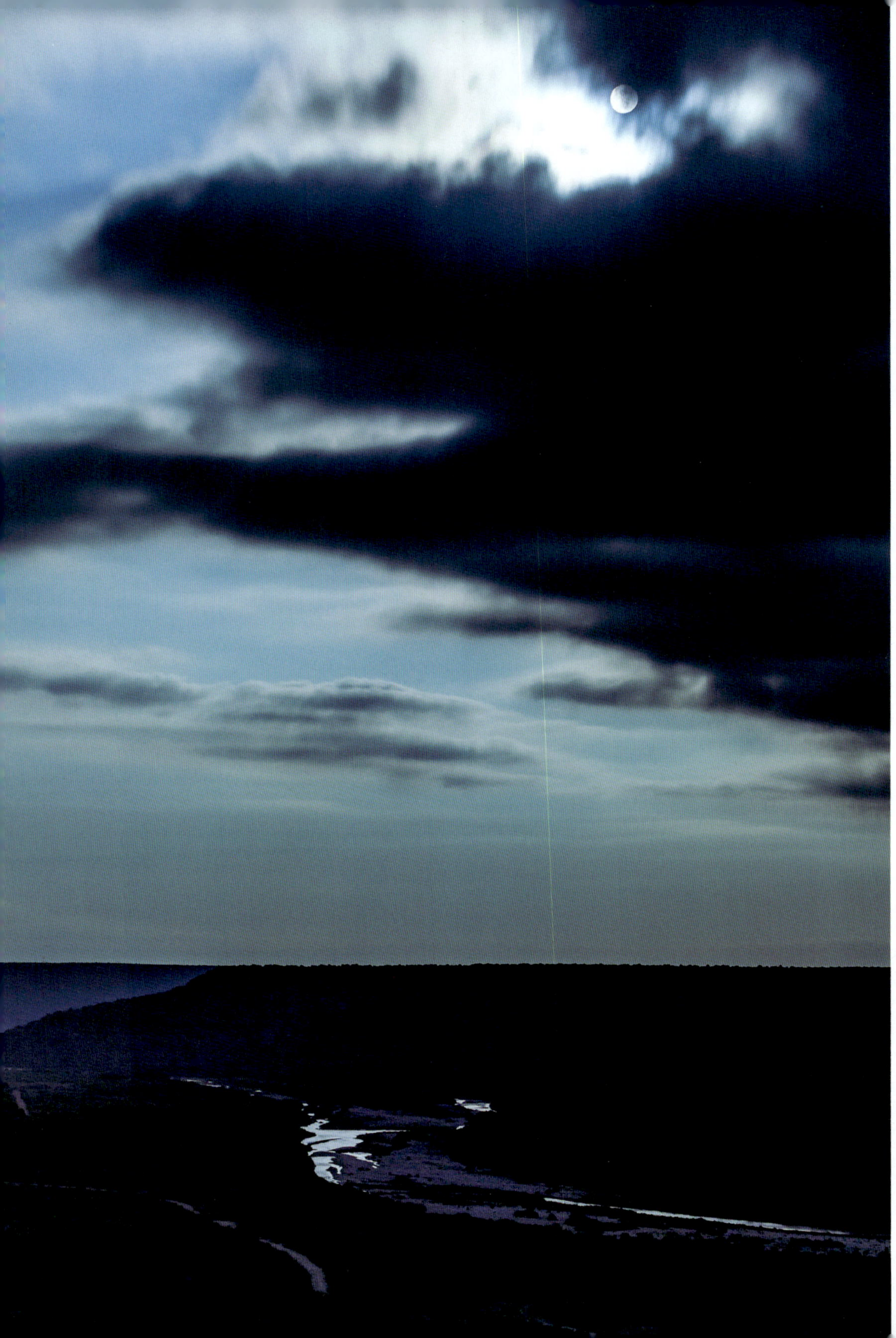

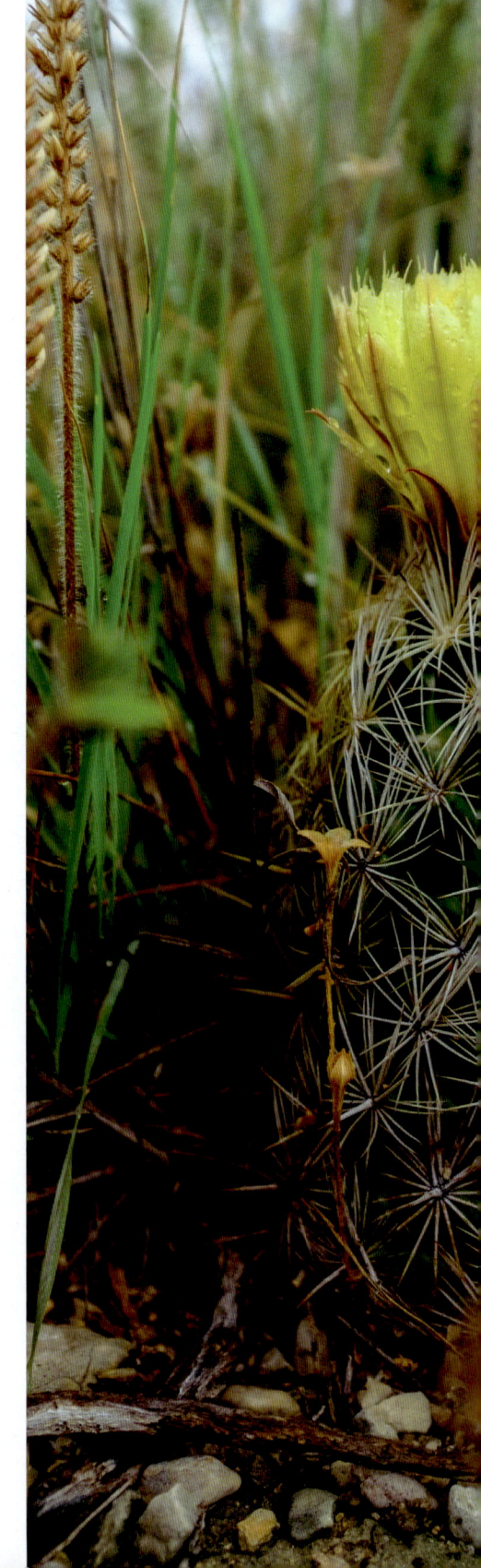

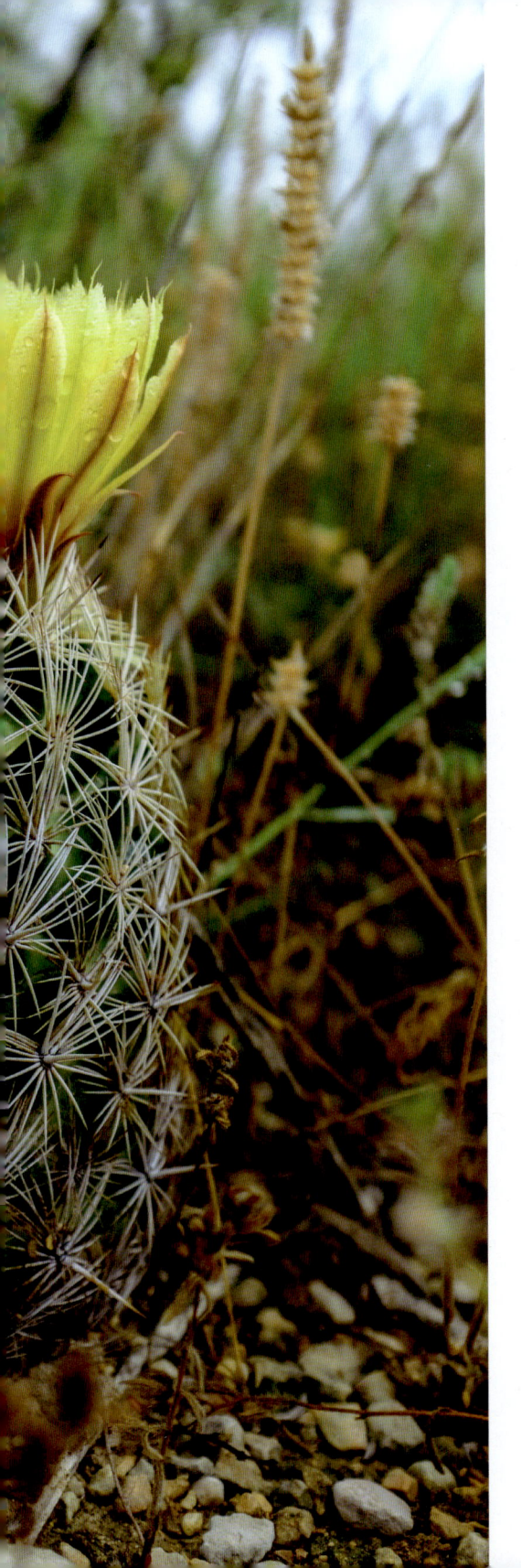

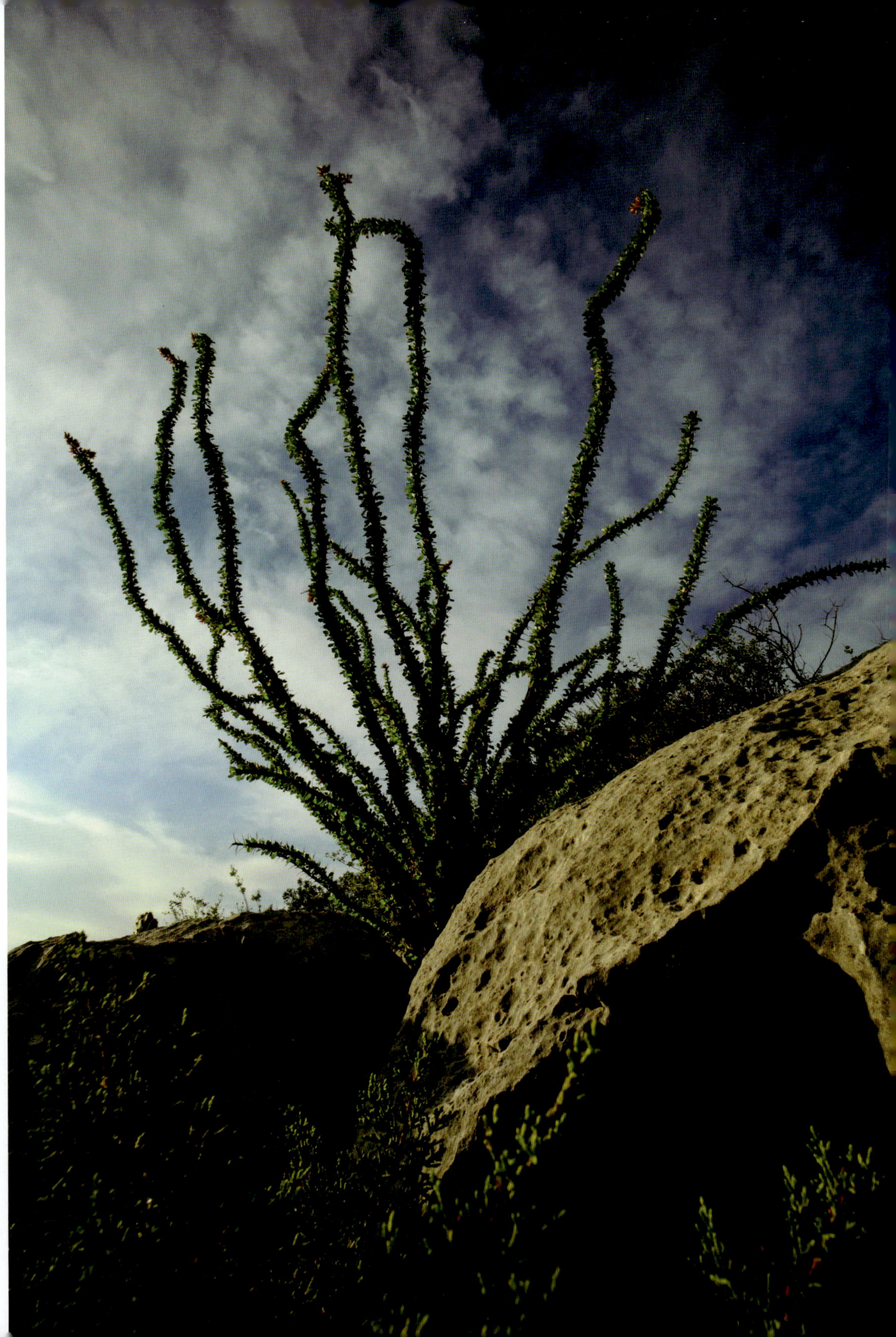

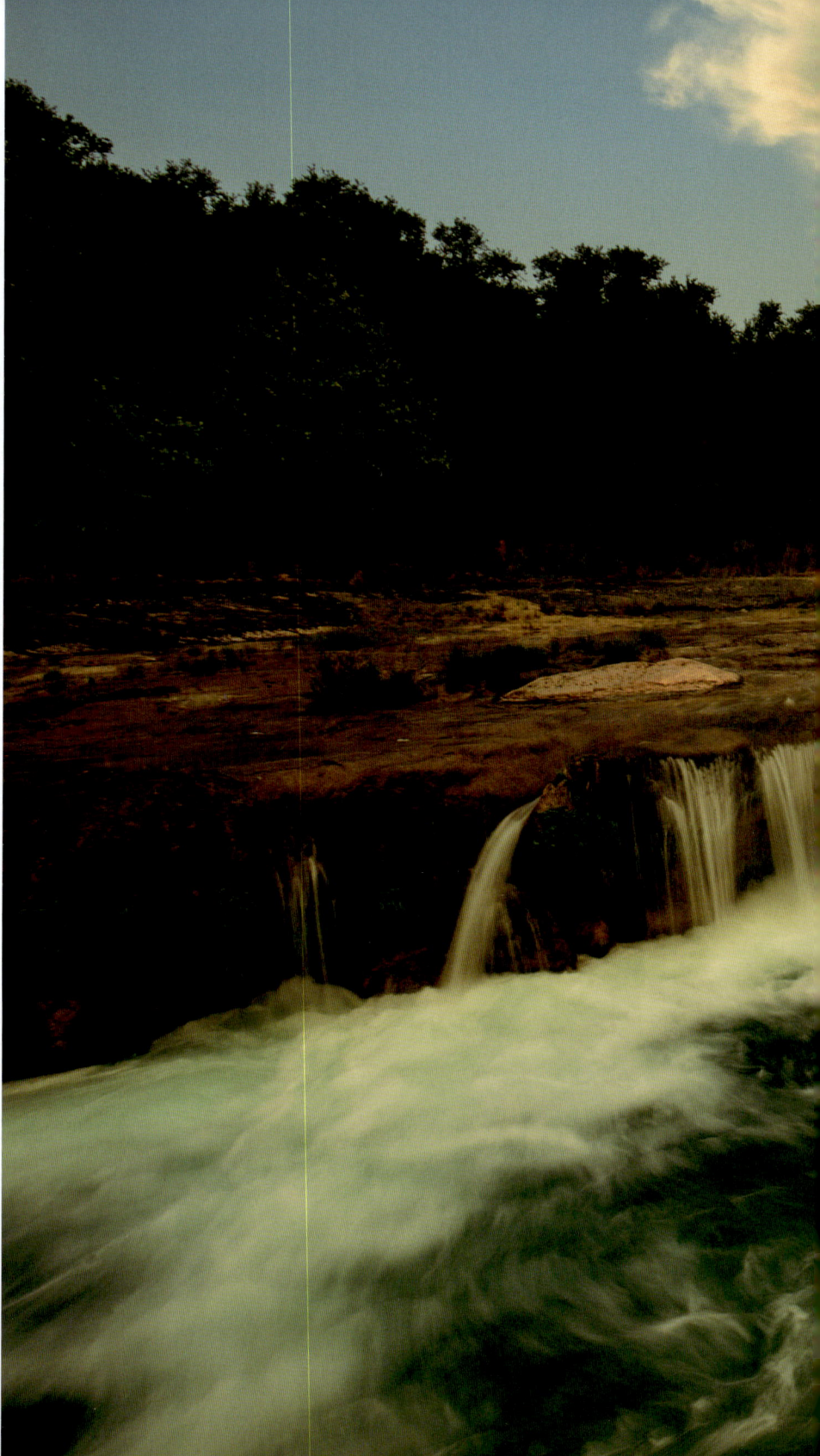

Punctuation on the Devils River

An hour off the paved highway, you have to take
a washboard dirt road past unattractive cactus,
sage and cedar scrub, and miles of hapless mesquite
until, after a few long barren washes, a river
in this wasteland overflows, and religiously
a thicket of little sycamores lets a lot of green light in.

We ford with a pickup the long flat, fat limestone shelf,
Up the bank in the oaks, asterisks of parasitic moss
like old, blind eyes just watch as we unpack.
The dark, little goodbyes of yesterday's rain
fade in the distance, move over another ridge,
another county, another heaven, under God,
divisible by doubts and wants.

Now the wet wind of low clouds racing boredom
and erasing mediocre plateaus tries to hide
four aoudads scampering the sheer rock face in mist.
This mist rises, and collecting drops seep down.
The biggest millipede in Texas, more than
the span of my entire hand, drinks tenderly
at the edge of a pool of dew, slow as a plateau crumbles.

At Dolan Falls, the shapely shelves hold
a different kind of book, limestone leaves whose language
erodes with the dew of ten thousand years.
In this month of May, ferns emerge in every crevice.
On a long flat shelf, three tinajas punctuate the morning
like nature's ellipses refusing conclusion,
and their distilled reflections of clouds lift.

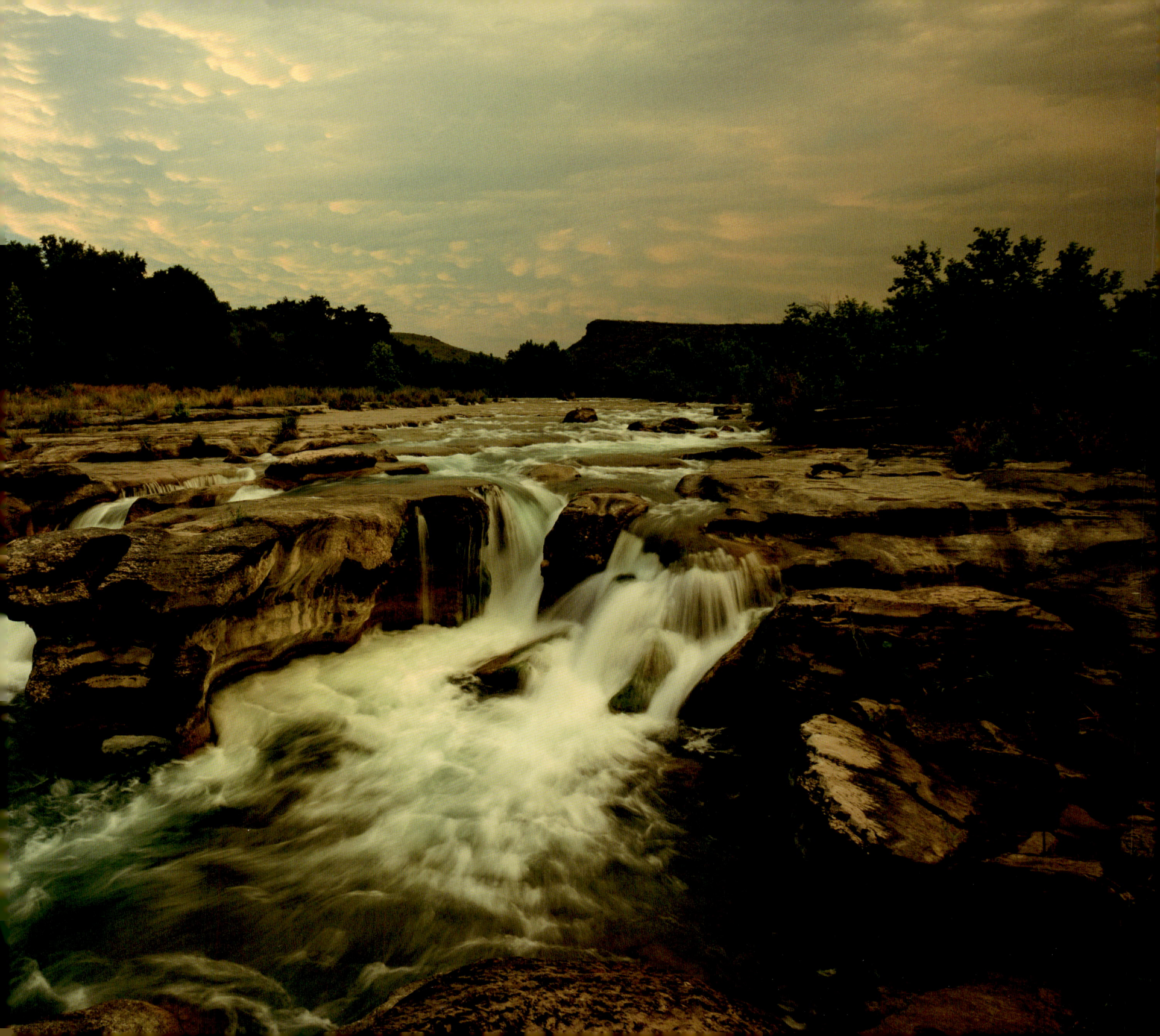

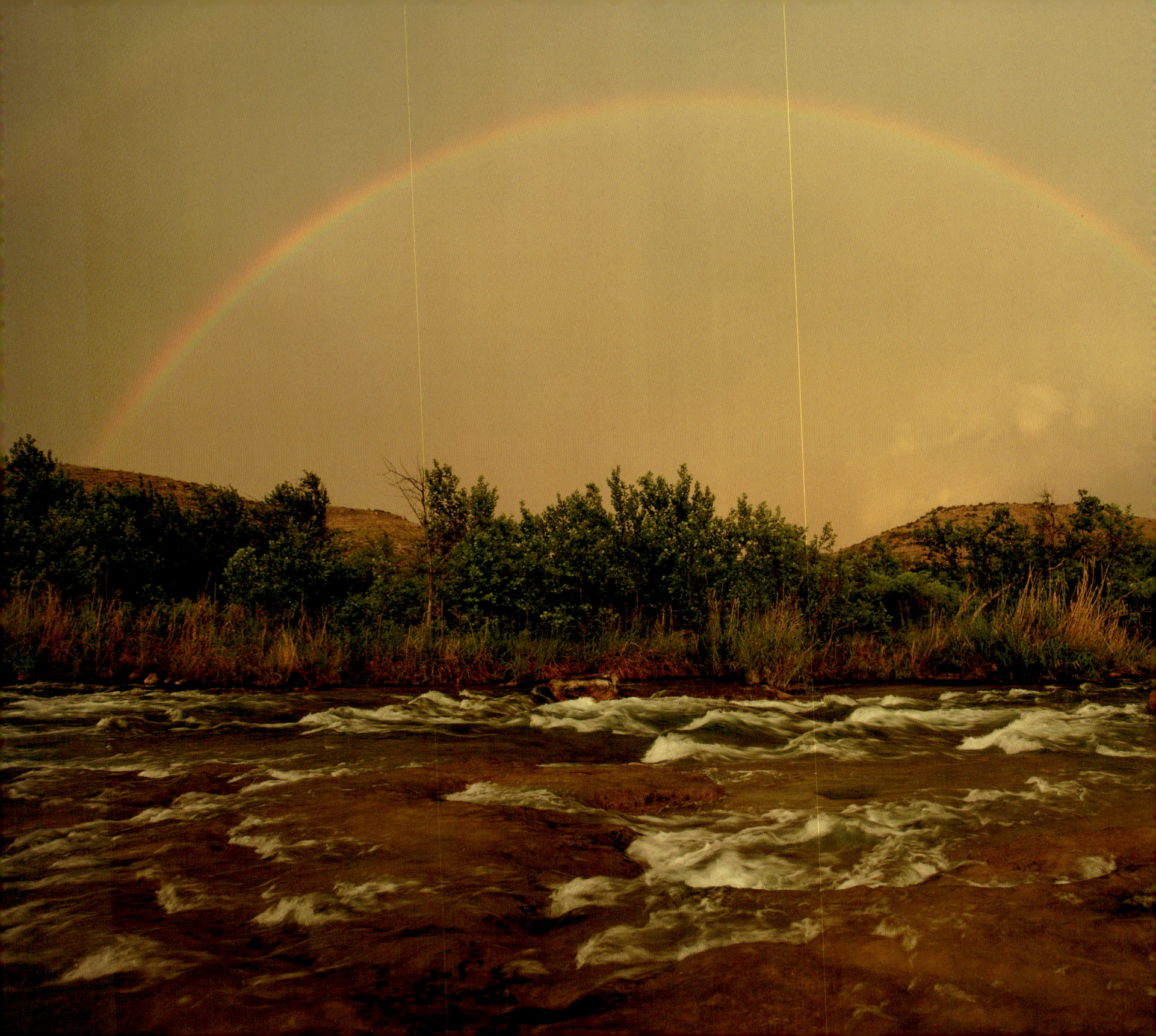

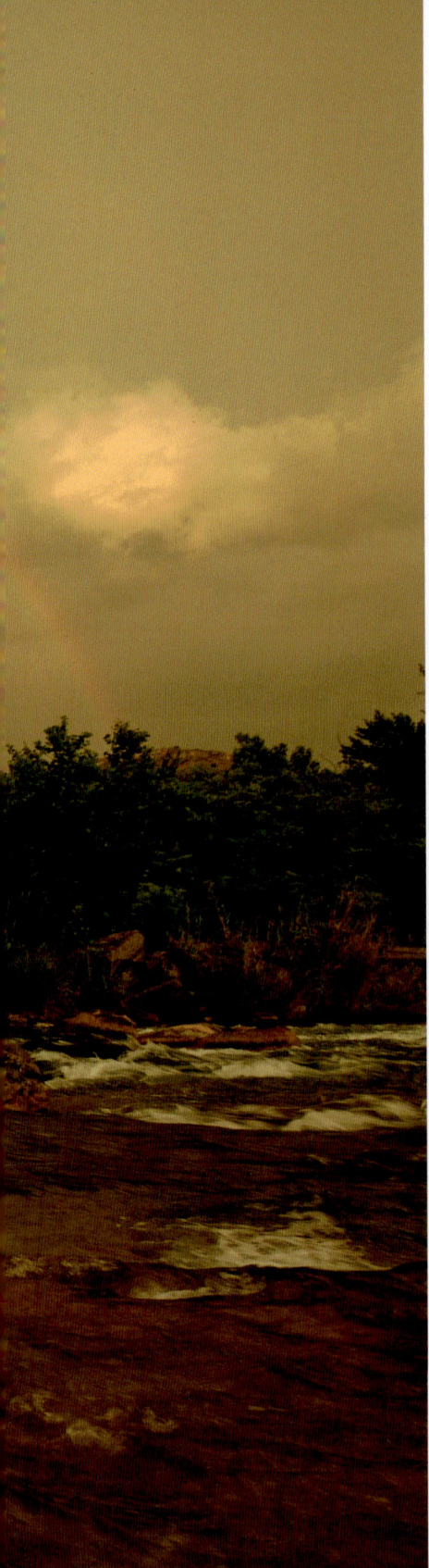

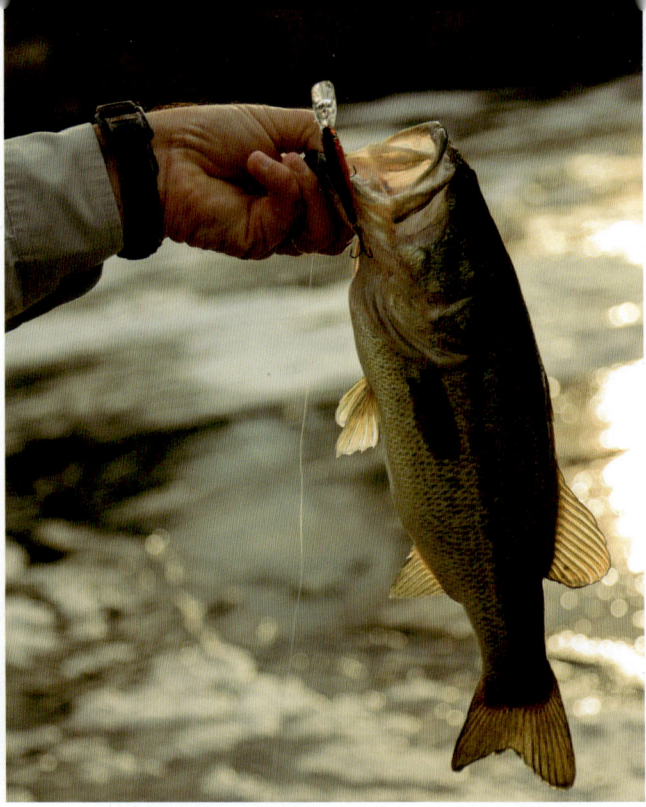

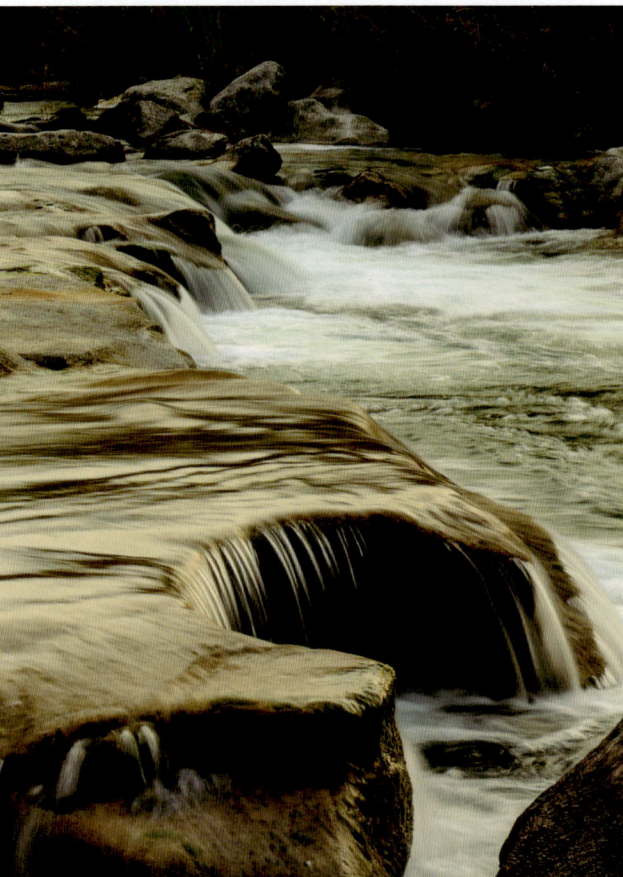

Let's not be too tender about Texas.
Water penetrates stone to death and dissolution.
After long droughts come floods,
and another limestone shelf the size of a tugboat
chases a giant white padlock in a Dali dream.
Suds below the falls the wind pushes
back upriver like dull weather memories.

And finally, the upside-down exclamation
of an angry smallmouth leaping for a moth
seems as possible as ice cream to a cowboy.

I wait on the comma of a big river eddy
like an eye waiting on light behind a black shutter
hopes an explosion will fall into an image.
I am always wanting that black aperture
of my form to flower geometrically empty
until I'm nothing and you are all. Period.
And like a psalm God swallows, I know
what light knows the Devil doesn't.

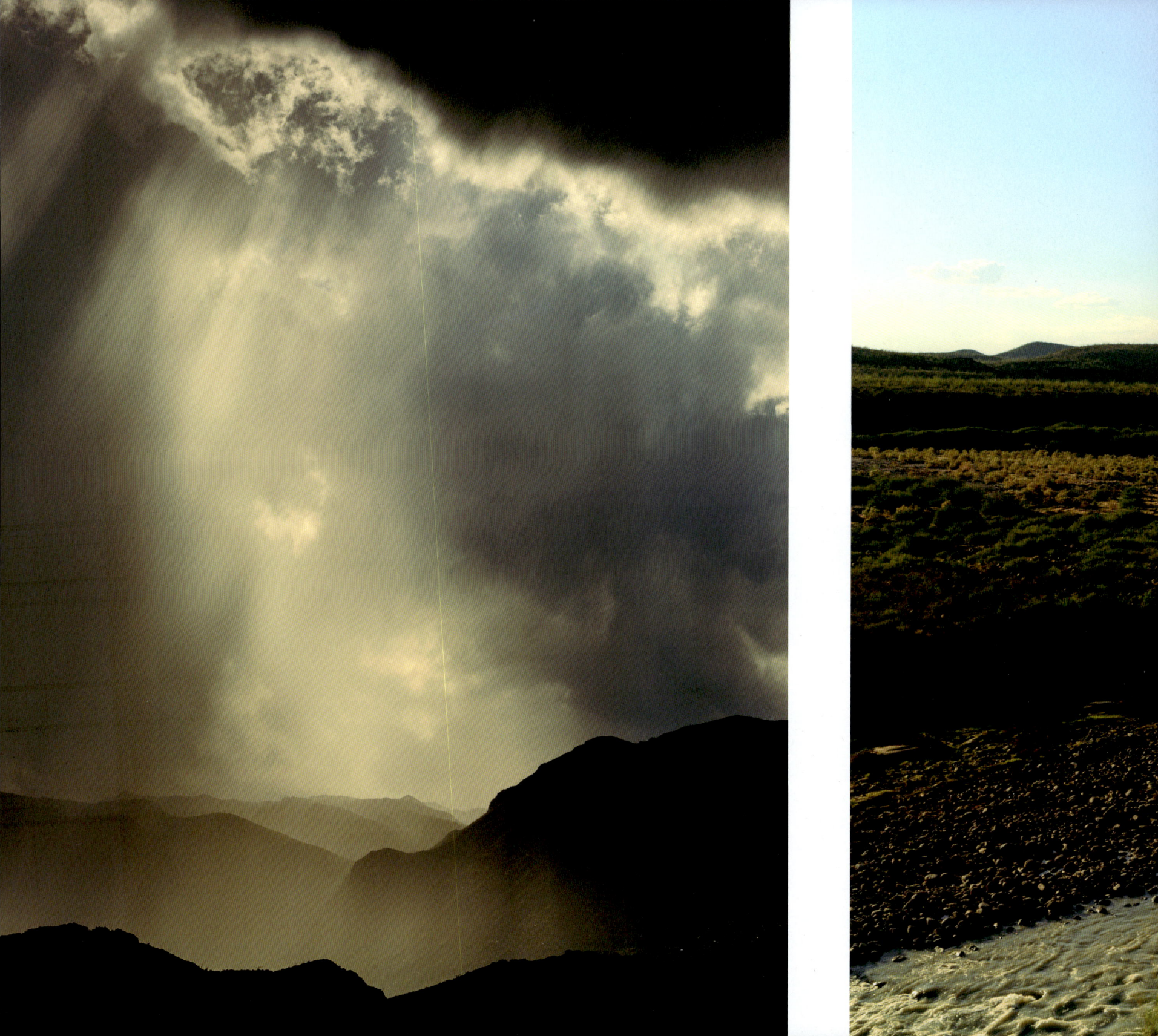

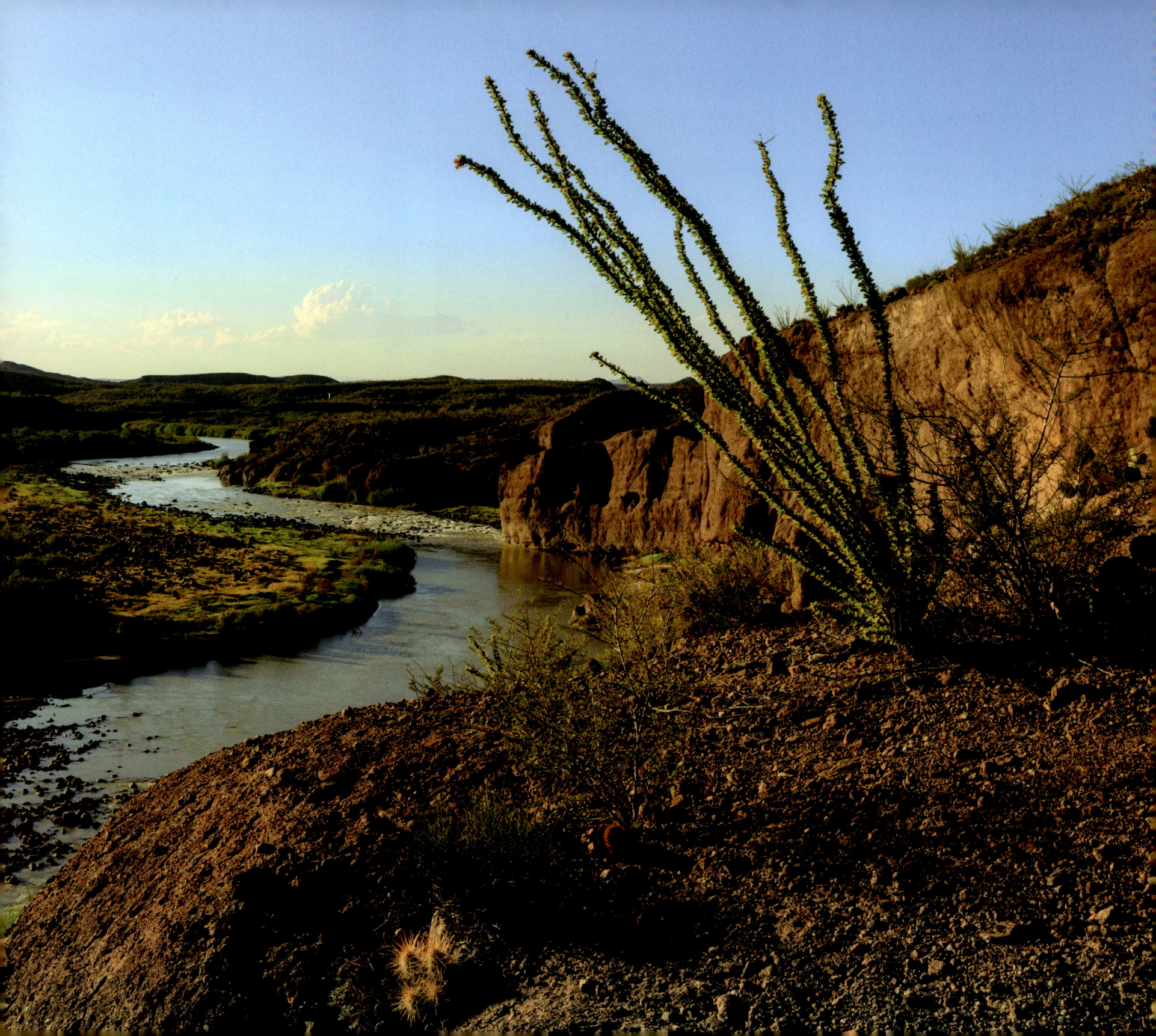

The Rio Grande (South)

Cascabel of liquid days
weaving inaudible Zs
in your long slow passages
where your scales
weigh in the balances
the light and grays
reflecting quartz and dust,
how do you fuse
two visions into one tongue
forked now and then
with such thirst
wandering through
this long brown chasm?

With rain you might wake
and wash the foothills,
for heaven's sake
rolling over stones,
the ocotillo jealous
of your distance, the roots
of juniper and willow
reaching to touch
the ragged hem
of your garment.
Iridescent,
as if risen,
you leave behind
your holy ghost.

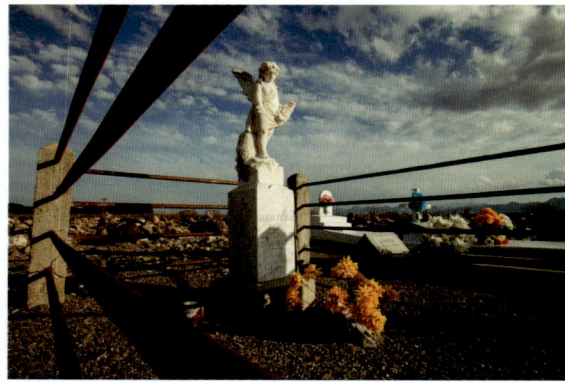

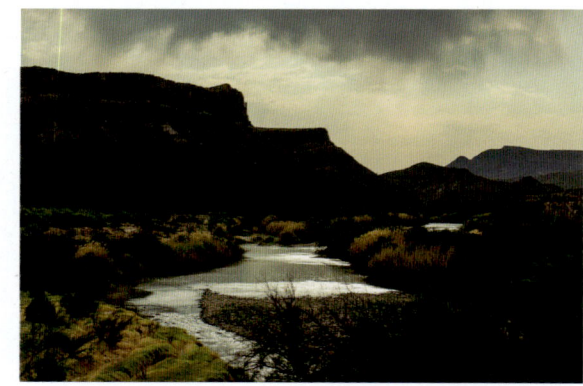

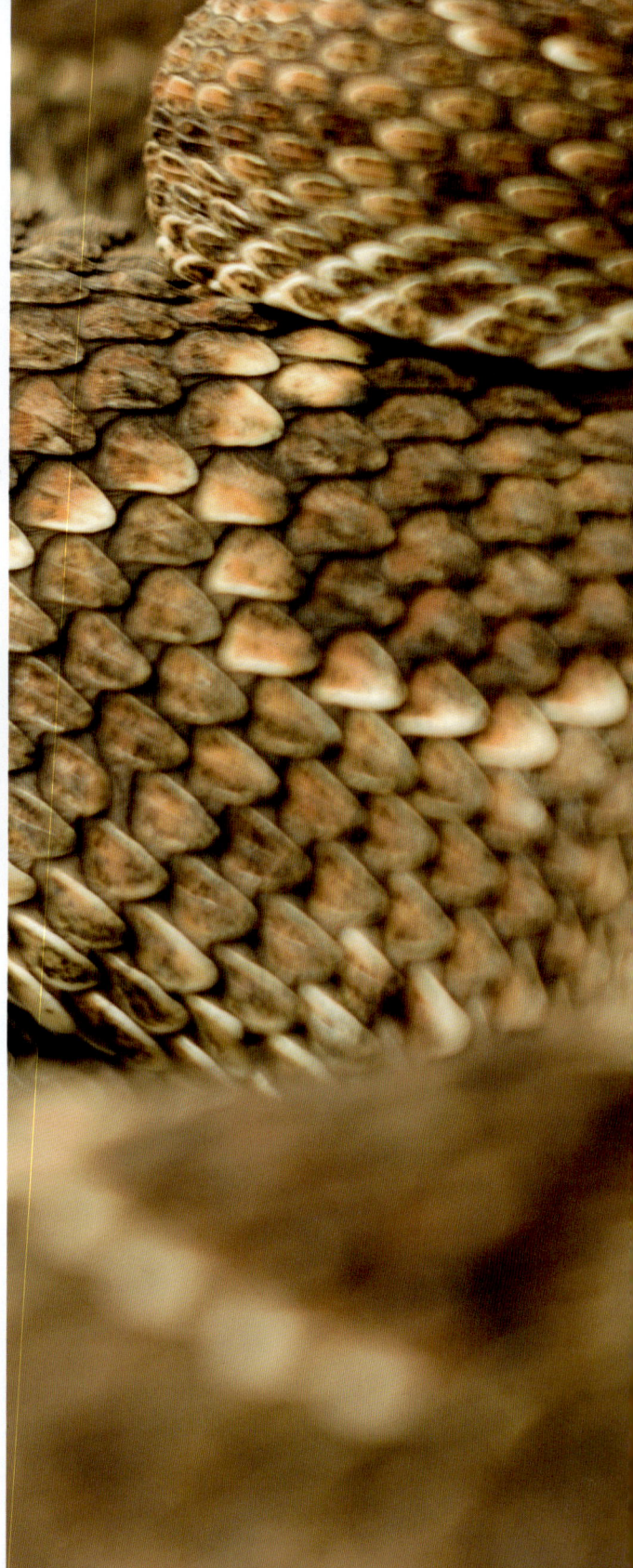

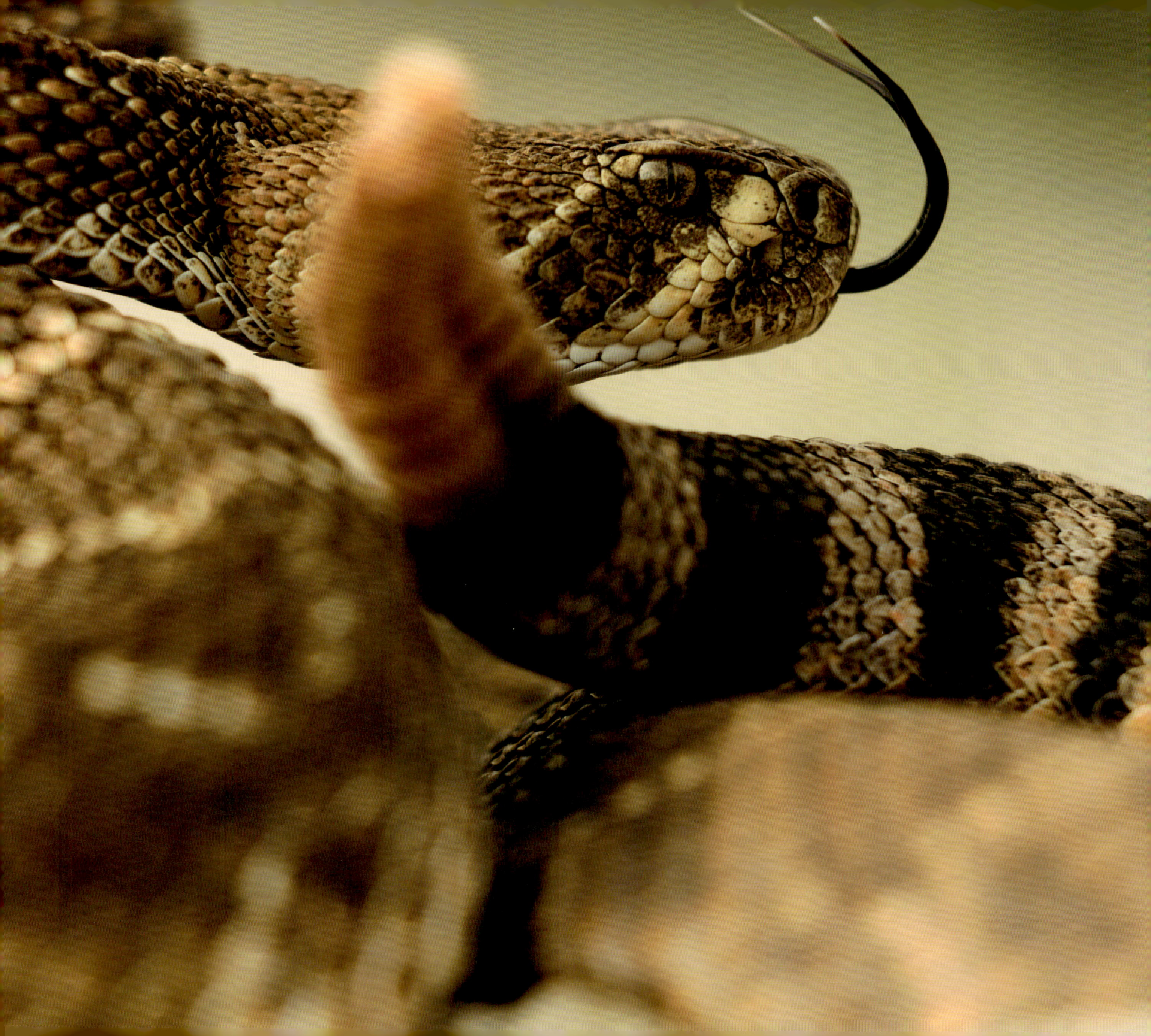

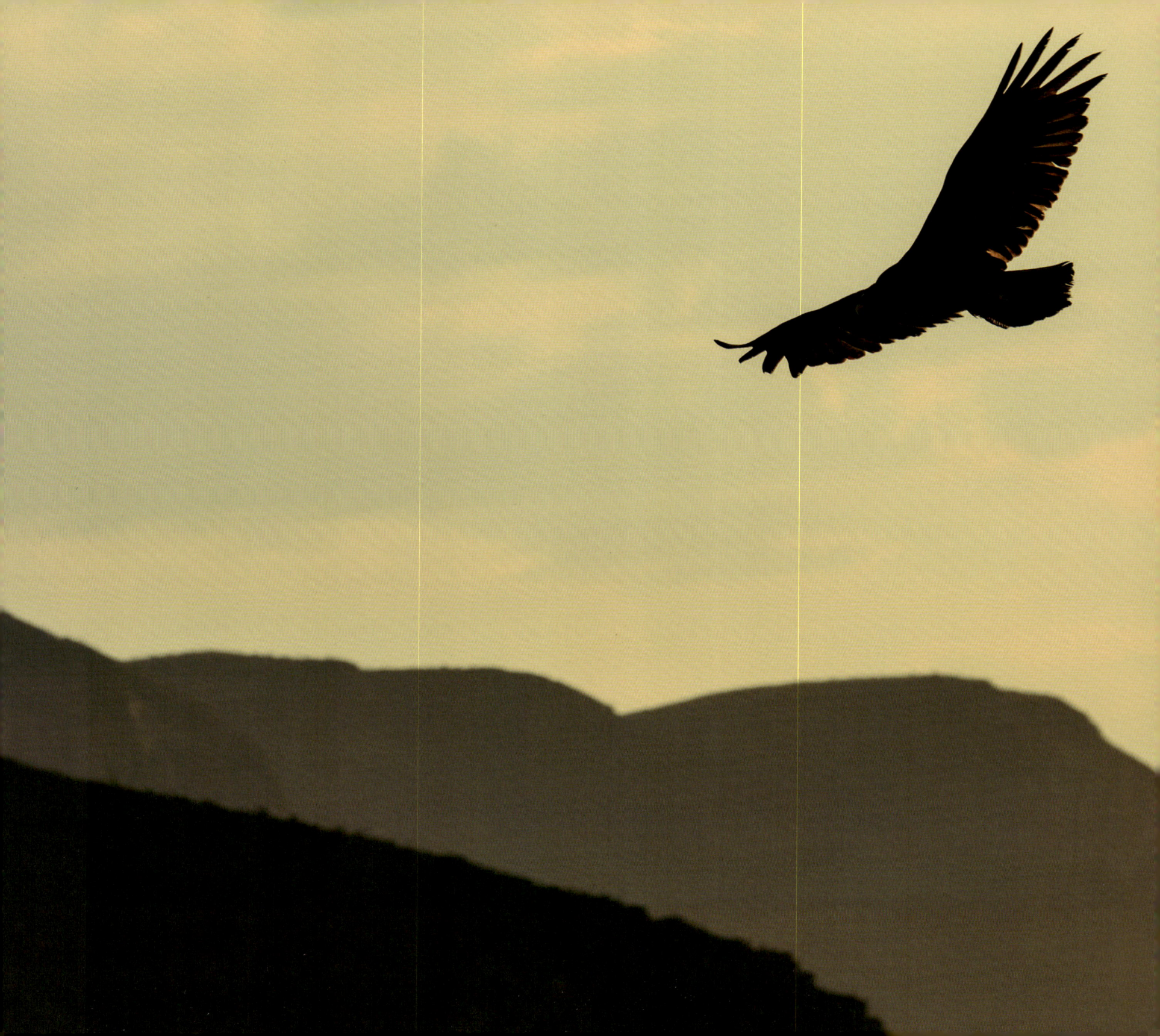

1. Moonlit movement along the Brazos River.

2. Moonlight reflections on the muddy banks of the Brazos near Rotan, Texas.

3. Red Creek drops into the Llano River during a springtime shower south of London, Texas.

4. Ice covers the landscape along the Brazos River near Knox City, Texas, after a bitter cold snap common in the Big Empty.

5. Golden waters of the Llano River at sunset.

6. The Rio Grande courses 564 feet below the top of the gorge it helped cut west of the Sangre de Cristo Mountains near Taos, New Mexico.

7. The Llano River flowing over pink boulders between Mason and Llano, Texas.

8. A lone windmill stands in Brazos River country on the 6666 Ranch, Guthrie, Texas.

9. Sunset along the Llano River, London, Texas.

10. An uncommon overcast sky sits atop the Rio Grande in Texas's Big Bend region.

11. Fourth of July celebrations at Buffalo Springs Lake, south of Lubbock, Texas.

12. Cathedral Peak, south of Alpine, Texas.

13. A dry Rio Grande near Presidio, Texas.

14. Drought relief and inspiration on the Llano River over Mason, Texas.

15. Sunset over Texas's Brazos River country near Guthrie, Texas.

16. Star trails over the Brazos near Waco, Texas.

17. Common sunflower in Arroyo Seco, New Mexico.

18. Morning light touches a bighorn ram among the sagebrush west of Taos, New Mexico.

19. Lightning strikes behind the Easter Pageant Cross in Junction, Texas.

20. A mid-autumn Rio Hondo flows out of the Taos Ski Valley into Arroyo Seco.

21. Columbia bottomlands along the Brazos River provide vital ecology to the area near Angleton, Texas.

22. Independence Creek is an ever-changing riparian ecosystem in the Chihuahuan Desert south of Sheffield, Texas.

23. Early morning sunrise along the Llano River near Junction, Texas.

24. Costilla Creek, a healthy tributary to the Rio Grande, northeast of Questa, New Mexico.

25. A dramatic rain shower moves across Marathon Basin in the Texas Big Bend.

26. Rainfall is a welcome sign for land and life of all kinds between northern New Mexico and southeast Texas.

27. Forest debris diverts runoff to the Rio Hondo, north of Taos, New Mexico.

28. Willow trees line the Brazos River at its exit into the Gulf of Mexico near East Columbia, Texas.

29. Monsoon season in the Big Bend near Shafter, Texas.

30. Llano River shallows, downstream from Castell, Texas.

31. The arid Chihuahuan Desert above Madrid Falls in Texas's Big Bend Ranch State Park.

32. Rocky cliffs west of Taos, New Mexico, fall into the Rio Grande Gorge.

33. A three-toed woodpecker moves among the evergreens in the Sangre de Cristo Mountains.

34. The Cimarron River sources its water originally from the canyons of the Sangre de Cristos.

35. Early morning fog amongst the sage mesas near the Sangre de Cristo Mountains.

36. New Mexican angling attire.

37. Fishing at the merger of Comanche Creek and Costilla Creek, below Comanche Point.

38. Colorful quaking aspens stand prevalent in the Valle Vidal, the "Valley of Life."

39. A frozen Williams Lake, a water source for the Lake Fork of the Rio Hondo.

40. Entrance to a lush field south of Arroyo Hondo.

41. The Milky Way high above Taos, New Mexico.

42. The Rio Pueblo, a benefactor of the Little Rio Grande, near Ranchos de Taos, New Mexico.

43. Centuries-old Anasazi pottery shards found along Pot Creek, south of Taos, New Mexico.

44. Beautiful fleabane in the Sangre de Cristo Mountains.

45. Monsoon season in the mountains north of Taos, New Mexico.

46. A Dolan Creek tinaja reflects a West Texas sunset.

47. A strawberry hedgehog cactus blooms high above Devils River country.

48. A bighorn ewe looks hundreds of feet down the Rio Grande Gorge near Taos.

49. The John Dunn Bridge crosses the Rio Grande, south of Arroyo Hondo.

50. A grown-over acequia gate off Embudo Creek near Dixon, New Mexico.

51. A Sangre de Cristo sunrise above Taos Pueblo.

52. Sagebrush populates the mesa between the Sangre de Cristo Mountains and the Rio Grande Gorge near Taos, New Mexico.

53. Late evening reflections along the Llano near Mason, Texas.

54. Rain falls on Colorado Canyon above the Rio Grande near Lajitas, Texas.

55. Ochre-colored canyon walls among the Sangre de Cristos.

56. A narrow band of the Red River, south of Questa, New Mexico.

57. Mesquite and cedar trees are a ready source for property boundaries along the Llano River.

58. Hunting for fish upriver from the Red River hatchery.

59. Cool spring mornings make for dense fog along the Llano River's small waterfalls.

60. Hilltop grasses blow in the wind high above the Llano River.

61. A dense pecan bottom sits just above the Llano near Junction, Texas.

62. The western stretches of the Llano are often lined by steep limestone cliffs.

63. Whitetail deer are more than common sights near the Llano.

64. Running through the heart of Texas Hill Country, the Llano is lined by colorful wildflowers throughout spring and early summer.

65. Scoured limestone rock riverbeds are revealed at lower levels on the Llano.

66. A low Llano River near Junction, Texas.

67. A prickly pear cactus takes root and prospers in the crook of a Texas Hill Country pecan tree.

68. A pair of mullein plants emerge from the gravel bank of the Llano near Junction, Texas.

69. Mid- and late-summer temperatures in the Texas Hill Country can be oppressive to the land and waterways.

70. A calm Sabinal River slowly meanders through wooded areas in the Texas Hill Country.

71. Evening light plays among the bald cypress trees lining the Sabinal River near Utopia, Texas.

72. Waterfalls create a pool on the Sabinal before the river runs underground.

73. Love Creek flows through dense Texas Hill Country cedar, mesquite, live oak, and bigtooth maple.

74. A thigh-deep pool on Love Creek just beyond a large limestone ledge.

75. Fallen bigtooth maple leaves stick to a craggy creek bed on Love Creek near Medina, Texas.

76. Low clouds over the steep hills surrounding a secluded Love Creek, north of Bandera, Texas.

77. Costilla Creek, northeast of Comanche Point in the Valle Vidal near Costilla, New Mexico.

78. Fish on the mind; stimulator.

79. A reddish egret stands silhouetted against a Laguna Madre sunset, north of the Rio Grande's exit into the Gulf of Mexico.

80. The Rio Grande snakes between Texas (right) and Mexico (left) north of Lajitas.

81. Dew-laden purple asters color the banks of Holy Ghost Creek.

82. Holy Ghost Creek falls into the Pecos River near Tererro, New Mexico.

83. Pronounced mesas overlook the Pecos River watershed south of Las Vegas, New Mexico.

84. Sunrise over an oilfield near Pyote, Texas.

85. Working pens west of the Goodnight-Loving Trail in eastern New Mexico.

86. Pecos River country along Interstate 40, west of Santa Rosa, New Mexico.

87. The Texas Trans-Pecos, the fringe of the Chihuahuan Desert, is known for its arid ecology.

88. A West Texas sunset over the oilfields south of Grandfalls.

89. Moon above the Llano River, near Yates Crossing east of Junction, Texas.

90. A juvenile brown trout in hand on the Red River near Questa, New Mexico.

91. The sun sets over arid Chihuahuan Desert plateaus along Independence Creek south of Sheffield, Texas.

92. Caves looking down on The Nature Conservancy's Independence Creek Preserve hold evidence of historic life in Texas's Trans-Pecos region.

93. Moonlight over Independence Creek.

94. A hedgehog cactus near Independence Creek blooms after a springtime shower.

95. A healthy ocotillo reaches for the heavens above Independence Creek.

96. A late spring thunderstorm moves over the Dolan Falls, the largest waterfall by volume in Texas.

97. Rainbow over the Devils River.

98. The Devils, an angler's paradise, supports largemouth, smallmouth, and Guadalupe bass.

99. The Devils River is assessed as some of the best water in Texas.

100. Sunlight breaking through ominous clouds above the Rio Grande opposite Fresno Canyon, north of Lajitas, Texas.

101. Ocotillo and a shallow Rio Grande near Presidio, Texas.

102. Redford Cemetery overlooks the Rio Grande southeast of Presidio, Texas.

103. The Mexican mountains northwest of Lajitas, Texas, drop into the shallow waters of the Rio Grande.

104. A Rio Grande resident, a western diamondback rattlesnake is poised to strike.

105. A turkey vulture rises on a thermal above the Rio Grande near Lajitas, Texas.

camera specifications

PHOTO NUMBER	CAMERA	LENS	ISO	SHUTTER SPEED (of a second)	APERTURE (f/)
1	Canon 5D Mark III	Canon EF 70-200mm f/2.8 L	400	25 seconds	16
2	Canon 5D Mark III	Canon EF 70-200mm f/2.8 L	400	30 seconds	11
3	Canon 5D Mark III	Canon EF 24-70mm f/2.8 L	100	20 seconds	22
4	Canon 5D	Canon EF 24-105mm f/4	100	1/40	4
5	Canon 5D Mark III	Canon EF 70-200mm f/2.8 L	50	1/5	32
6	Canon 5D Mark III	Canon EF 24-70mm f/2.8 L	200	1/10	8
7	Canon 5D Mark II	Canon EF 17-35mm f/2.8 L	50	3.2 seconds	22
8	Canon 5D Mark II	Canon EF 400mm f/5.6 L	100	1/800	5.6
9	Canon 5D Mark III	Canon EF 300mm f/4 L	200	1/1600	4
10	Canon 5D Mark III	Canon EF 24-70mm f/2.8 L	200	1/30	16
11	Canon 5D Mark III	Canon EF 17-35mm f/2.8 L	100	20 seconds	8
12	Canon 5D Mark III	Canon EF 70-200mm f/2.8 L	100	1/125	22
13	Fujifilm X100S		200	1/40	16
14	Canon 5D Mark III	Canon EF 24-70mm f/2.8 L	800	15 seconds	2.8
15	Canon 5D	Canon EF 17-35mm f/2.8 L	100	1/30	4.5
16	Canon 5D Mark II	Canon EF 24-105mm f/4	200	286 seconds	4.5
17	Canon 5D Mark III	Canon EF 400mm f/5.6 L	400	1/1000	5.6

18	Canon 5D Mark III	Canon EF 400mm f/5.6 L	1600	1/1600	5.6
19	Fujifilm X-T1	Fujinon XF 14mm f/2.8	200	6.5 seconds	5.6
20	Canon 5D Mark III	Canon EF 24-70mm f/2.8 L	100	0.5 seconds	22
21	Canon 5D Mark III	Canon EF 17-35mm f/2.8 L	200	1/60	16
22	Canon 5D Mark III	Canon EF 70-200mm f/2.8 L	100	1/50	22
23	Canon 5D Mark II	Canon EF 70-200mm f/2.8 L	50	0.5 seconds	32
24	Canon 5D Mark III	Canon EF 24-70mm f/2.8 L	200	1/100	16
25	Canon 5D Mark III	Canon EF 17-35mm f/2.8 L	100	1/160	16
26	Canon 5D Mark III	Canon EF 70-200mm f/2.8 L	100	1/125	8
27	Canon 5D Mark III	Canon EF 70-200mm f/2.8 L	100	1 second	25
28	Canon 5D Mark III	Canon EF 17-35mm f/2.8 L	200	1/160	11
29	Canon 5D	Canon EF 17-35mm f/2.8 L	50	1/60	8
30	Canon 5D Mark III	Canon EF 17-35mm f/2.8 L	100	2.5 seconds	22
31	Canon 5D	Canon EF 17-35mm f/2.8 L	100	1/25	22
32	Canon 5D Mark III	Canon EF 24-70mm f/2.8 L	100	1/8	22
33	Canon 5D Mark III	Canon EF 17-35mm f/2.8 L	200	1/5	22
34	Canon 5D Mark III	Canon EF 70-200mm f/2.8 L	100	1 second	25
35	Canon 5D Mark III	Canon EF 300mm f/4 L	400	1/160	4
36	Canon 5D Mark III	Canon EF 17-35mm f/2.8 L	100	1/160	4.5
37	Canon 5D Mark III	Canon EF 17-35mm f/2.8 L	100	1/60	16
38	Canon 5D Mark III	Canon EF 70-200mm f/2.8 L	200	1/5	22
39	Canon 5D Mark III	Canon EF 17-35mm f/2.8 L	100	1/100	16
40	Canon 5D Mark III	Canon EF 24-70mm f/2.8 L	100	1/100	8
41	Canon 5D Mark III	Canon EF 17-35mm f/2.8 L	3200	30 seconds	2.8
42	Canon 5D Mark III	Canon EF 17-35mm f/2.8 L	50	1/8	22
43	Canon 5D Mark III	Canon EF 24-70mm f/2.8 L	200	1/400	2.8
44	Canon 5D Mark III	Canon EF 24-70mm f/2.8 L	400	1/1600	2.8
45	Canon 5D Mark III	Canon EF 70-200mm f/2.8 L	400	1/125	16
46	Canon 5D Mark II	Canon EF 17-35mm f/2.8 L	100	1/6	8
47	Canon 5D Mark III	Canon EF 14mm f/2.8 L II	100	1/40	16
48	Canon 1D Mark IV	Canon EF 400mm f/5.6 L	400	1/640	5.6
49	Canon 5D Mark III	Canon EF 17-35mm f/2.8 L	400	1/200	8

50	Canon 5D Mark III	Canon EF 24-70mm f/2.8 L	200	1/50	8
51	Canon 5D Mark III	Canon EF 70-200mm f/2.8 L	100	1/30	4
52	Canon 5D Mark III	Canon EF 24-70mm f/2.8 L	100	1/50	16
53	Fujifilm X-T1	Fujinon XF 55-200mm f/3.5-4.8	800	1/55	8
54	Canon 5D Mark III	Canon EF 400mm f/5.6 L	200	1/1600	8
55	Canon 5D Mark III	Canon EF 70-200mm f/2.8 L	100	1/160	5.6
56	Canon 5D Mark III	Canon EF 17-35mm f/2.8 L	100	1/320	5.6
57	Canon 5D Mark II	Canon EF 17-35mm f/2.8 L	100	1/60	9
58	Canon 5D Mark III	Canon EF 70-200mm f/2.8 L	200	1/640	2.8
59	Canon 5D Mark II	Canon EF 24-105mm f/4	50	0.3 seconds	22
60	Canon 5D Mark II	Canon EF 70-200mm f/2.8 L	400	1/500	2.8
61	Canon 5D Mark III	Canon EF 17-35mm f/2.8 L	100	0.5 seconds	22
62	Canon 5D Mark III	Canon EF 17-35mm f/2.8 L	100	1/13	22
63	Canon 1D Mark IV	Canon EF 400mm f/2.8 L	100	1/1000	2.8
64	Canon 5D Mark II	Canon EF 70-200mm f/2.8 L	100	1/320	2.8
65	Canon 5D Mark II	Canon EF 17-35mm f/2.8 L	100	1/40	13
66	Canon 5D	Canon EF 24-105mm f/4	100	1/20	22
67	Canon 5D	Canon EF 70-200mm f/2.8 L	100	1/125	3.2
68	Canon 5D Mark III	Canon EF 24-70mm f/2.8 L	200	1/50	11
69	Canon 5D Mark II	Canon EF 100-400mm f/4.5-5.6 L	100	1/500	8
70	Canon 5D Mark II	Canon EF 24-105mm f/4	100	0.6 seconds	22
71	Canon 5D Mark II	Canon EF 24-105mm f/4	100	1.6 seconds	22
72	Canon 5D Mark II	Canon EF 24-105mm f/4	100	25 seconds	22
73	Canon 5D Mark III	Canon EF 17-35mm f/2.8 L	100	0.4 seconds	22
74	Canon 5D Mark III	Canon EF 24-70mm f/2.8 L	100	1/4	22
75	Canon 5D Mark III	Canon EF 24-70mm f/2.8 L	400	1/50	5.6
76	Canon 5D Mark III	Canon EF 400mm f/5.6 L	200	1/200	5.6
77	Canon 5D Mark III	Canon EF 24-70mm f/2.8 L	100	1/1250	4
78	Canon 5D Mark III	Canon EF 24-70mm f/2.8 L	200	1/250	2.8
79	Canon 5D Mark II	Canon EF 70-200mm f/2.8 L	800	1/2500	5.6
80	Canon 5D Mark III	Canon EF 17-35mm f/2.8 L	200	1/30	16
81	Fujifilm X-H1	Fujinon XF 16mm f/1.4	200	1/35	2.8

82	Fujifilm X-T2	Fujinon XF 10-24mm f/4	200	0.6 seconds	16
83	Canon 5D Mark III	Canon EF 400mm f/5.6 L	200	1/1600	5.6
84	Canon 5D Mark III	Canon EF 70-200mm f/2.8 L	200	1/125	2.8
85	Canon 5D Mark III	Canon EF 17-35mm f/2.8 L	100	1/60	16
86	Canon 5D Mark III	Canon EF 24-70mm f/2.8 L	100	1/200	8
87	Canon 5D Mark III	Canon EF 17-35mm f/2.8 L	400	1/10	8
88	Canon 5D Mark III	Canon EF 17-35mm f/2.8 L	200	1/30	8
89	Canon 5D Mark III	Canon EF 70-200mm f/2.8 L	100	1/5	22
90	Canon 5D Mark III	Canon EF 70-200mm f/2.8 L	100	1/2500	4
91	Canon 5D Mark III	Canon EF 17-35mm f/2.8 L	100	1/50	5.6
92	Canon 5D Mark III	Canon EF 17-35mm f/2.8 L	100	1/50	11
93	Canon 5D Mark III	Canon EF 70-200mm f/2.8 L	800	5 seconds	5.6
94	Fujifilm X100S		800	1/1200	4
95	Canon 5D Mark III	Canon EF 17-35mm f/2.8 L	200	1/160	16
96	Canon 5D	Canon EF 17-35mm f/2.8 L	50	1/4	22
97	Canon 5D	Canon EF 17-35mm f/2.8 L	50	1/15	10
98	Canon 5D Mark II	Canon EF 24-105mm f/4	100	1/400	4
99	Canon 5D Mark III	Canon EF 70-200mm f/2.8 L	100	1/4	32
100	Canon 5D Mark III	Canon EF 70-200mm f/2.8 L	200	1/2500	8
101	Canon 5D Mark III	Canon EF 24-70mm f/2.8 L	100	1/80	13
102	Canon 5D Mark II	Canon EF 17-35mm f/2.8 L	100	1/80	16
103	Canon 5D Mark III	Canon EF 70-200mm f/2.8 L	200	1/500	11
104	Canon 1D Mark II N	Canon EF 70-200mm f/2.8 L	50	1/320	3.5
105	Canon 5D Mark III	Canon EF 70-200mm f/2.8 L	100	1/640	9

about the authors

JEROD FOSTER is a natural history and travel photographer whose work has appeared in *Texas Highways, Texas Parks and Wildlife, The New York Times,* and *The Texas Tribune.* He has authored seven books on photography education and is associate professor of practice in the College of Media and Communication at Texas Tech University.

JOHN POCH is the author of five collections of poetry, including the forthcoming *Texases* (WordFarm Press, 2019). His poetry has been published widely and has won many prizes including the Nation/"Discovery" Award, the Donald Justice Prize, and The New Criterion Poetry Prize. He is professor in the Department of English's creative writing program at Texas Tech University

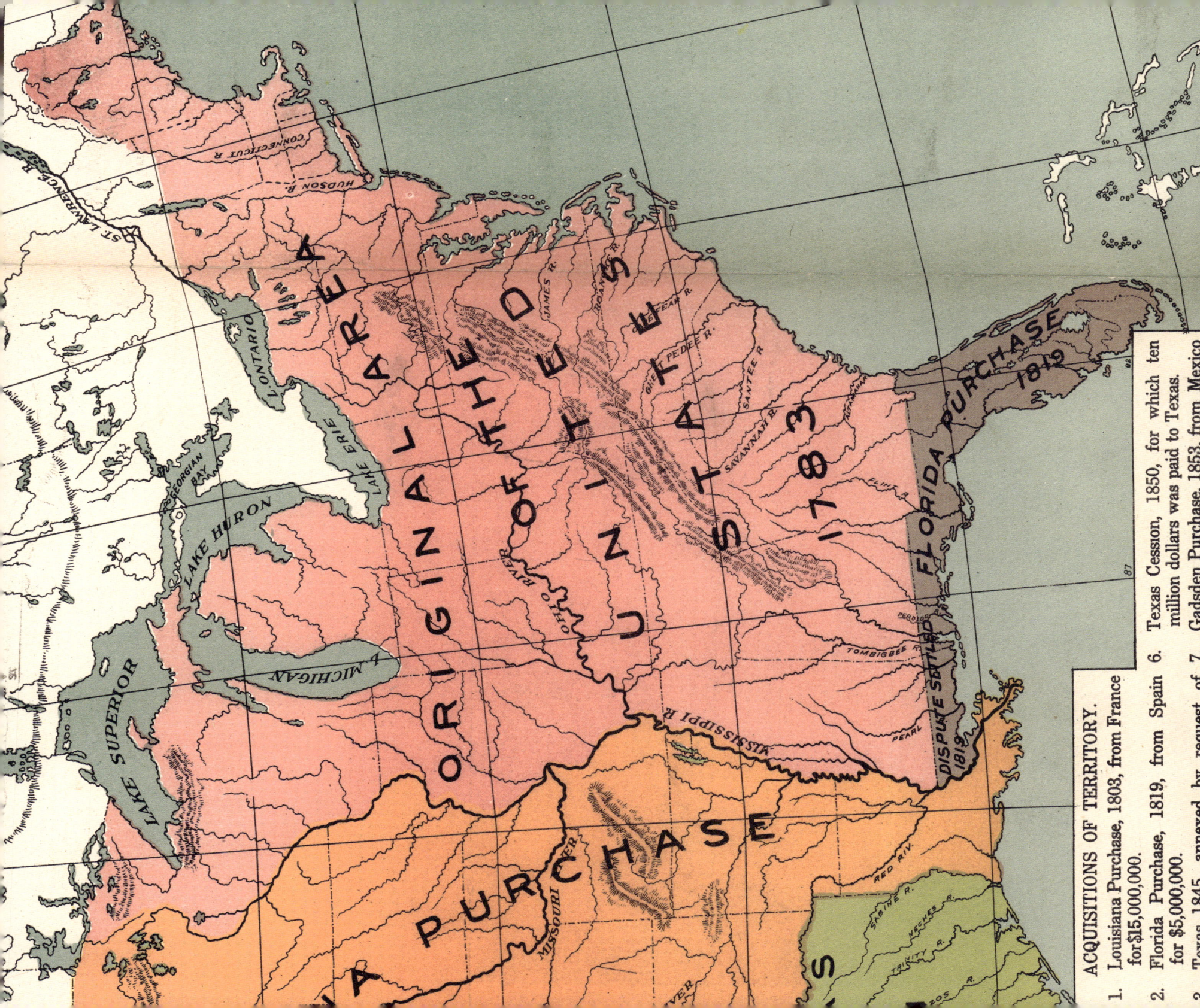

ORIGINAL AREA OF THE UNITED STATES 1783

FLORIDA PURCHASE 1819

DISPUTE SETTLED 1819

LOUISIANA PURCHASE

LAKE SUPERIOR

LAKE HURON

L. MICHIGAN

GEORGIAN BAY

LAKE ERIE

L. ONTARIO

ST. LAWRENCE R.

CONNECTICUT R.

HUDSON R.

JAMES R.

ROANOKE

NEUSE

CAPE FEAR R.

PEDEE R.

SANTEE R.

SAVANNAH R.

FLINT

TOMBIGBEE R.

PEARL

GEORGIA

MISSISSIPPI R.

OHIO R.

MISSOURI R.

RED RIV.

SABINE R.

NECHES R.

TRINITY R.

BRAZOS R.

ACQUISITIONS OF TERRITORY.

1. Louisiana Purchase, 1803, from France for $15,000,000.

2. Florida Purchase, 1819, from Spain for $5,000,000.

3. Texas, 1845, annexed by request of

6. Texas Cession, 1850, for which ten million dollars was paid to Texas.

7. Gadsden Purchase, 1853, from Mexico